COMING INTO THE LIGHT:
THE WORK, POLITICS AND RELIGION
OF WOMEN IN ULSTER

1840–1940

Published 1994
The Institute of Irish Studies
The Queen's University of Belfast,
Belfast

This book has received support from the Cultural Traditions Programme
of the Community Relations Council, which aims to encourage acceptance
and understanding of cultural diversity.

British Library Cataloguing-in-Publication Data. A catalogue record for
this book is available from the British Library

ISBN 0 85389 539 2

Printed by W & G Baird Ltd., Antrim
Cover designed by Rodney Miller Associates

COMING INTO THE LIGHT: THE WORK, POLITICS AND RELIGION OF WOMEN IN ULSTER

1840–1940

edited by

JANICE HOLMES AND DIANE URQUHART

The Institute of Irish Studies
The Queen's University of Belfast
1994

ACKNOWLEDGEMENTS

This collection is the product of the efforts of numerous individuals. A special word of thanks is extended to Dr. Mary O'Dowd for her enthusiasm and guidance during the early stages of this project. Credit must be given to Paul Marley for designing the maps, graphs and tables in chapter seven. Eileen Black, of the Ulster Museum, directed us towards our choice of cover illustration. Kate Newmann, of the Institute of Irish Studies, made numerous helpful and encouraging editorial suggestions. We are grateful for their personal kindness as well as their specialist expertise.

On a personal level, we would like to thank Eric and Betty Urquhart, Tom and Susan Holmes, Eoin Magennis and Gill McIntosh. Their contributions have not gone unappreciated.

CONTENTS

INTRODUCTION

JANICE HOLMES AND DIANE URQUHART

'To a great extent the standard of a nation's civilisation may be guaged by the position occupied by its women, the manner in which they are treated, the education they receive, the influence they possess, the freedom accorded them.'[1]

This collection of historical articles follows in the footsteps of other recent contributions to the field of Irish women's history. Maria Luddy and Cliona Murphy's *Women surviving*, Margaret MacCurtain and Mary O'Dowd's *Women in early modern Ireland* and the recent article in *Irish Historical Studies* entitled 'An agenda for women's history in Ireland'[2] have questioned the priorities of the historical establishment. The quality of this research has begun the process of challenging the ongoing perception of Irish history as political history. Certainly women's history in Ireland should have moved beyond the stage where it needs to justify itself. These essays have emerged out of an environment which is becoming more receptive to the concept of women's history.

The position of a historian examining Ulster within the context of Irish history is a complex one. All-Ireland studies have traditionally paid lip-service to the province's unique regional, industrial and religious composition. Women's history in Ireland has struggled with similar tendencies. Little historical attention has focused on the role of women in the north, although Ulster's distinct social, economic and political character has shaped their lives fundamentally. Ulster women have been living in the shadows of historical obscurity for too long. This collection is an attempt to bring them into the light.

As with any research into women's history, the articles in this collection have grappled with the scarcity of source material - if not in quantity, at least in quality. Looking at historical events from a female perspective involves the creative use of existing material or the innovative assessment of new sources. Alternative approaches become necessary in order to piece together a coherent picture of female experience. Brigitte Anton's work on the Young Ireland movement has involved the painstaking process of recreating the identities of several Ulster women who wrote for *The Nation*. Their previously anonymous contributions can now be credited with having a significant role in the creation of an Irish nationalist ideology.

Ulster women were not immune from the standards of femininity and respectability that were prevalent in nineteenth-century Britain. Division between the public and private, with women participating only in the latter, was a standard to which all women were urged to conform. How women operated within these constraints is remarkably complex. Andrea Ebel Brożyna has examined the role of temperance literature in the construction of female piety. Although women participated in the public sphere through their temperance work, they were reluctant to challenge traditional stereotypes. Belfast's temperance literature reflects this ambivalent position in its portrayal of women as either moral crusader or drunken reprobate. Similar tensions emerge in Janice Holmes' work on women in the Ulster revival of 1859. An examination of working-class women's ecstatic religious behaviour reveals that only during a time of religious upheaval and emotional chaos did women experience an expansion in their male-defined gender roles. Women embraced religion for its potential to bring them into the public sphere of religious activity. However, as they were denied access to denominational power structures, their influence remained a spiritual one.

Other articles in this collection focus, not on male constructions of femininity, but on history from a female perspective. Such research allows different issues to be discussed and different images to emerge. Diane Urquhart's article reveals an entirely new perspective on Ulster unionism. Examining the Ulster Women's Unionist Council, Urquhart has discovered that women constituted a significant political force within popular unionism, an influence which has been ignored in most unionist historiography. Women's pivotal political work on a mass scale highlights their importance to the movement and alters modern conceptions of its agenda.

Pioneering research into women's history in Belfast has been conducted by Alison Jordan. Her book on Margaret Byers, an early advocate of female education, and her publication on the role of women in Belfast's charitable institutions, illustrate Ulster women's active participation on a number of different levels.[3] In this collection her analysis of the Belfast Ladies' Institute shows women participating fully in the campaign for the admission of women to Irish tertiary and secondary education. This middle-class organisation was successful in its efforts to prove that women were as intellectually capable as men, at a time when women's higher education was still a controversial issue.

Another theme running through this collection is the tension between the public and private arenas. Women both reinforced these societal stereotypes and challenged them. Margaret Neill's analysis of the female homework industry shows that women's waged employment brought the public and private spheres together. Work performed in the home allowed women to fulfill the basic economic function of providing for their families. In doing so, they could work without challenging traditional domestic stereotypes of women as mothers and guardians of the home.

Women's lives are characterised to a certain degree by the stresses and strains of contradictory expectations. Women themselves both challenge and reinforce restrictive perceptions of their designated role within society, be it in religion, politics or work. This is evident in the research Marie O'Connell has conducted into nuns in Ulster. These women encountered the liberating tendencies of a conventual life but at the same time experienced the restrictive nature of a church which was essentially conservative and male dominated. O'Connell has revealed the extent of the convent network in Ulster and the breadth of its social and educational involvement in the local community. Her analysis once again adds a new dimension to a field which has largely ignored the Ulster dynamic.

Much of the research contained herein prompts almost as many questions as it answers. However, by focusing on the political, religious and social aspects of the female existence, we hope we have revealed some of the more important defining features of women's lives, perhaps outlining new areas of research. Women's lives were complex and riddled with contradictions, stresses and ambivalence. Yet women were able to overcome these obstacles to achieve better lives for themselves, for their families and for their country. The women who appear in these pages have exhibited a strength of character, a resilience to change and a diversity of experience which provide more than enough justification for the continued study of women's history.

[1] Crissie Doyle, *Women in ancient and modern Ireland* (Dublin, 1917), p. 3.
[2] Maria Luddy and Cliona Murphy, (eds.), *Women surviving: studies in Irish women's history in the nineteenth and twentieth centuries* (Swords, 1990); Margaret MacCurtain and Mary O'Dowd, (eds.), *Women in early modern Ireland* (Dublin, 1991) and Margaret MacCurtain, Mary O'Dowd and Maria Luddy, 'An agenda for women's history in Ireland, 1500–1900', in *Irish Historical Studies* 28, no. 109 (May 1992), pp 1–37.
[3] *Margaret Byers: pioneer of women's education and founder of Victoria College, Belfast* (Belfast, n.d.) and *Who cared? Charity in Victorian and Edwardian Belfast* (Belfast, n.d.).

PART I
WORK

HOMEWORKERS IN ULSTER,
1850–1911

MARGARET NEILL

I

The production of goods in the home was an integral and essential part of the linen and cotton industries from the 1840s to the early 1900s. Despite industrialisation, homework remained both a major source of employment for women and an important aspect in the overall economic structure of Ulster. In 1911, the committee of inquiry into the linen and cotton making-up trades in Northern Ireland concluded that homework was an indispensable part of the machinery of production.[1] Yet this important area of work has been largely neglected and marginalised by historians. Even when researched the tendency has been to analyse homework as part-time or seasonal, work which was, on the whole, fitted in and around women's domestic chores.[2] Similarly, the low and irregular wages earned from homework are often portrayed as being merely a supplement to a husbands's wage, or 'pin money'.[3] There is, however, a wealth of evidence to show that this is an extremely misleading and one-sided interpretation of the labour of homeworkers.

The terms homework and outwork are often confused and used interchangeably by contemporaries and historians. They were, however, two different forms of industrial organisation. Homework, as the name implies, was work, usually piecework, done in the home of the workers. The materials or goods were distributed either directly by the management from the factory or workshop door, or indirectly through a series of agents distributed throughout the country districts. In rural districts the main method of distribution was through agents who were usually small shopkeepers.[4] The shirt industry, based in Londonderry, also used outstations. These were depots specially set up throughout the different districts; a certain day, or days, being set aside each week for the distribution and collection of unmade and completed goods.[5]

After the completed goods were returned and examined the worker was paid in coin or in goods of equivalent value. All work was paid by the piece and deductions were made from the wage for any flaws, stains or late deliveries.[6] Agents generally received ten per cent commission on all the goods completed and returned to the manufacturer.[7] Very importantly, the piece-rate for all work was set by the manufacturer and not the agent. One of the few exceptions to the system of commission was the knitting industry which was situated in west Donegal. In this industry the yarn was obtained from the mill by merchants and given out to be knitted in the homes of the workers. The merchant/shopkeepers made their profit from the difference between what they paid for the yarn and the payment they received from the wholesaler for the finished articles.[8]

Outwork was the process whereby a subcontractor, called a middleman, took the work out at a given rate from the manufacturer or clothier. The middleman employed workers, often his family, in his home or a small workshop to do the work. The middleman could sublet part or all of the work to other subcontractors. The crucial point is that not all outworkers were homeworkers. Many worked in small factories, regulated workshops and unregulated workshops in the home. In contrast to homework the piece-rates were always set by the middleman/subcontractor and not the manufacturer. The middleman made his profit out of the difference between what he paid to the manufacturer and the wages paid to his employees.[9] Outwork was a system which was extensively associated with the ready-to-wear industries in Britain and Ireland, for example, the boot and shoe trades, tailoring and dressmaking. The evidence suggests, however, that outwork was much less extensive in Ireland than in Britain.[10] It would appear that the vast bulk of the work put out by manufacturers in Ulster was in the form of homework. To avoid any confusion the terms homework and outwork will be used only in the context of the above definition.

II

Homework encompassed a wide variety of industries: dressmaking, glovemaking, lace, knitting, clothing, to name but a few. Despite the diversity of occupations most homework was based on the sewing and needlework trades, or what can be loosely referred to as the 'sewing trades'.[11] As sewing and needlework were regarded as 'women's work' the labour force was predominantly female. Prior to 1850 the work in the ready-to-wear trades and the making-up industry was all done by hand. Following the application of the sewing machine to various sectors of the sewing trades in the 1850s, the industry underwent a degree of mechanisation and centralisation of production.

However, the mechanisation of industry was an uneven process, taking place in different industries at different times and at varying rates. Consequently, many parts of the production process continued to be performed by hand throughout the nineteenth century. In dressmaking and millinery, and nearly all finishing processes in the tailoring and shirt trades, most work was done by hand until the early 1900s.[12] In the linen and cotton making-up industry there was still a vast array of hand work, for example, scalloping, clipping, thread-drawing, embroidery, sprigging and vice-folding.[13] In addition, many of the small delicate industries lent themselves to hand work. For instance, the Irish lace industry, of which Carrickmacross is perhaps the most famous, was established and developed as a hand industry.[14]

Certainly the sewing machine had a radical impact on production. In the 1860s and 1870s large stitching factories and warehouses were established in towns such as Belfast, Lurgan and Londonderry.[15] For instance, between 1855–78 the shirt industry established several large concerns in Londonderry. By 1871, 2,229 operatives were employed in sixteen concerns, with another twenty smaller factories employing roughly between fifty to one hundred persons each.[16]

The initial belief that more and more workers would be drawn into these factories proved to be unfounded.[17] Both manufacturers and the workers themselves were quick to realise the adaptability of the sewing machine for use in the home. Hand and treadle machines, mostly the latter, were introduced into the home in large numbers from the 1860s onwards. The shirt manufacturers of Londonderry were hiring out new and second-hand machines to their homeworkers in the early 1860s. Some manufacturers even gave out machines free of charge on the condition that a certain number of garments were produced each week.[18] Most machines, however, were purchased from machine manufacturers under easy instalment agreements or hired for approximately 1s. to 1s.6d. a week. Between 1874 and 1900, 3,572 sewing machines had been sold in the area controlled by the Londonderry branch of the Singer manufacturing company.[19]

Homework survived and expanded largely because it provided considerable cost savings to the manufacturer. Under industrialisation the production process was sub-divided into minute tasks, with each worker only assigned one operation. As most tasks were easily and quickly learnt, requiring little or no supervision, they could be performed by women, children and the elderly. This added to the existing pool of surplus female labour which enabled manufacturers to keep labour costs to a minimum.[20] Wages paid for work put out were always lower than those paid to factory workers, even when the same work was being done. In addition, the employer made savings on capital investment in buildings and machinery, supervision, training, heating, light and other overhead costs.[21]

Homeworkers were also outside of the protection of the factory and workshop acts. Hence a home labour force enabled manufacturers to avoid restrictive legislation on hours and health. The flexibility which this afforded the manufacturer was of the greatest importance, particularly in the linen making-up industry where rushed orders to America were common. In order to facilitate the dispatch of these orders homeworkers often had to work from early in the morning until late into the night.[22] In addition, home labour was particularly suited to the cyclical peaks and troughs of the linen industry and the seasonality of trades such as dressmaking and tailoring. Home labour could be easily expanded in times of increased demand, at little or no cost to the employer other than wages. Equally, in times of recession they could be dispensed without any great loss to the employer. All of these factors combined to make homeworkers a very attractive proposition to employers.[23]

Considering the economic advantage, it is not surprising that the ratio of homeworkers to factory workers ranged between three to one and four to one. This ratio would appear to have applied wherever industrialists combined home and factory labour. In 1863, for instance, in the Londonderry shirt and collar industry, Robert Sinclair employed 500 factory workers to 2,000 outside workers; at Welch and Margeston the proportion was roughly 200 factory workers to 900 homeworkers.[24] Despite the boom in the shirt industry and the establishment of new large premises in Londonderry, the ratio between factory and homeworkers remained basically unchanged at least until the 1900s. In 1889 the Inspector of Factories was able to report that one firm in Londonderry was employing 1,200 inside and 3,000 outside workers. Two other firms employing about 600 each inside were giving work to 1,500 and 2,000 respectively through their stations.[25]

The above figures were, however, based on the names on the manufacturer's wage books. In nearly all home industries it was common practice for one or two persons to register with an employer and collect work for two, three or more members of the family.[26] The ratio of homeworkers was, therefore, undoubtedly even greater than that quoted above. The ratio of factory to homeworkers was not unique to

Ireland. In the early 1890s, Miss Collet reported that in Bristol three quarters of the work of clothiers was done in the home, with the ratio between factory and homeworkers in the industry being about five to one. However, in individual firms the ratio was sometimes as great as twelve to one.[27]

It is important to understand that the two systems of production were neither separate or competing sectors of industry, but interrelated parts which, taken together, formed a complete system.[28] For example, in the handkerchief industry, work was often handed out late in the afternoon, or after the factory had closed, to the thread-drawers who were the first link in the chain of production. This work usually had to be returned the next morning, often before the factory opened, so that the stitchers could complete the next stage; the handkerchiefs then went back out to be embroidered in the home before being returned for the final stages of production. If domestic production was not completed on time then workers in the factory would have been slack or idle and vice versa.[29] As the above evidence demonstrates, to understand any part of the system it must be seen in relation to the whole industry.

As noted by Schmiechen, many historians tend to view homework in the clothing and other industries as uneconomic, wasteful and incompatible with the demands of an expanding consumer market.[30] However, contemporaries had a very different perspective on its economic significance. Many industrialists clearly believed that they could compete effectively with home and foreign competitors by utilising home labour. In many cases manufacturers found that they could obtain equal or greater productivity by increasing their home labour force. In 1907 Miss Martindale described the increase in demand for embroidered goods including tablecloths, ladies underwear, napkins and handkerchiefs. This expansion in consumer demand was largely met by increasing both the volume of work to homeworkers and the number of homeworkers themselves.[31]

Flexibility of production, surplus labour and substantial savings on capital expenditure all combined to ensure that manufacturers retained a firm commitment to both homework and the contracting out of work.

III

As noted previously, homework was not one single industry, but a large and varied group of industries, each with its own occupational subdivisions. This section looks at the distribution of industries throughout Ulster.

The embroidery and sprigging industry was based in Belfast but provided employment for women throughout the counties of Antrim, Down, Donegal, Fermanagh and Tyrone.[32] Sprigging, often referred to as white embroidery, was the working of a pattern with a needle on white work. This industry had its roots in the sewed muslin industry which was established in Donaghadee in 1829. Under the system of agents working for the large Glasgow houses the industry rapidly expanded into several counties in Ulster. By 1849 the muslin industry was reported to be employing a total of 150,000–180,000 persons and expending £400,000 annually in wages. By the 1850s this had risen to £1,400,000. Despite the collapse of the muslin industry in the 1860s and early 1870s, the embroidery industry re-emerged in the 1880s–90s under the huge demand for embroidered linen and cotton goods. By the early 1900s it was estimated to be still expending a quarter of a million pounds in wages.[33]

The shirt industry was established in the city of Londonderry in the 1840s and by the 1860s it had extended into counties Londonderry, Donegal and Tyrone. The industry was of the greatest importance in Donegal and Londonderry. In 1901 the occupation of shirtmaker and seamstress accounted for 40.2 per cent and 34.8 per cent respectively of the total numbers of females in employment.[34] In Donegal the greatest concentration of shirtmakers was along the Innishowen peninsula, where one quarter of those enumerated in the census lived.[35] By 1889 the shirt industry had an annual turnover of £1,000,000, one quarter of which was wages. A decade later the industry was still estimated to be expending £209,209 annually in wages.[36]

The town of Lurgan, County Armagh, was the chief centre of the handkerchief industry. After Belfast, it was reported to be the most important industrial town in Ulster. The handkerchief industry provided employment for thousands of women in the districts of Lurgan, Portadown, Dromore and Banbridge. In 1887, Mr. Woodgate, factory inspector, reported that every female whether married or not was supplied with ample means of work in thread-drawing, veining, hemstitching and folding.[37]

The town of Glenties and adjacent neighbourhoods, the Rosses, Dungloe and Bunbeg in County Donegal were the chief centres for the machine and hand-knitting industries.[38] Although the knitting industry was one of the poorest paid, it provided essential employment in districts noted for their extremes of poverty. Similarly, the homespun Irish tweed industry of Mayo, Kerry and Donegal was for the most part based in south west Donegal in the districts of Carrick and Ardara. Like the handloom linen industry, homespun provided employment for the whole family: the wool being carded, dyed, spun and woven by the household.[39]

In the 1890s the quality of homespun was improved with the assistance of the Congested District Board and the Irish Industrial Council. Despite this there was little development in the industry in the 1900s. Wages remained a pittance with women earning about 7d. for two days work carding and spinning. In 1897–8 only £5,200 was expended in wages for the industry in Ardara and Carrick.[40] In the early 1900s it was estimated that about 1,000 families were involved in homespun industry around Carrick and Ardara.[41]

The lace industry dated from about the period of the Famine. Under the influence of lady philanthropists, an occupation previously undertaken by ladies was transformed into employment for the peasantry. At the turn of the century the Irish lace industry underwent a revival under the influence of the Irish Lace Depot, the Irish Industrial School and the Congested District Board. Lace was produced partly in the homes of the workers. While there was employment in lace production in counties Sligo, Donegal and Down, the industry was largely concentrated in Armagh, Fermanagh and Monaghan.[42]

IV

Despite the data in the occupational returns of the decennial census, and the official lists of homeworkers sent to the local district councils, it is impossible to assess with any accuracy the size of the home labour force. Under the Factory and Workshop Act (1901) employers were required to send lists of outworkers and homeworkers twice yearly to the local district council. The object of this was to ensure that the names and addresses of outworkers were available for inspection by the public health officer. However, this section of the Factory and Workshop Act was not applied to the making-up of clothes until 1907, and to the making-up of household linen goods until 1911.[43]

Quite apart from the late application of the act to significant areas of homework in Ulster, this legislation proved to be grossly inadequate. Only a few of the larger towns such as Belfast, Lurgan and Londonderry actually made any attempt to comply with it. Even then, the returns represented only a fraction of the total number employed. In Lurgan, where literally thousands were employed, a return of 1,400 employees was made. The act was ignored to such an extent that even when the commissioners for the 1911 linen inquiry dispatched circulars to all the local district councils in Ulster, almost none replied. The best the commissioners could state was that homeworkers probably outnumbered the 22,000 employed in factories and workshops in the linen making-up trade, but this estimate was based on inadequate census data.[44]

There is evidence that the census tended to omit work done in the home, as well as other forms of part-time and seasonal labour. Many women did not report themselves as employed to the enumerators. This was partly because they did not see their work as 'real work' and partly because of a traditional fear of officialdom. When other contemporary sources are used to supplement the census figures, it is clear that there was a gross underenumeration of women employed in the home.[45]

While we are unable to estimate accurately the total numbers of women employed in homework, contemporary reports, especially those of the lady inspectors, enable us to see the extent of work that was conducted in certain rural dis-

tricts. It would appear that wherever a homework industry
was established it generally expanded rapidly to employ thousands in the surrounding districts. For instance Donegal,
despite its remoteness, was a major employer of homeworkers
in the last quarter of the nineteenth century. As we have seen,
this county had home industries in sprigging, knitting, homespun and shirt making. Miss Martindale reported the proliferation of agents over a wide area of Donegal, especially the
embroidery and sprigging industry in the southern part of
the county which ran roughly from Ballyshannon to
Glencolumbcille and as far north as Ardara.[46]

Agents nearly always worked for several firms and each agent
was capable of supplying work to hundreds of people. In
Ballintrae one agent had six hundred names on his books and
another in Donegal had seven hundred names. One sprigging
agent in Donegal had paid £1,100 in wages in six months for
one Glasgow firm alone. In Ardara, two tweed merchants
employed several hundred women each for embroidery and
knitting.[47] It is important to remember that women who regis-
tered with an agent usually collected work for others in the
family, hence increasing the number of homeworkers still
further. According to the lady inspectors, agents were dotted
all over even the smallest districts. For instance, Killybegs had
seven agents and another two nearby; Kilcar, about six miles
away, had another six agents.[48] Mr. McNeilis, secretary to the
Glenties Poor Law Union, estimated that 75 per cent of
the holdings of the Union were valued under £4 a year. The
poverty of the people was extreme, and both men and women
were compelled to supplement their income by whatever other
means available. McNeilis estimated there were about 180
agents employing about 12,000 families, four or five to a
family, in sprigging, knitting and drawn thread work.[49]

Not all of the women on an agent's books would
necessarily have worked all year round. Most, especially in
trade booms, would probably have been able to obtain work
at some time of the year. Consequently, their employment
should have been recorded in the census. Contemporary
investigations demonstrate the vast gap between the economic reality and the data in the census. For example, the

number of females recorded under the main categories in Textile and Fabrics in the 1901 census for County Donegal were: embroidery, 903; woollen manufacture, 565; fancy goods, 1,626.[50] If a low average of one hundred persons per agent was taken then the total of 903 embroiders would equate with only nine sprigging agents for the whole of Donegal. As the evidence clearly demonstrates this is a gross understatement of both the number of agents and home-workers for County Donegal.

V

A feature of homework from its early beginnings and throughout the period, was that it was not confined to work-ing-class women. In towns throughout Ulster homeworkers were described as widows and spinsters who were dependent upon it for their livelihood; married women whose husbands were on low or irregular wages or who were out of work. By far the largest section worked to supplement a low wage. This class of women were, for the most part, compelled to work out of sheer economic necessity. There were also women in 'better circumstances', the wives of skilled workers, artisans and small tradespeople whose husbands earned a regular and relatively high income.[51] This particular group of women was referred to by Clementina Black as Class D or 'reprehensible women' who could have afforded to live upon their hus-band's wages, but yet chose to engage in paid homework.[52] The money Class D women earned was commonly referred to by contemporaries as 'pin money' or 'pocket money'.

In the country districts homeworkers were mainly the wives and daughters of small holders and farmers and agricultural labourers.[53] The economic class of rural homeworkers ranged from the very poorest labourers to relatively well off tenant farmers. Some of the tenant farmers were described by Miss Collet as being 'according to Irish ideas, very well off'.[54] Therefore the home labour force was not confined to lower class women. According to Mr. George Ward, executive sanitary officer of Belfast, some homeworkers lived in 'very respectable localities'. The rental of their houses ranging from 2s.6d. and 3s.6d. for working-class housing to as much as £30 a year.[55]

This social and economic diversity was largely due to the perception of homework as a relatively respectable occupation. Firstly, sewing and embroidery were part of the womanly accomplishments, a genteel art learned and practised since childhood. Secondly, work was performed in the home and largely hidden. It was, therefore, possible to disguise the amount of hours spent each day on paid work. Homework could be portrayed as something which was secondary to women's role as housewives and mothers; it was performed only when they had some spare time from their family duties.[56] Thirdly, because they worked at home they were not associated with the loose, rough and immoral behaviour attributed to factory women.[57]

On one hand, these women were deviating from those codes of behaviour expected of 'respectable women'. On the other hand, they could be seen as largely conforming to the norm expected of them from upper and middle-class society, still socially dignified, outwardly demure, fulfilling their role as housewives and mothers and dependent on their husbands. This image of respectability was almost certainly a central factor in the relative lack of social condemnation of homework. Consequently, it became a desirable and acceptable occupation for women of a higher economic and social class.

Low hourly rates, combined with the erratic nature of work, compelled women to work long, excessive hours to earn a wage that was on or below the poverty line. In general, wages of 3s. to 6s. a week were earned in most homework trades, including thread-drawing, clipping, folding, scalloping and embroidery. Even good workers employed in relatively well paid sewing machine work could only expect to earn a net wage of 8s. to 9s. per week.[58] On such wages, women living on their own, or with a family to support, suffered the worst extremes of poverty. The long hours and poor standard of living is well illustrated in the testimony of the women themselves to the government's official inquiry into the linen making-up trades.

Mrs. S. had worked as a thread-drawer in Lurgan for fifteen years; she was married to a weaver and had several children, the eldest of whom was thirteen. Her husband left for work at six o'clock and after preparing breakfast for the family she regularly began work at eight o'clock and worked constantly through the day until ten or eleven o'clock at night. If there was a rush order that had to be completed for the next morning, she had to stay up to complete it no matter what the hour. The eldest child of thirteen worked with the mother until about seven at night. The only breaks Mrs. S. took in her long day were to prepare the dinner and tea for the family which took about two hours for dinner and one hour for tea.

Mrs. S.'s husband earned 12s. a week. The combined wage of the mother and child averaged 6s. to 7s.6d. a week. All of the husband's wage and that of the child were handed over to Mrs. S. who took charge of all the expenditure. She stated that the total weekly income of 18s. to 19s. was spent on the household, mostly on food and rent. There was nothing left for what she referred to as 'any extras'.[59]

Mrs. H. performed the very heavy work of clipping threads from large valances and sheets. Her two eldest boys, aged eleven and nine, worked alongside her. The boys were usually woken at six o'clock in order to get at least three dozen done before breakfast at eight She stopped work to prepare breakfast for her husband and resumed work immediately afterwards, continuing until ten or eleven at night. The boy of nine usually worked until seven o'clock, but when the situation demanded it he was compelled to work until one in the morning. In common with many women the only break in the day was for the preparation of meals. In addition to clipping, the large and heavy parcels of work had to be carried to and from the factory on a daily basis. On arrival at the factory the parcels had then to be carried up and down six flights of narrow stairs. Mrs. H. was not in good health and was unable to carry the parcels herself; the task was therefore always done by her young sons.[60]

For their work, Mrs. H. and her two children earned about 6s. a week and her husband earned between £1 and 30s. a week.[61] For a working-class man in Ireland this was a relatively fair wage. Yet the labour of the mother and the children was believed to be essential to sustain the family. Very importantly, the higher wage of the husband did not allow work to be done on a casual basis. In common with those wives economically worse off than herself, she worked long, uninterrupted hours on a regular basis throughout the year.

Widows and deserted wives were regarded as being among the worst cases of homeworkers. These women were often either the sole support of their families or the chief breadwinner. Similarly, women with husbands who were out of work for long periods of time and in poor health had the burden of supporting themselves, their husbands and their children, and sometimes had also to meet the extra expenses of doctor's visits or medical bills. For example, Mrs. J.'s husband had been unable to work for a long time because of ill-health. She had five children, the eldest of whom was a daughter of ten years of age. She had no alternative but to keep the eldest girl off school to help with the clipping and scalloping. The girl worked the same long hours as her mother from early morning until late into the night, sometimes till two o'clock in the morning. In addition, the daughter helped to look after the younger children.[62] The only break from the daily toil was if work was scarce. The mother stated that she was unable to allow her daughter any playtime. The only break her mother could give her was a short walk for some fresh air on Sundays. The most Mrs. J. was able to earn was 5s.3d. a week. The only assistance she had was some charity to help pay the 3s.6d. rent.[63] Apart from this the whole family was supported on her meagre earnings. At most she was feeding and clothing two adults and five children on roughly 9d. a day, or 9d. per head per week.

Some homeworkers literally led a hand to mouth existence. For example, Mrs. C.C., a widow, collected 6d. worth of work in the morning and worked constantly top-sewing handkerchiefs. During their school dinner break, her children clipped what was sewn. Work was then resumed until about four o'clock when the children came home from school. The children returned the day's work and brought back another 4d. or 6d. worth to complete that night. During February 1911 her weekly earnings were 4s.9d., 2s.8d., 3s.5d. and 3s.7d. In addition, she had 3s.6d. a week assistance from charity.[64]

Despite the obvious extent of her poverty, Mrs. C.C. was more fortunate than others in a similar position. According to Miss Galway in Belfast some of the elderly homeworkers and young widows found it impossible to sustain themselves without charity. Only a tiny minority of those in need actually received any grants from friendly societies and charities.[65] Without additional assistance, sometimes even with charity, some women and their families had to do with less food when there was no work and sometimes they were unable to eat at all.[66]

There is unfortunately no way of knowing how numerous this section of homeworkers was. Surveys undertaken show a high percentage of women heading households in certain areas. In 1897 a survey by the Women's Industrial Council showed over 40 per cent of homeworkers were the sole bread-winners. According to Booth's survey in 1901, 20 per cent of dressmakers, shirtmakers and seamstresses were heads of households. In a small sample of industries, Clementina Black found 28.4 per cent of women workers supported a family, and another 64.5 per cent of them worked because of their husband's inadequate wage.[67]

The evidence clearly shows that the women who suffered the greatest economic pressure were deserted wives, widows, spinsters, and wives with husbands on very low and irregular wages. The poverty of the poorest sections of homeworkers was undoubtedly worsened by the erratic nature of wages. Due to a variety of factors all homeworkers suffered some degree of fluctuation in their wages. Wages were reduced when women had to work on poorer paid articles or when there was a shortage of work. Mrs. Y., for instance, received 9d. a dozen for sewing coloured pinafores and aprons, but on the coarser white work she only received 5d. a dozen.

It has to be remembered that although the drop in wages was often slight, for the poorest women even 1s. would have been a substantial decrease. Any reduction in income for women on or below subsistence level, even for a short time, was potentially very serious indeed. When sufficient money was not earned to cover the cost of food and rent many home-workers survived by extending their debt with the agent/shopkeeper. In many areas throughout Ulster it was common practice for these individuals to pay women in goods from their shop. When the price of goods purchased by homeworkers exceeded their wages they could either pay the difference in cash or have it credited to them.[68]

Although these running accounts were often vital for the survival of families, they were also an added burden. When available, extra hours had to be worked in order to reduce the debt or prevent it from rising to a level which would have been beyond their means to repay. The longer the drop in wages the greater the debt and the greater the need to work longer, uninterrupted hours. The system of truck and running debt also placed the women very much at the mercy of agents. It was claimed that agents could induce workers to take work that was badly paid because they were in his debt.[69] Thus, even when there was an abundance of work, women could not always choose the well paid work.

Clearly the main priority for the poorer sections of homeworkers was to spend as much time as possible on their waged work. Hence there was only a minimal amount of time spent on cooking, cleaning and child care. A working day of fourteen to sixteen hours, five and a half or six days a week was common, those who earned the least per hour being habitually driven to work more hours. Poverty compelled them to rush their housework to enable them to spend an extra few minutes at their trade and earn an extra farthing.[70]

It would appear that generally two to three hours a day were spent on cooking and cleaning. In some cases women who did not have husbands to prepare mid-day meals for, chose to work on rather than take even a short dinner break. The heavier tasks of scrubbing and washing were, for the most part, done on Saturday afternoons.[71] However, as the above evidence demonstrates, not all women could afford to take even this time off at week-ends for household chores. Time not spent on sewing, for example, could not be exclusively devoted to household duties. Those without children had to collect and return the work themselves. Even in towns where women generally lived fairly close to the factory office this could take up an hour or more every day. In rural districts, Miss Squires found that it was not uncommon for women to walk a fourteen to eighteen mile round journey to their agent.[72]

For the poorest workers, even a day's illness was not affordable.[73] Many women continued to work at sewing and embroidery when they had sore eyes and failing sight, even though they knew the work had not only ruined their health but would continue to make it worse. Some like Mrs. L. were fortunate in that when her sight had almost 'given up on her' and her 'constitution got run down' she was able to find a job working as a charwoman.[74] However, because she had to support her children and a sickly husband she had been unable to resign when her health began to fail. Nor was she able to reduce her heavy workload. On the contrary, she had been compelled to work long hours into the night to sustain the family.[75] Her case is illustrative of the thousands of women who suffered ill-health and were unable to get additional support from family or charity. All too often sickness or physical disability meant that more hours had to be worked to compensate for the reduced rate of output. Only when their children grew up could these women relax.

These homeworkers worked out of financial necessity. Although small, their earnings were absolutely essential to obtain the basic necessities of food and shelter. The economic pressures of work prevented a domestic ideology from dominating their daily lives in the same way as that of the middle classes. Despite this, the evidence suggests that they did derive at least part of their identity from their domestic and familial role. Many of the women appear anxious to stress their attention to meal preparation and other household duties. At the same time they often expressed pride in their economic role. Most women were anxious to emphasise that the family simply could not have existed without their work. If the work was cruel and hard on them and their children, they had no alternative but to keep working, otherwise the family would have been destitute. Women would have perceived this as a failure in their role as mothers and carers of their children. Mrs. J., for instance, who worked herself and her children seven days a week, expressed pride that her work kept the family from being maintained by charity. As she was receiving assistance with the rent she wanted to prove that she was doing what she could, 'so it is not all charity'.[76] From the perspective of married homeworkers, status and pride was obtained from working. In contrast to middle-class ideology, work, pride and being a good wife and mother were to a large extent interrelated.

A small section of homeworkers were drawn from the ranks of a relatively higher social stratum: women from a 'better class' who were not compelled to work out of the the same financial necessity as their poorer counterparts. It was claimed that women in Class D generally worked to add to their comforts and to maintain a better standard of living or to have money which was their own and which they could spend or save as they wished.[77] Because they did not work out of financial necessity some historians and contemporaries have assumed that their work experience, and their concep-tualisation of their economic role, was distinctly different. It is argued that they not only worked considerably fewer hours in the day but also on a much more irregular basis. This projects an image of women working at a more leisurely pace, stopping and restarting their waged work in a somewhat casual manner. Thus Cohen suggests that their waged work was done when and if it could be fitted in and around their housework.[78] Closely connected to this argument is the view that these women derived their identity from their domestic role.[79] Waged work was secondary and peripheral to their lives having little or no impact on their status or identity.

Attempting to assess the extent to which women divided their time between waged work and housework is fraught with difficulties. Not all the responses from women were as detailed as those given to the 1911 linen inquiry. The middle-class investigators assumed that women would be able to state clearly the number of hours generally allocated to domestic work, waged work and leisure. However, the responses from many women were 'exceedingly vague' as to the division of their day. While some women could give a rough idea of the time spent on housework, many others were less forthcom-ing. Miss Collet complained of the extent to which women stated that they 'sat constantly', or 'more or less constantly', without any attempt to define what that meant.[80]

What can be deduced from the evidence, however, is that these women generally began waged work about eight or nine in the morning. Like their poorer counterparts, they usually continued to do waged work until ten or eleven o'clock at night. It would appear, however, that some women may have taken more time off during the day to cook and clean, or at least slightly longer breaks at meal times. It is necessary to stress, however, that these breaks were not substantial: at most five or six hours out of an estimated fourteen or fifteen hour working day.[81]

Work was still central in the sense that it took up the greatest part of their day. The evidence suggests that work was, for the most part, performed on a regular basis throughout the year.[82] Nevertheless, whenever these women were employed they also had to work long hours to earn a decent wage. One of the most obvious reasons for this was the low hourly pay rates of 1d. to 2d., and even these low rates were only possible if work was carried out at a fast pace. Women working for a few hours a day and at a less sustained pace would only have earned about 1s. to 2s. per week. Investigators found that in most instances where women's wages were low it was not as a result of intermittent and casual labour by the women, but because of abominably low piece-rates, lack of work, or because of a disability.[83] Secondly, it was standard practice, irrespective of the industry, for the distributor to set a time and a date for the return of the work.[84] In country districts work was usually collected once or twice a week; in towns, work was often collected on a daily basis and had to be returned early the next morning. Homework and factory production were closely interdependent and late deliveries from the domestic producers often meant that workers in the factory were slack or idle. The fining system was a way of ensuring women returned their work on time.

Rushed orders, common to the linen and cotton trades, enforced additional pressure on women and agents to meet deadlines. The amount of rushed orders varied; they could be handed out two or three times a week and then maybe not for three months. The pressure of such a system on agents and homeworkers is clear. It was reported that the towns and villages were filled with women who sat up late into the night, in order to meet the dispatch of these orders by steamer to America. Agents who could command the greatest number of women prepared to work late into the night had the best chance of securing large orders from the factories.[85] As they received a ten per cent commission it was in their best interests to secure women they could rely on. Women who gave housework priority over their homework would not be considered for regular work and in many cases were taken off the books altogether. One agent stated that for ten years he had adopted a policy of terminating the employment of women he considered to be bad workers.[86] Within the pressurised nature of homework there was still some room for women to take out small amounts of work and earn a few pence a day. While others worked only when their husband's income was reduced, the evidence suggests that they comprised only a small minority of homeworkers.

It is generally accepted that the poorest women were motivated to work out of financial necessity. However, it is seldom considered that the 'better off' sections of homeworkers could have been equally motivated by necessity. Historians have tended to uncritically apply an absolute definition of 'financial necessity' to their analysis of women's work. From this perspective the wage of 'better off' women was 'pin money' and as it was not essential, these women were unlikely to be motivated to work long hours. What has been overlooked is that 'necessity' was a relative term. The definition varied from person to person and from one social group to another.[87] For some women it was essential to work to maintain the outward symbols of respectability which differentiated them from lower social groups. There were a wide variety of occupational subdivisions within the working classes, each with its own distinct notions of status. Thus many upper working-class females saw it as a necessity to have a better standard of dress and housing than the poorest sections of society. Other women felt more money was essential to avoid debt or provide a better education for their children.[88]

It was clearly important for people to maintain a particular social status. For example, one woman lived with her widowed father, his means being sufficient to maintain a decent standard of living. She worked to have money of her own and 'to keep both the house and herself in a respectable appearance and clean beyond reproach', and in the words of another woman, 'to keep yourself respectable and your family as it should be'.[89] Hence those women who wanted to maintain a certain standard of housing and appearance were prepared to work to obtain it. Consequently, although women in better economic circumstances informed investigators that they would have preferred to give up their waged work, they also were extremely reluctant to relinquish waged work and the benefits it brought. While some displayed a degree of shame regarding their waged work, others were proud of their economic contribution to the family.[90]

Often the poorest homeworkers had little or no alternative but to work. Women in better economic circumstances did have an alternative as they could have tolerated a reduced standard of living. In actively choosing employment, their work was a positive response to their social and economic situation. In contrast to the perception of their work as 'reprehensible', it was a means they adopted to attain or maintain respectability. Unlike social observers and historians, they did not necessarily see their work role and their domestic role in any contradictory way. They saw themselves as better mothers because they worked and were able, therefore, to provide a better standard of life for themselves and their family. Hence women tended to emphasise the fact that without their work the family would be worse off economically and socially.[91]

Homework is of the greatest importance because it demonstrates the acceptance of work beyond the narrow confines of lower working-class districts. Even amongst the skilled working classes and small tradespeople, waged work, marriage and respectability were not mutually exclusive. Thus, the traditional view that the skilled working classes internalised in an unmodified form the values of upper and middle-class society has to be challenged.[92] On the one hand, their identity was to a large extent located in the feminine virtues of home and family. On the other hand, they rejected the norms of behaviour on work and in so doing constructed their own cultural values which attached importance and status to waged work. As with the lower working classes, their ideologies and values were frequently altered in response to economic pressures.

VI

As an exhausting and time-consuming occupation homework left little individual time for domestic or farm duties. The burden of a woman's double responsibilities was undoubtedly increased by the fact that the home was also the workshop. This meant that small houses, already cramped and overcrowded, were littered with parcels of work, sheets, wool or whatever material was being worked on. The greater the number of homeworkers, the greater the volume of work and subsequent litter and confusion. One of the worst problems was the paper with which large valances and other items were stuffed. This all had to be removed before work could begin, hence floors were often strewn with paper.[93]

Other tasks such as thread-drawing created their own extra work load. Thread-drawing could be done more speedily if linen was dampened. Hence it was common for the cloth to be wet with a mixture of tallow and water, thus softening it. After thread-drawing was completed the handkerchiefs, tablecloths and sheets were hung on lines in the kitchen or scullery to dry. These then had to be taken down, folded and parcelled for return to the agent.[94] All this not only added to the workload of women, but also increased the untidy appearance of the houses and reduced the living space for the family.

Two ways in which women managed their excessive workload was by utilising the labour of elderly and young family members and by making co-operation a fundamental principle of their labour. One of the main features of the evidence is the extensive use of child labour which prevailed throughout the period. It would appear that wherever homework was established, the use of child labour from the ages of six and seven years of age was commonplace. Systematic investigations found that boys and girls often worked before and after school until late into the night.

In the districts of Lurgan, Portadown and Dromore the employment of mothers and children in the home was extensive. Mr. McCaffrey, district inspector for national schools, reported that children generally worked before and after school in Lurgan and the surrounding districts, chiefly at thread-drawing and clipping. As in other areas, some children were also kept off school two or three days a week to work. He described the common scene of women and children crowded around a table in the middle of a small kitchen drawing threads and hem-stitching until late into the night.[95]

The use of boys as well as girls in homework appears to have been fairly common. Until the age of about thirteen, homework was often performed by both sexes. The need to earn a few extra pence overrode any notions of what was 'girl's work' or 'boy's work'. Children assisted in whatever way they could. If they could not sew, embroider or knit they could still be used for a multitude of other tasks. They could carry work to and from the distribution centre, clip and fold or prepare work to be sewed on machine, to name but a few.[96] As in the case of Mrs. C., children could sometimes add two or three shillings to a week's wage. Often they worked long hours to earn a few extra pence themselves or to enable their mothers to do so. Sewing-machine work had many preparatory hand stages, such as the folding-in of straps and tucking-in of corners. By getting their children to do this work, mothers were able to work continuously at the machine and increase their total earnings.

Children's earnings were incorporated into the wages of their mothers or older sisters. Due to the nature of their assistance it would undoubtedly have been impossible in many instances to even estimate the actual value of their work. Because of the excessive use of children it is impossible to discuss the work experience of women, especially mothers, without reference to their contribution. Moreover, children's labour points to the existence of a family based system of labour and a collective wage.

One of the most significant factors of homework in Ulster

was the extent to which adult women co-operated over the production of goods and the very low percentage of women who worked alone. The lady inspectors visited approximately 1,700 homes in London, the provinces and Northern Ireland for the 1907 select committee on homework. Out of 737 homes visited in rural areas and small urban districts throughout counties Down, Londonderry, Tyrone and east Donegal, only 27 per cent of women were found to be working alone. This contrasted sharply with 69 per cent in London and 75 per cent in the provinces.[97] The percentage of women working alone in Ulster would undoubtedly have been reduced further if the labour of children had been taken into account.

It was common for two, three and sometimes more members of the family to be homeworkers and these women normally co-operated closely with each other with regard to both their paid and unpaid labour. The evidence suggests that mothers and daughters, grandmothers, aunts and nieces formed a sort of combined work unit. The common practice was for one member of a family to register with an agent and collect and return the work for several members of the household. When the completed work was returned payment was based on the total output of the household. This practice applied whether or not the members of the household were performing the same or different tasks at different piece-rates.[98]

Within this system of payment it was still possible for each person to estimate their own particular output and earnings. The lady inspectors found that in households where several members worked, little or no attempt was made to estimate how much each person earned. In the majority of cases they found it extremely difficult to obtain even a rough estimate of individual weekly earnings. Indeed, the problem was so extensive that the inspectors were forced to base their approximation of earnings on women who worked alone.[99] Wage differences certainly existed between individuals within each household. Some women would have been working on much higher paid work, while some were capable of greater output than others, but the fact that so many women made little or no attempt to ascertain their individual wage, strongly suggests that wage differences between individuals were not regarded as a problem. Distinctions were not made between the wages of each person because the important issue was the family's total wage.

Homework output varied according to the different levels of ability of family members. The elderly, those disabled by poor eyesight, rheumatism or some other form of ill-health, could not produce work at the same rate as the skilled, fit worker. By being flexible a family was able to maximise output. Homework lent itself well to this flexible work approach. Many tasks were simple, easily learnt and suited to the young and the elderly. Hence they could be sub-divided and allocated according to the abilities of individuals. For instance, children, the elderly or the physically disadvantaged could perform tasks of clipping, thread-drawing and preparatory hand work for sewing machines.

Another method of maximising production was to divide a larger task into its smaller parts. Co-operation over tasks was particularly beneficial where women were disadvantaged by age or ill-health. Miss I., for instance, lived with her niece and both women worked at lace clipping and top-sewing from nine in the morning until eleven at night. As the niece had much better eyesight, she did all the finer work while her aunt did the coarser work. However, because the niece was not very strong, the aunt carried the work to and from the distributor.[100] In slower months they could only earn 5s. or 6s. between them, but when the work was plentiful the niece was able to earn more than the aunt. It seems they pooled their wages and the aunt's pension and shared the costs of rent and food.[101] The mutual advantages of co-operating in this way are obvious. On her own, the niece would have had great difficulty obtaining work and the inability of the aunt to do fine work would have reduced her income. As in many similar cases the paramount issue was the need to earn as much as possible in order to survive or maintain a certain standard of living. Widows and unmarried women benefited greatly from living with female relatives or sharing the costs of rent, food and heating because a subsistence wage was paid to most homeworkers.

The same co-operation and flexible approach to labour is

evident with regard to the allocation of household and farm tasks. On the small farms and holdings women still performed a multitude of tasks including care of poultry, pigs, milking, dairying, planting and lifting potatoes, cutting and carrying turf and assisting during the main harvests.[102] In some families one or two women devoted themselves almost entirely to sewing or embroidery and the rest were employed mainly on farm and household duties. In other families the women spent part of their time attending to tasks on the farm and working in the fields, the priority allocated to each task obviously varied according to the needs of the household.[103] In peak harvest seasons more time would have been allocated to field labour. In districts such as the Rosses and Glenties the majority of men worked as migratory labourers in the Scottish and English harvests, leaving women to manage all the necessary work on the family smallholding. As a result of their added outdoor tasks, agents expected a drop in the homework output of women during the summer months.[104]

Similarly, in urban areas, women tended to adopt the arrangement which best suited their own particular circumstances. It was reported that when a mother or sister was allocated the main household tasks the others concentrated on homework throughout the day. Meals were often their only break. Such a division of labour allowed the family to increase its earnings.[105] The women who focused primarily on cooking and cleaning made an indirect contribution to the earnings of the household. Moreover, the evidence also shows that there was an overlap of duties between the women of a given household. Those who concentrated on waged work also helped with the heavier domestic tasks, like washing, when they had spare time. Likewise, the women who focused on household chores often helped with the parcelling or folding aspects of homework.[106]

VII

The experience of homeworkers was strikingly different from that of factory workers. Their work was not marked by a clear separation between home and work and the wage was often earned collectively. The hours of the clock did not define the beginning and end of the working day. Consequently, their daily lives were not lived in separate compartments of waged work, domestic work and leisure. Homework was an industry which had a great deal of continuity with the pre-industrial past where work was performed in the home, largely on a collective basis, and all members of the family contributed what they could to the economy of the household.

Homework was for the most part sweated labour with women being compelled to work long hours for low wages. Moreover, the system of truck in Ireland tended to place women very much at the mercy of agents. Only in trade booms, such as the early 1900s, were women able to exercise any choice as to the type and class of work they performed. Homework was an important part of the economic infrastructure of Ulster, particularly in rural districts. It injected cash into districts and stimulated growth. Money was, for the most part, spent within the locality, the purchase of groceries and other household goods stimulating the growth of small agent/shopkeepers and raising the general living standard of the community.

The evidence shows that waged work remained a central feature of the lives of many working-class women. Very importantly, the wages of wives and children remained essential for the survival of the family. We should not allow twentieth century conceptions of 'real work' or a 'real wage' to detract from the economic importance of homework industries to both women and manufacturers. Homework was at times erratic, but it was waged work and as such should not be excluded from studies of the labour market.

[1] *Committee of inquiry into the conditions of employment in the linen and other making-up trades in the north of Ireland.* Report and evidence, p. vi, H.C. 1912–13, [Cd. 6509], xxxiv, p. 365. Hereafter *Inquiry into the linen making-up trades.*

[2] Marilyn Cohen, 'Working conditions and experiences of work in the linen industry: Tullylish, County Down' in *Ulster Folklife* 30 (1984), p. 15.

[3] *Inquiry into the linen making up-trades,* p. v. Similar references to 'pin money' can be found in the *Report of the select committee on homework, together with the proceedings of the committee, minutes of evidence, and appendix,*

pp 1–232, H.C. 1907, (290), vi. Hereafter cited as *Report of the Select committee on homework* 1907.

[4] *Inquiry into the linen making-up trades,* p. vi, qq 5176, 5254–55.

[5] *Minutes of evidence taken before the truck committee* vol. iii – minutes of evidence (days 38–66) and index, p. 249, H.C. 1908 [Cd. 4444], lix, p. 533. Hereafter cited as *Evidence, truck committee* 1908, vol. iii.

[6] *Inquiry into the linen making-up trades,* p. xviii, qq 450-54, 1117–19, 1204-10, 1890-93.

[7] *Evidence, truck committee* 1908, vol. iii, p. 249.

[8] *Minutes of evidence taken before the truck committee,* vol. ii, minutes of evidence (days 1–37), q. 1713. H.C. 1908 [Cd. 4443], lix, p. 147. Hereafter cited as *Evidence, truck committee* 1908, vol. ii.

[9] *Copy of the report of the board of trade on the sweating system in the East End of London by the labour correspondent of the board,* pp 5-6, H.C. 1887 (331), lxxxix, p. 253. See also Shelley Pennington and Belinda Westover, *A hidden workforce: homeworkers in England, 1850–1985* (London, 1989), pp 82–7.

[10] *Fourth report from the select committee of the House of Lords; together with the proceedings of the committee, minutes of evidence, and appendix,* qq 26648–49, H.C. 1889 (331), xiv, pt. I, p. 1.

[11] For the different types of homework performed by women see Pennington and Westover, *Hidden workforce,* pp 44–70.

[12] Ibid., p. 34.

[13] *Inquiry into linen making-up trades,* pp v-vi.

[14] *Irish rural life and industry, Irish international exhibition: home industries section* (Dublin, 1907), pp 128–40.

[15] *Report of the chief inspector of factories and workshops to her majesty's principal secretary of state for the home department, for the year ending 31 Oct. 1885,* p. 6, H.C. 1886 [Cd. 4702], xiv, p. 797; *Report of the chief inspector of factories and workshops to her majesty's principal secretary of state for the home department, for the year ending 31 Oct.1887,* p. 23, H.C. 1888 [Cd. 5328], xxvi, p. 395.

[16] Jennifer Grew, 'The Derry shirt industry, 1831-1913', unpub. M.Phil. diss., University of Ulster (1988), pp 112–14.

[17] *Children's employment commission,1862.* Second report of the commissioners with appendix, pp 59–61, H.C. 1864 [Cd. 3414], xxii in Irish University Press series, *Industrial Revolution: children's employment,* vol. 14 (1864). Hereafter cited as *Second report of the children's employment commission.*

[18] Grew, *Derry ,* pp 105–6, 189.

[19] Ibid., pp 105–6 and *Report of select committee on homework* 1907, q. 680.

[20] Pennington and Westover, *Hidden workforce,* p. 35.

[21] Ibid., pp 32–9.

[22] *Inquiry into the linen making-up trades,* qq 324-33.

[23] Ibid., p. vi.

[24] *Second report of the children's employment commission,* pp 58–9.

[25] *Report of the chief inspector of factories and workshops to her majesty's principal secretary of state for the home department, for the year ending 31 Oct.1888,* p. 146, H.C. 1889 [Cd. 5697], xvii, p. 359.

[26] *Report of the select committee on homework 1907,* qq 655–57.

[27] *Royal commission on labour. The employment of women: reports by Miss Eliza Orme, Miss Clara E. Collett, Miss Mary E. Abraham and Miss Margaret Irwin (lady assistant commissioners), on the conditions in various industries in England, Wales, Scotland and Ireland,* p. 34, H.C. 1893–4 [Cd. 6894–xxiii], xxiii, pt. I, p. 845.

[28] For the interdependence between large centralised industries and home-work in Ireland see W.H. Crawford, *Industries of Ireland one hundred years ago: industrial and commercial life in the north of Ireland, 1888–91* (Belfast, 1986). For England see James A. Schmiechen, *Sweated industries and sweated labour: the London clothing trades, 1860–1914* (London, 1984), pp 24–44.

[29] *Inquiry into the linen making-up trades,* qq 324–33.

[30] Schmiechen, *Sweated ,* p. 34.

[31] *Evidence, truck committee 1908,* vol. iii, p. 248.

[32] *Inquiry into the linen making-up trades,* p. v.

[33] Ibid., p. vi; Grew, *Derry ,* pp 67–76.

[34] *Census of Ireland 1901.* Pt. I. Area, houses and population: also the ages, civil or conjugal condition, occupation, birthplaces, religion and education of the people. Vol. iii. Province of Ulster, no. 4. Co. Donegal, pp 90, 103, H.C. 1902 [Cd. 1123-iii], cxxvi, p. 503; Census 1901. Vol. iii. Province of Ulster, no. 7. County and city of Londonderry, pp 50, 52, 65, 78, H.C. 1902 [Cd. 1123–vi], cxvii, p. 325.

[35] Grew, *Derry,* p. 140.

[36] Ibid., pp 151, 186.

[37] *Report of the chief inspector of factories 1887,* p. 23, H.C. 1888 [Cd. 5328], xxvi, p. 395.

[38] *Evidence, truck committee 1908,* vol. iii, p. 248.

[39] *Irish rural life and industry,* pp 142–56.

[40] *Seventh report of the Congested Districts Board for Ireland, of proceedings under the Congested Districts Board (Ireland) Acts, 1891–1896* (54 & 55 Vic., ch. 48, sec. 41), pp 33–4 H.C. 1898, [Cd. 9003], lxxii, p. 481.

[41] *Evidence, truck committee 1908,* vol. iii, q. 17,735.

[42] James Brennan, 'The modern Irish lace industry' in W. P. Coyne (ed.), *Ireland industrial and agricultural* (Dublin, 1902), pp 433–35; see the *Reports of the Congested District Board for Ireland* for an account of the establishment of industrial classes.

[43] *Inquiry into the linen making-up trades,* p. xix.

[44] Ibid., p. v.

[45] Schmiechen, *Sweated,* pp 37–44; Elizabeth Roberts, *Women's work, 1840–1940* (London, 1988), pp 11–21.

[46] *Evidence, truck committee 1908,* vol. iii, pp 2848–49; *Royal commission on labour: the employment of women. Miss Orme and Miss Abraham's report on the condition of women in Ireland,* pp 327–28.

47 *Royal commission on labour,* ibid.

48 *Evidence, truck committee* 1908, vol. iii, p. 248.

49 Ibid., qq 15648–62, 15676–82, 15747–53.

50 *Census of Ireland 1901,* pp 102–3. For a discussion of the under-representation of women's work in the census see Roberts, *Women's,* pp 18, 20–1, 40–1 and Schmiechen, *Sweated,* pp 48, 68–9.

51 *Inquiry into the linen making-up trades,* p. v.

52 Clemintina Black (ed.), *Married women's work: being the report of an inquiry undertaken by the Women's Industrial Council (incorporated)* (London, 1915), p. 7.

53 *Inquiry into the linen making-up trades,* p. v.

54 *Report of the select committee on homework* 1907, q. 748.

55 *Inquiry into the linen making-up trades,* qq 1653–55.

56 Wanda Neff, *Victorian working women: an historical and literary study of women in British industries and professions* (London, 1929), pp 129–33.

57 *Children's employment commission,* 1862. Fifth report of the commissioners, with appendix, pp 189, 191, 194, H.C. 1866 [Cd. 3678], xxiv, p. 1. Testimony from employers and workers shows the prejudice and hostility against the 'mere scum' of the factory girls.

58 For an example of the better paid work see *Inquiry into the linen making-up trades,* qq 4072–4114, 4343–69.

59 Ibid., qq 2524–72.

60 Ibid., qq 1748–87.

61 Ibid., q. 1787.

62 Ibid., qq 1845–68.

63 Ibid., qq 1867–84.

64 Ibid., qq 4253–58.

65 Ibid., pp 29-30, case 24.

66 For the poverty of many families see *Report of the interdepartmental committee on the employment of children during school age, especially in street trading in the large centres of population in Ireland, appointed by his excellency the Lord Lieutenant of Ireland, together with minutes of evidence and appendices,* H.C. 1902 [Cd. 1144], xlix, p. 209.

67 Schmiechen, *Sweated,* pp 70–1.

68 *Inquiry into the linen making-up trades,* p. xviii; *Evidence, truck committee* 1908, vol. ii, pp 80–2; vol. iii, pp 250–53.

69 Hilda Martindale, *From one generation to another, 1839–1944: a book of memories* (London, 1945), pp 130–31.

70 Black, *Married,* p. 3.

71 *Inquiry into the linen making-up trades,* p. 30, case 121.

72 *Evidence, truck committee* 1908, vol. ii, q. 1697 and vol. iii, p. 249.

73 Black, *Married,* p. 3.

74 *Inquiry into the linen making-up trades,* qq 1956–80.

75 Ibid.

76 Ibid., qq 1867–68.

[77] Black, *Married*, p. 7.

[78] Cohen, *Working*, p. 15.

[79] See Roberts, *Women's*, pp 72–3.

[80] *Report of the select committee on homework* 1907, q. 660; *Evidence, truck committee* 1908, vol. iii, p. 249.

[81] See *Inquiry into the linen making-up trades*.

[82] The majority of women would appear to have worked throughout the year. When they did not it was usually because of a shortage of homework or because of other farm duties during harvest.

[83] See Clemintina Black, *Sweated industry and the minimum wage* (London, 1907).

[84] This system applied to homework in England, Scotland and Ireland.

[85] *Inquiry into the linen making-up trades*, qq 325–27.

[86] *Evidence, truck committee* 1908, vol. ii, q. 4406.

[87] The relative nature of 'necessity' was a factor which struck Black in her investigations.

[88] Black, *Married*, p. 7.

[89] Ibid., p. 113.

[90] Ibid., p. 7.

[91] Ibid., pp 7, 13.

[92] For an account of domestic ideology see Roberts, *Women's*, pp 11–18; Joanna Bourke, 'The best of all home rulers: the economic power of women in Ireland' in *Irish Economic and Social History*, xviii (1991), pp 34–47. Bourke supports the idea that the lives of women, including the working classes, were dominated by the concept of domesticity.

[93] *Inquiry into the linen making-up trades*, qq 1748–54.

[94] Ibid., qq 2111–13.

[95] Ibid., p. 125, qq 4100–7.

[96] The evidence of both the mothers and the social investigators to the linen inquiry clearly shows that the labour of children was commonplace.

[97] *Select committee on homework* 1907, q. 648.

[98] Ibid., qq 655–56.

[99] Ibid., qq 656–57, 829.

[100] *Inquiry into the linen making-up trades*, qq 1803–33.

[101] Ibid.

[102] For a description of the work of women on farms, especially smallholdings, see *Reports of the Congested Districts Board*.

[103] *Inquiry into the linen making-up trades*, p. v.

[104] *Tenth report of the Congested Districts Board for Ireland, of proceedings under the Congested Districts Board (Ireland) Acts, 1891–99, for the year ending 31 Mar. 1901*, p. 44, H.C. 1902 [Cd. 681], lx, p. 1.

[105] *Inquiry into the linen making-up trades*, qq 277–80, 319–23.

[106] Ibid., qq 4348–67.

'OPENING THE GATES OF LEARNING': THE BELFAST LADIES' INSTITUTE, 1867–97[1]

ALISON JORDAN

I

The growth of towns and cities in Britain throughout the nineteenth century has been well documented, as have the social developments of this time. One such development was the provision of public, organised education for both sexes of the lower and middle classes. During the 1850s and 1860s there was increasing interest in the question of higher education for women in England and Ireland. In Ireland there were several reasons for this. A system of national (that is primary) education supported by government funds had been established in Ireland from 1831. National schools operated in all parts of the country providing free elementary education in even the most remote villages. This system provided equitable education for both girls and boys, primarily from the lower classes.

In the nineteenth century intelligent and interested middle-class women were growing increasingly concerned by the lack of serious education for girls and were determined to press for a remedy. Throughout Ireland there were endowed schools for middle-class boys. These schools, such as the Royal Belfast Academical Institution and the Royal schools in Armagh and Dungannon, bridged the gap between primary and university education for boys. However their sisters were much more limited in their educational opportunities.

The nineteenth century was a time of rapid and wide-spread urbanisation. When a woman remained single, a family business declined or the male head of household died, the city based family, including its women, had to find paid work to support themselves. Girls who had little or no formal education could not compete successfully in the search for 'respectable' jobs. In addition, even those who had attended seminaries for young ladies had no proof of their academic achievement as there were no public examinations. Women who had left school and had not secured a formal occupation often wished to continue their education. This desire was prompted because women wanted not only to occupy their time, but also to expand their knowledge.

This situation provided an impetus for the foundation of the Ladies' Institute in Belfast in 1867. Similar institutions already existed in the cities of Great Britain and in the two large conurbations in Ireland, Dublin and Belfast. Dublin expanded only slightly in the nineteenth century, but Belfast followed the same pattern of industrialisation as cities like Manchester and Glasgow. Belfast was a rapidly developing port, market town and commercial centre with expanding numbers of middle classes. Indeed, Belfast grew at a faster rate than any other British city, having a population of less than 20,000 in 1800 which had increased to 349,000 by 1900.[2]

The six enthusiastic women who founded the Ladies' Institute were Mrs. Bushell, Mrs. McIlwaine, Mrs. J. Scott Porter, Mrs. Duffin, Miss Stevelly and Miss Cunningham. They all came from prominent and prosperous local families who supported the idea of higher education for women. For example, Mr. Bushell was a stockbroker and wine and spirit merchant, Rev. William McIlwaine was rector of St. George's, High Street, Belfast, Rev. J. Scott Porter was the minister of Second Presbyterian Church, Belfast (Unitarian), Mr. Duffin owned a flax spinning mill, and Professor Stevelly was a lecturer at Queen's College, Belfast.[3] The same class of women remained the leading figures in the institute throughout its existence. Many held the position of lady superintendent for years, indeed Mrs. Duffin was still on the committee at the last meeting in 1897. However, this was exceptional service, as it was usual for women to hold office for a shorter time. For instance, some women had to resign when their husbands left Belfast, as Professor Thomson did in July 1873[4], Mrs. J.J. Murphy had to resign as she could not manage to attend meetings in March 1878[5], while others merely lost interest. The ordinary members of the institute were also largely middle-class, being the wives and daughters of clergymen, insurance agents, distillers and textile manufacturers.

II

The Belfast Ladies' Institute's declared objective was essentially 'to provide advanced classes for ladies of a higher class than hitherto attempted in the neighbourhood'.[6] This experiment in education was an ambitious attempt to broaden the opportunities for local young women. The institute aimed to employ professors of Queen's College, Belfast[7] and offer a high standard of teaching. Moreover they planned to hold tests at the end of each session to provide proof of women's academic achievement. The Ladies' Institute was efficiently organised with elected officers and members.[8] In an attempt to stimulate interest in the project, Hariot, Marchioness of Dufferin and Ava, was chosen as president and Ladies Lurgan, Adair, Annesley and Cairns were invited to be vice-presidents.[9] Inviting Lady Dufferin to accept the presidency, the lady superintendents outlined the development of the institute, 'so as to admit the co-operation of all ladies in Ulster who were interested in the subject'.[10] Any lady could become a member on the payment of a minimum of 5 shillings[11], provided she was proposed, seconded and accepted by two-thirds of those present at the institute's meetings. There were originally six lady superintendents, whose numbers rose to eight in 1870 and eventually to ten in 1871. These officials were expected to be present at all meetings of the institute, both committee and general, which were held monthly. It was estimated that there were approximately seven committee meetings held over a period of six months. Committee meetings were often held in the homes of the institute's lady superintendents, like Mrs. Porter's in College

Square East, Mrs. Burden's at College Square North, Miss Isabella Tod's at Claremont Street or Mrs. Duffin's at Strandtown Lodge.

In spite of the prevailing feminist spirit of the society, their treasurer was always male and the organisation did rely on men to preside at open meetings, as it was almost unheard of for women to take such a public role at this time. In 1870, for example, Lord Dufferin was asked to take the chair at a meeting of the institute. Invitations were sent to the Bishop of Down, Connor and Dromore, the mayor of Belfast, the professors of QCB and to other prominent businessmen. Indeed the support of Belfast's business and professional community was a vital ingredient in the success of the Ladies' Institute. The ladies were also very appreciative of the support they received from the president of QCB who delivered the inaugural address of the institute in 1870 and offered to prepare a pamphlet on the 'Higher Education Of Women'.[12]

It was essential to secure suitable premises both for the institute's committee meetings and classes. Such accommodation was difficult to find in Belfast. The museum in College Square North, owned by the Belfast Natural History and Philosophical Society,[13] was the favoured venue of the institute. Indeed the BNHPS proved very helpful to the Ladies' Institute, as the museum was often made available free of charge.[14] The Ladies' Institute lectures were normally held on two days per week for two hours on Monday and Thursday afternoons. At one time a room was allocated for the ladies' 'disrobing' in the museum. However it was decided that this was unnecessary and that the hall would be sufficient.

During the first session in 1867–68 five subjects were offered to the 187 students enrolled.[15] Professor Nesbitt taught English language and literature, Professor Thomson took physical geography, Rev. Dr. J.S. Porter taught politics and historical geography, Mr. Wild took French language and literature and Dr. Hodges taught economic science.

It must have been difficult to hold scientific classes in a building not specifically designed for this purpose. Indeed, William Darragh, the institute's porter, was given a substantial bonus of £1 for 'the trouble connected with the chemistry classes'.[16] Cookery classes were also hard to accommodate. In 1873 the secretary was deputed to enquire about the use of the Music Hall in May Street, Belfast, however it was decided that the Minor Hall of the Ulster Hall was best suited for this purpose.[17] With regards to art tuition, it was hoped that lectures could be held in the Government School of Art, housed in the north wing of the Royal Belfast Academical Institution. In some cases the subjects offered for classes depended on the availability of lecturers, their willingness to teach, and the popularity of specific courses. The lady superintendents were eager to have a wide range of topics, interestingly, often with a scientific bias. A survey of proposed courses over the years shows this clearly. The main standby of the Ladies' Institute, 1867–97, was English language and literature. This was traditionally the most popular area of women's interest and these classes were always fully subscribed. Other regular offerings were English history, German and French language and literature, Latin and botany. It was proposed that these educational staples should be supplemented with lectures in astronomy, numerology, physiology, theory of music, chemistry and zoology. Not all of these suggestions materialised. It was not possible to run classes in geometry in 1872[18] and the theory and practice of arithmetic in 1876[19], as insufficient numbers of girls were interested. Local physicians, Dr. Redfern, Prof. Cummings and Dr. Browne were asked to consider giving talks on the laws of health but this topic was not pursued. Given the low level of educational standards for women in the mid-nineteenth century it is understandable that the Ladies' Institute should try to lift the intellectual aspirations of their students. However it is difficult to see any practical advantage of some subjects. If the intention was to provide extra skills to facilitate female employment, numerology and astronomy would appear to have little application, except, of course, for teaching. These were not usual topics of study in a ladies' seminary. It was more likely that in offering these subjects the organisers wanted to destroy the common perception that young ladies could only expect to acquire the ability to play a little, sing a little, do some painting on satin or velvet and appear to advantage at a concert or ball.[20]

Disappointingly, the Ladies' Institute had to rely on men to teach the academic classes, for there simply were insufficient educated women in Belfast to undertake such a programme of slightly esoteric subjects at a sufficiently high level. This very factor highlighted the deep need for the actual existence of the institute and for its development. Most of the lecturers were professors at QCB or local personalities in science or the arts. For example, Professor Younger of Nottinghill was a regular contributor to the English history programme while Dr. Andrews, vice-president of QCB, taught chemistry classes, Dr. Hodges of the Chemico-Agricultural Society lectured in the session 1867–68 and Mr. Nixon was clearly a man of many talents, being capable of teaching both arithmetic and English classes. One important teacher was Dr. Wyville Thomson, the eminent zoologist. Thomson was knighted in 1876 and was professor of mineralogy, geology and natural history and later the scientific head of the 'Challenger' expedition which conducted deep sea diving explorations. Thomson was a firm supporter of the Ladies' Institute.[21] Another notable was the Belfast naturalist, Robert Patterson, who gave papers on zoology to the institute from 1870 until his death in 1872.[22]

There were two other courses of a less academic nature, cookery and art. These subjects attracted substantial numbers of female students. The only classes run by a woman were, perhaps not surprisingly, cookery lectures. These were conducted by Mrs. Price, the holder of a certificate from the Government School of Science and Art at Kensington. Mrs. Price was also employed at the Ladies' Collegiate school.[23]

III

The examinations which professors held for the institute may have been proof of academic achievement, but they possessed only limited recognition. Girls holding these end of session certificates found that they were not widely accepted outside Belfast or Ulster. As a result the lady superintendents realised that their classes required official recognition if they were to be of real value to their students. Therefore, at a meeting in 1869, the committee, with the addition of Professor Nesbitt and Professor Wyville Thomson, resolved to hold a general meeting of all the ladies associated with the enterprise. The purpose of this gathering was to draw up a memorial to be forwarded to the senate of the Queen's University of Ireland[24] asking that examinations for women be instituted. The ladies were encouraged in this endeavour as Cambridge University and Trinity College Dublin had already drawn up plans for such tests. Indeed it was pressure from leading girls' school principals, such as Miss Frances Buss of the North London Collegiate school and Miss Dorothea Beale of Cheltenham Ladies' College, which helped to persuade Cambridge to. open the higher local examinations to girls in 1868.[25]

Mrs. Margaret Byers, principal of the Ladies' Collegiate school in Belfast had tried previously, without success, to persuade Cambridge to open an examination centre in Belfast where her pupils could sit for the examinations. The Cambridge university authorities believed that Belfast was too far from Cambridge to make this feasible.[26] A similar petition had also been sent to Trinity College Dublin. However the ladies of the institute really desired QCB, one of the three constituent colleges of the Queen's University of Ireland[27], to establish examinations, as this would be most convenient for their students. The ladies knew and accepted the fact that girls would only be awarded certificates, not degrees, as this was the practice in other universities. However they were still enthusiastic that the tests should be held. The memorial from the institute was drawn up on 5 October 1869:

We, the undersigned superintendents and visitors of the Ladies' Institute, Belfast feeling a deep interest in the management of the education of Women, beg to bring under your consideration the great want which is felt in this country of such examinations as would furnish a real test of their attainments. Such examinations with the certificates of proficiency which would be awarded at them by creating a higher standard of knowledge would raise the intellectual tone of girls' schools generally and would supply parents with a means of judging as to the efficiency of the education given in them. They would be especially valuable in the case of Ladies who have adopted or intend to adopt teaching as their profession; they would make it easier to form a just estimate of the qualifications of such persons, and would tend to give to solid knowledge and real mental cultivation, the advantage they ought to possess over showy but superficial accomplishments.

We beg that, taking into account the want thus generally and increasingly felt you will follow the precedent set by the Universities of Cambridge and Dublin and appoint a committee of members of your University, to construct and carry out under your sanction and control a system of Examinations for Irish Ladies, and to grant Certificates to such Candidates as shall be judged to deserve them[.][28]

This memorial forwarded by the Ladies' Institute to the senate of the university was successful and a scheme of examinations for women was drawn up in 1869.[29] Immediately the lady superintendents began to alter and modify their existing plan of tests[30] to comply with the new Queen's examinations. It was fortunate that the institute's lecturers were already chosen from QCB, thus guaranteeing their high educational standards. The secretary of the institute was deputed to draw up circulars to publicise this new system. The first examinations were to be held in 1870 and in January of that year the secretary of the institute wrote to the university asking for details of when the examination regulations would be available. This was to allow the Ladies' Institute to plan for the exams and organise a post mortem after the completion of the first tests in order to evaluate the overall success of the scheme.[31]

There were two sections of university tests, junior and senior. Some subjects were compulsory, for example, English literature and arithmetic. Others were optional, such as music. Pupils who passed the junior section could then enter for the senior division. Examinations were normally held in June each year. This was convenient for girls who attended either boarding or day schools in Belfast which had collegiate or university departments and who went home for the holidays in the summer. The prime advantage in these Queen's examinations was that monetary prizes and scholarships were awarded and the most successful candidates could win up to

£50. These prizes gave substantial encouragement for girls to continue their education in several ways. Each year a list of the prizewinners was published in the local newspapers.[32] Male alumni of QCB who sat on a committee of the university offered a prize to the ladies taking exams. The institute found this recognition of their right, as women, to share the educational advantages then enjoyed, particularly encouraging.[33] In addition to money prizes, honours certificates were given for conspicuous merit, and there were also girls who passed and received a university certificate without rating special mention. At first it was the policy of the senate of QUI to maintain as much privacy as possible when issuing results. Candidates were known by numbers, not names, so examiners could not identify them and no class lists were published. However when some prizes were obtained in the second year of these exams it was decided that the senate should announce the winners of three prizes. Further, in 1873, those taking honours were announced, and in 1874 the names of all successful candidates were given, though with only limited detail. No information was published as to where the young ladies had been educated, though there was some demand for this, as it was undertaken at Cambridge as a matter of course. Thus it is impossible to ascertain how many girls taking Queen's examinations were taught at the Ladies' Institute.

Early disclosures of honours and details of the subjects taken were requested by some women candidates who were anxious to learn of their own position. For example, Miss M. T. Reid complained in 1874 that regulations for the university examinations were issued too late to make it possible to distribute study over the time allowed without undue haste. She pointed out that for English literature the book titles of Spalding's *Literature,* Marsh's *Lectures,* Morrow's *Accordance with Hamlet* and 'long and tedious notes', thirty of Bacon's essays and Hall's *English Poets* with copious notes about the given poets were only issued in February. As Reid emphasised, it was unreasonable to expect anyone to prepare honestly and without cramming for a June examination.[34]

Over the years the Ladies' Institute corresponded with Queen's senate over changes in the university examinations.

These requests were usually sympathetically regarded. For example, in 1875 the ladies asked the university senate to allow senior candidates to take obligatory subjects in one year and optional ones in the following year. In addition, they requested that the marks gained be held over to the second year to enable subjects to be dealt with separately, that French or Latin be added to the list of junior section compulsory subjects and that a detailed report be compiled annually comparing each year with the last.[35] The senate agreed to these proposals. They also agreed to add a new subject, the 'theory of music' to the senior course. This particular topic was on the list of subjects tested by other universities and was regarded as being of special value to ladies intending to become teachers. It was also believed to be important from a scientific point of view – and thus attractive to the lady superintendents of the institute who were always enthusiastic to promote science. Indeed, they commented that study of musical theory would 'correct the exceedingly superficial habits of thought in regard to education which is particularly so in the study of music'.[36] This provides an example of the institute's efforts to prove young ladies were able to cope with the study of serious subjects. The senate accepted the new course and in addition added 'perspective' to the test in art. Again in 1877 the Ladies' Institute had to approach the senate when they discovered that the certificates of the QUI examinations for women were were not accepted by the London School of Medicine for Women as an entry qualification. This was a major problem for any Ulster girls who hoped to take up medicine as a profession, for the London school was the only educational establishment which admitted women to medical training. It was vital therefore that the Irish certificates should be recognised. The members of the senate wrote to the General Medical Council in response to the institute's protest. The ladies also wrote to Sir Dominic Corrigan, the QCB representative on the General Medical Council, in October 1877, to highlight:

. . . a matter which is of much importance to those Irish Ladies . . . preparing to study medicine at the London School of

Medicine for Women. Its arrangements are governed by the rules of the British Medical Council. The regulations of the Council acknowledge the certificates of the Oxford and Cambridge local Examinations . . . and this applies to women as well as to men. The Queen's University of Ireland does not hold local Examinations for men, which we presume is the reason that no reference to the Queen's University is made . . . But the effect is to place women who are holders of Queen's University certificates at a very great disadvantage in entering upon the study of medicine . . . The educational value of their certificates is widely known and recognised in England as well as in Ireland . . . any difficulty in the recognition of these certificates will have a most injurious effect upon the progress of general as well as medical education of women . . . [it] is not consistent with the high status of the Queen's University . . . We feel confident . . . that you will do what lies in your power to remove this unexpected obstacle in the path of educational progress.[37]

In answer to these protests it was agreed that Irish qualifications were acceptable, providing that they complied with the Council's recommendations – which they did.[38]

In 1879 the Queen's University was dissolved and was replaced by the Royal University of Ireland[39] which, unlike its predecessor, was a purely examining body with no colleges attached, demanding no lecture attendance. 'The most important aspect of the new RUI was that women were admitted to degrees on the same terms as men'[40], something which was of great value in the moves towards educational equality for women. Girls could now matriculate and take Bachelor and Master of Arts degrees. The Ladies' Institute continued its classes but it now faced competition from girls' schools such as the Ladies' Collegiate, whose principal, Mrs. Margaret Byers, established a separate university department to prepare her students for degrees.[41] The institute continued to be responsible for holding university examinations and Miss Connery, the institute's secretary, was recommended as a superintendent for the RUI.[42]

As a result of running the university tests, the ladies of the institute had become very conscious of the lack of adequate teaching for girls and campaigned to rectify this situation. Writing to the committee of graduates of QCB in August 1873

the institute emphasised the practical difficulties their organisation faced with regards to increasing awareness of university examinations for women, and of their hopes of further
co-operation with QCB:

. . . the Lady Superintendents are met by many obstacles – the diffi-
dence of candidates – unaccustomed to such an ordeal – the uncertainty of teachers to the fitness of their pupils – and the want of
appreciation of the value of such tests on the part of parents. All
more, however, spring chiefly from ignorance as to the aims of the
Examinations, and also of their mode of working. Nothing has
tended more to dissipate that ignorance than the attention awakened by the prizes given to distinguished candidates . . . the difficulty which surrounds all efforts . . . are so numerous that such an
association as the Ladies['] Institute often finds it hard to know
what steps are correct to take. It is evident, however, that the best
hope of success lies in strengthening the bond now formed with the
Queen's University. The University as the recognised head and
guider of education, ought to take the lead in opening the gates of
knowledge to a larger part of the community hitherto all but wholly
excluded . . . your interest in the Examinations which are the first
distinct help offered to women by the Universities, is of the best
auging for the future.[43]

   In essence, the ladies of the institute wanted girls to be
admitted to university classes.[44] This, of course, was now more
difficult to attain due to the closure of QUI and its replace-
ment with a non-collegiate body. Subsequently, the Ladies'
Institute concentrated its efforts on achieving the admittance
of women to existing Queen's colleges, emphasising the need
for universities to do more than hold tests. Writing to Dr.
Henry, QCB president, in September 1873, they stressed:

. . . for a considerable time past a feeling has been gathering
strength, that more might be done by the Universities for the
Education of Women than the instruction of special Examinations,
valuable as they are. As long as the means of good teaching is so
scanty, and so irregularly distributed, tests of instruction are only
applicable to a very limited number.
   The only effective remedy is to admit Ladies to share the best
teaching, that of the Universities themselves. The necessity of work-

ing up to the Collegiate standard would raise the efficiency of schools for girls, as the experience of the Queen's College shows that it has already done so in the case of boys . . . there is nothing in the constitution of the Queen's University to prevent it from being opened to women . . . [this] would be an immediate boon to Ladies, and a further benefit of inestimable value to such women of every rank . . . if the Queen's University takes a lead in a movement which all the Universities must join, but which at present is surrounded with difficulties enough, it will add to the lustre which it has already in its brief but honourable existence.[45]

In addition, there was a bequest in existence from Mr. John Stuart Mill which would be paid to any university which would admit girls.[46] This was an added attraction to the authorities. However, the request of the Ladies' Institute was deferred indefinitely. In 1870 the question of admitting women had come before Queen's Academic Council and Dr. Andrews, vice-president of the college and a supporter of the institute, suggested that women could be permitted to attend lectures if the professors concerned were satisfied that 'the discipline and instruction of the classes would not suffer'.[47] A considerable amount of discussion took place over this matter and although there was some support, it was impossible to convince some of the professors that the admission of girls was either desirable or practicable. There was little chance that Queen's would be a pioneer in the field of university education for women.

Pressure from the Ladies' Institute continued. Professor Nesbitt proposed a motion regarding the admittance of women to QCB during a convocation meeting in November 1873[48], and, in the same year, when there was already interest in the provision of the University Education (Ireland) Bill, the institute itself forwarded another memorandum to the senate. Sir Thomas McClure MP, whose sister was a superintendent, and Mr. Pim MP, whose wife served on the institute's committee, both supported the cause of the ladies:

. . . there is need for further help from the Universities. The Examinations *test* teaching but do not *give* it.
    To obtain teachers capable of really raising the level of culture among Ladies . . . more efficient aids are necessary. Only the more

distinguished scholars are able to go forward from the schools to the University Examinations, and this process is far too slow to make any wide impression. Those institutions which have a higher status than that of schools, from their voluntary and amateur character, have but an uncertain existence. Without public or permanent schools, without intellectual training and nurture of the universities it is an impossible thing for women to have such an education as it is now acknowledged they ought to have. As the Universities not only offer the highest kind of instruction which the time affords, but naturally take the lead in all educational movements, it is to them we look to take the first step in extending to women a share of the national provision for education . . . The Queen's University is less hampered by old rules and traditions than others, and it is more in harmony with the wants of our time. . . . [In] examining our claim, the difficulties of our position, the total inadequacy of any private effort to remove those difficulties, and the ease with which you could place within our reach advantages, hitherto withheld, you will deem it expedient to throw open to women your graduate degree examination.[49]

The ladies of the institute anticipated the potential objections to men and women attending 'sensitive' classes together and offered to compromise. The institute wrote to the university, stating that, 'if medical classes should be formed we wish to state our conviction that separate instruction in these subjects is *absolutely necessary* of course under the same university function'.[50] The senate, on considering this application, referred the matter to the law officers of the crown to ascertain whether they possessed the power to take this decision. However the reply informed the senate that this was outside their jurisdiction.

In 1874 the whole question of the legality of admitting women to QCB was taken up in an effort to clarify the position of the girls who had been trying to gain admission. A memorial was again prepared but the fall of Gladstone's government meant that it was never forwarded.[51] Throughout these discussions it was emphasised that supporters of higher education for women in no way wished to *compel* universities to admit female students. Indeed, a letter from Isabella Tod to the institute in April 1874 underlined this:

I hope the Ladies fully understand that such an enabling Bill would not oblige either Irish University to take any steps in regard to it unless they pleased and if they did take steps, they would be at liberty to do so in whatever way, and to whatever degree approved itself to their respective Governing Bodies. The sole result of such an enabling Bill would be to recover actual legal restrictions, and to enable any University to do what it thought right, without being hindered by rules made under different circumstances.[52]

In 1882 the Belfast institute again wrote to the president of QCB, to request his known sympathy for their efforts to advance the cause of higher education for women, especially to those who had passed the university's matriculation test and who subsequently required tuition for bachelor of arts degrees. While there were some ladies' schools offering advanced classes, the institute firmly believed that the honours classes of QCB were 'in the highest degree desirable' for their students.[53] This time the institute was successful, and the first women were accepted to the classes for arts degrees in 1882. This breakthrough was not achieved solely through the petitioned demands of the Ladies' Institute, though these were significant. However, by the 1880s it was becoming harder to justify the exclusion of women from higher educational establishments, as primary and secondary schools were educating and examining both sexes equally. It is also possible that as there were no compulsory attendance requirements at RUI, QCB was glad to have a number of intelligent young women to swell their student numbers. Certainly during the 1880s some of the principals of girls' schools feared that they would suffer from 'poaching' by the men's colleges. Further progress was forthcoming in 1889 when women were admitted to QCB medical lectures and in the following year to classes in all faculties. In 1895 the government altered the statutes of RUI to make women equal to men in the competition for scholarships and exhibitions. Only a small number of girls went to QCB, and far larger numbers continued to attend the collegiate departments of girls' schools. This is clearly illustrated in the tables of returns of graduate numbers 1891–1900:

Graduates	Colleges	Category
95	Victoria College Belfast (Ladies' Collegiate)	Female
84	Alexandra College Dublin	Female
20	Loreto Convent Dublin	Female
19	Queen's College Belfast	Mixed
17	St. Mary's College Dublin	Female
17	Magee College Londonderry	Mixed
2	Queen's College Cork	Mixed
1	Queen's College Galway	Mixed[54]

The headmistresses' fears of 'poaching' would appear to have been unjustified on the basis of these figures. Although only a very small number of women took advantage of the new openings in higher education, these women were of considerable significance as pioneers and as role models for younger girls.

IV

The concerns of the Ladies' Institute were not confined to tertiary level educational provisions for women. Although the teaching focus of the organisation was on girls aged approximately sixteen to eighteen, who had already been educated, either at home with a governess or in one of the numerous ladies' seminaries, the committee was also interested in teaching standards, as this had an important impact upon subsequent academic attainments. The report of the Endowed Schools' Commission of 1868 highlighted the unsatisfactory state of education for upper and middle-class girls in England. Although no report was produced, provisions were no better in Ireland. The Ladies' Institute was well aware of the inadequacy of existing secondary schools which were, in their opinion, amateur. The institute fully recognised the need for a system of state supported public schools. They therefore petitioned the house of commons in June 1873. According to the existing provisions, only girls in the national school system had the opportunity to take public tests. By not offering exams at a secondary level the ladies were concerned about the resulting poor quality of education for girls. The lack of such secondary level testing reinforced their 'belief that these tests have brought out very

forcibly the want of adequate means of study for girls . . .
there are no public endowments in Belfast available for girls
for any Education other than primary'.[55] In 1878 Disraeli's
government reacted to demands for secondary education in
Ireland by introducing the Intermediate Education (Ireland)
Bill which proposed to set up a system of education which
would attract public funds. The supporters of higher education for women were delighted by this suggestion, which
would provide educational grounding for girls, until they
learnt the terms of this bill only applied to boys. Fearing that
the girls of Ireland would not benefit from the intermediate
system, the Ladies' Institute drew up another memorial
addressed to the Lord Chancellor, Lord Cairns, and to James
Lowther, the Chief Secretary for Ireland. Dated 25 June 1878,
it stated:

. . . the education of women of the middle and upper middle classes
is now recognised as a matter of national concern, as well as that of
men of those classes. The welfare of the country largely depends
upon the enlightenment and well applied energy of those who have
it in their power to influence those beneath them in the social scale,
that for this end, – even more than for the great professional and
industrial interests involved, – it is needful that the means of higher
education should be brought within the reach of these classes.

Inadequate, however, as the provision for secondary education
for boys has hitherto been in Ireland it has been still more inadequate for girls. The endowments of which they can claim a share are
few and scanty; and the whole support of higher education has
been left to private enterprise, which is necessarily local and limited
in its range, even when most deservedly successful.

We have upon previous occasions brought this subject before
gentlemen filling the office of Chief Secretary for Ireland, but no
opportunity so favourable as the present has presented itself for taking any satisfactory action upon it.[56]

This question was so important that the Ladies' Institute
sent a deputation of Irish women to London to lobby Lord
Cairns.[57] The meeting with Cairns was organised by Isabella
Tod, with the assistance of J.P. Corry, a Belfast member of
parliament. This facilitated an opportunity for the women to
present their case and highlight the successes girls had

achieved in the university certificate examinations. The Lord
Chancellor, impressed by the strength of their arguments,
subsequently admitted girls under the provisions of the act.
Corry, a strong supporter of education for girls, was delighted
that the Intermediate Education Act had been extended to
'the whole instead of the half of the young people of
Ireland'.[58]

The Ladies' Institute was apprehensive that the commissioners of education would be reluctant to implement this
act. Therefore, in the event of any delay, the women planned
to send a deputation to Dublin to press for action and to hold
a public meeting.[59] Their concern was unfounded as Mrs.
Byers of Victoria College, Belfast, and Mrs. Jellicoe of
Alexandra College, Dublin, ensured that their pupils took
the examinations in the first year.[60] This act was a landmark
in women's education. Although girls and boys were examined in separate sections, the tests were of equal difficulty and
were marked on the same level. For the first time large numbers of female students showed that they were as academically
competent as boys. The university examinations were significant, but never involved a substantial proportion of the
population. With the Intermediate Education Act female
education expanded widely through the middle classes, and
the Ladies' Institute played a crucial part in this achievement.

V

Although they experienced some practical difficulties, on the
whole the institute was a successful organisation. During the
institute's first session, 1867-68, there had been over 180
students enrolled and the professors from QCB had earned
substantial payments from fees. Therefore, the lady superintendents were shocked to receive a letter from Professor
Younger in September 1868 withdrawing his agreement to
hold classes in the new sessions.[61] His decision had been
prompted by a warning from the president of QCB, Dr. P. S.
Henry, that delivering lectures to the Ladies' Institute could
forfeit Younger's 'claim to a lecturing pension'.[62] The president claimed that he had not realised the extent of the

commitment required to teach at the Ladies' Institute. The lady superintendents replied that Professor Thomson and Professor Nesbitt had previously been allowed to lecture without complaint. Furthermore the professors were impossible to replace at such short notice. As a result the planned lectures would have to be suspended, thus damaging a 'valuable educational institution which is conducted in the same way as Queen's College and University'.[63] In response, the ladies therefore requested the president to reconsider the situation. It was vital that this issue should be settled promptly and a favourable decision reached in order to maintain the institute's educational credibility. It was also essential that the QCB professors with their high teaching status should continue to lecture. Moreover, it was bad for the whole enterprise to be faced with uncertainty and the possibility of cancelling classes which had already been advertised and paid for. However, the president of Queen's simply ignored the problem for some time. The ladies circulated copies of the president's letter to the professors to inform them of the potential risks of fulfilling their teaching agreements with the institute. This was a controversial issue, as the president of Queen's faced considerable opposition from the gentlemen whose families were involved with the institute, and whose views were solicited on the issue. For example, Mr. Dunville and Mr. Duffin formed a deputation to visit the president. On 29 September 1868, the president wrote officially to the institute, stating that had he been fully consulted he would have only permitted staff to teach their own subjects and not deliver more than twenty-five lectures. Henry concluded that if these conditions were met, he would not interfere further, but he hoped that all future plans would be submitted to him first.[64]

This did not conclude the issue. Professor Wyville Thomson wrote to QCB's president from the Commission of Science and Art in Dublin. Thomson had received a letter from Miss Connery of the Ladies' Institute explaining the problem. Thomson emphasised that the Ladies' Institute was a popular, useful body which brought college staff into contact with a cross-section of Belfast's populace. Further,

Thomson highlighted the fact that a number of influential people supported the institute and that it was part of a wider educational movement already in existence in Edinburgh, Dublin and in other leading cities. In conclusion, Thomson felt that the president's right to interfere in the spare time of his staff was questionable:

I am entitled, when my college work for the day is done, to give a lecture if I choose at the Ladies' Institute; to give a lecture in the Museum to working men; to write an article for a journal, or take a hand at whist. At what point the President imagines his contract to end I am at a loss to imagine.[65]

The correspondence between Thomson and the Queen's president continued, until the former advised Dr. Henry that it was not advisable to interfere with the agreements made with the Ladies' Institute and that professors should only be reprimanded, or reported to the government, if they were neglectful of their duties. In October 1868 the president conceded.[66] However, it was an unfortunate consequence of this dispute that the institute's classes for the 1868 session had to be cancelled. Fees already paid were refunded, but the existence of the institute was not seriously imperilled.

The institute faced similar difficulties with the Government School of Art in October 1872 over teachers' contractual arrangements, which led to the suspension of classes on the history and principles of art.[67] In the following year the institute had to renegotiate their arrangements with the BNHPS over the use of the museum premises.[68] This was amicably resolved, and by March 1874 committee meetings of the institute were again being held in the museum free of charge.[69] These episodes provide an interesting example of the influence of the lady superintendents, an influence which led to victory over important figures, like the president of QCB.

VI

By the 1880s the whole *raison d'etre* of the Ladies' Institute was called into question.[70] The organisation had questioned their future position as early as February 1878, discussing:

. . . the desirability of resuming lectures under the auspices of the Institute. Although the subjects formerly lectured upon are now generally included in the curriculum of schools, the ladies were agreed that there were other subjects which might be advantageously taken up by them.[71]

The whole situation of girls' education and its perceived importance had changed. Now women were admitted to all educational establishments, the need for lectures had virtually disappeared. Intermediate examinations had stimulated the opening of secondary schools throughout Ireland while the existence of collegiate departments in colleges and the opening of the QCB classes to girls, had removed the necessity for outside bodies. In the 1880s meetings of the institute were only held annually and were, on occasion, not held at all, reflecting a decline in their activities. By 1883 the committee of the institute was forced to admit their inability to organise a memorial scholarship for the late Mrs. Jane McIlwaine, who had been one of its founders. A group of former pupils of the Ladies' Collegiate school had formed an association to encourage girls to attend the collegiate department of their old school and the Ladies' Institute believed this group were in the best position to fund raise. The institute resolved to give a corporate subscription to McIlwaine's memorial 'to show that our valued friend was adequately appreciated in Belfast.'[72]

The final meeting of the Belfast Ladies' Institute was held in April 1897. Lady Ewart took the chair and, with only three other members present[73], it was agreed that the remaining funds of the institute should go to the Isabella M. S. Tod Memorial Scholarship. Their last resolution was that as 'the object for which the Ladies' Institute was founded having been accomplished by the attainment of higher education for women it is now unanimously resolved that the association should be formally disbanded'.[74]

The Ladies' Institute performed an important function in Ireland, with aims similar to British organisations. Indeed there were links between women's educational reform movements in Britain and Ireland. For example, the Women's

Education Union and the Edinburgh Association for the Improvement of the Education of Women corresponded with the Belfast institute. As early as January 1872, Isabella Tod proposed and Anna Wellard seconded a motion, 'that the Ladies' Institute should be connected with the National Union for the Improving the Education of Women of all classes.'[75] On 25 August 1874 the institute held a meeting at the Ladies' Collegiate School, Belfast, in connection with the National Union for the Improvement of the Higher Education of Women, chaired by Lord Waveney, and addressed by Mr. G. Johnston Stoney and Mrs. William Grey, who travelled to Belfast as representatives of the Union.[76] In May 1880 the superintendents of the Ladies' Institute attended a meeting of the Committee of the Society for School and University Education of Women in Ireland and were instructed to 'use their own judgment, and act as circumstances may suggest'.[77] Similarly in May 1882 Isabella Tod was awarded travelling expenses by the Ladies' Institute to enable her to go to London 'on important business about girls and the Intermediate Education Board.'[78] All these organisations succeeded in expanding the educational horizons of middle-class women. The members of the Ladies' Institute were strong and influential advocates of the advancement of women's social position, and collectively formed a significant pressure group. The organisation played a vital role in determining women's right to education in the developing nineteenth-century city of Belfast.

[1] The editors are grateful to the estate of Alison Jordan for granting us permission to publish this article posthumously.

[2] Ian Budge and Cornelius O'Leary, *Belfast: approach to crisis* (London, 1973), p. 28.

[3] Information complied from *Belfast Street Directory* 1870, 1871.

[4] Minute book of the Belfast Ladies' Institute (hereafter MBBLI), 30 July 1873.

[5] Ibid., 15 Mar. 1878

[6] Ibid., 19 Nov. 1869.

[7] Hereafter QCB.

[8] No records exist of complaints regarding the organisation's efficiency.

[9] MBBLI, 19 Nov. 1869.

[10] Ibid.

[11] Ibid. The institute seemed to experience few serious financial difficulties. During the first year of operation there was sufficient support to generate receipts of £350, with expenses of £100 to cover heat, lighting, cleaning, advertisement of lecture programmes and payment of wages. MBBLI, 7 Jan. 1868. As the subscribers, committee and students of the institute were mostly middle class, they were able to sustain the organisation while it was perceived as useful, however as interest declined, the amount of money held by the treasurer fell. For example, in 1882 there was only £60 in the institute's capital account, with the balance in hand being £9 17s.7.5d. Ibid., 30 May 1882.

[12] Ibid., 17 Nov. 1870. The institute donated £4 towards the cost of publishing and printing this pamphlet, which included the QCB president's address.

[13] Hereafter BNHPS.

[14] MBBLI, 19 Nov. 1869.

[15] Ibid.

[16] Ibid., 21 Apr. 1871.

[17] Ibid., 7 Aug. 1873.

[18] Ibid., 18 Dec. 1873.

[19] Ibid., 21 Jan. 1876.

[20] Margaret Byers, *Money rewards in girls' schools*, paper delivered to the AGM of the Irish Schoolmasters' Association, Dublin, 28 Dec. 1883.

[21] D.J. Owen, *History of Belfast* (Belfast, 1921), p. 406.

[22] MBBLI, 11 Apr. 1872. For example, see the later discussion of Thomson's defence of the Ladies' Institute in 1868.

[23] *Report of the Ladies' Collegiate School*, 1874–75.

[24] Hereafter QUI.

[25] A.V. Clarke, *History of the Cheltenham Ladies' College* (London, 1953), p. 41.

[26] Byers, *Girls' education*.

[27] The other two colleges were situated in Galway and Cork.

[28] MBBLI, 5 Oct. 1869. The memorial was signed by A.J. Bushell, Jane McIlwaine, Anna Hicks, Margaret Porter, Jane Taylor, Sarah Pim Bruce, Jane Mullan, Charlotte W. Morgan, Margaret Davison, Anna Georgina Dunville, Theodisa Duffin, Anne Cunningham, Jane McGee, Eliza Sinclair, Anna Smith, ? Patterson, ? Murphy. Christian names of the latter two women are unknown.

[29] T.W. Moody and J.C. Beckett, *Queen's Belfast, 1845–1949* (London, 1959), p. 267.

[30] MBBLI, 19 Nov. 1869.

[31] Miss Isabella Tod, one of the most active superintendents of the institute, was responsible for assessing the examination scheme.

[32] There was no overall list of awards in order of merit produced by the university, as it was found impracticable to deal with the large numbers of students involved and to distinguish between optional and compulsory subjects.

[33] MBBLI, 25 Aug. 1874.

[34] Ibid.,15 Sept. 1874.

[35] Ibid., 5 Oct. 1875.

[36] Ibid., 26 Oct. 1877.

[37] Ibid.

[38] Ibid., 5 Feb. 1878. The institute resolved to prepare a paragraph for publication in the press on this issue.

[39] Hereafter RUI.

[40] P.J. Dowling, *A history of Irish education* (Cork, 1971), p. 172.

[41] For further information see Alison Jordan, *Margaret Byers: pioneer of women's education and founder of Victoria College, Belfast* (Belfast, n.d).

[42] MBBLI, 30 May 1882.

[43] Ibid., 23 Aug. 1873.

[44] Ibid., 22 Sept. 1873.

[45] Ibid.

[46] Ibid.

[47] Moody and Beckett, *Queen's*, p. 211.

[48] MBBLI, 3 Nov. 1873. The institute wrote to Nesbitt to thank him for his attempt.

[49] Ibid., 22 Sept. 1873. This memorial was signed by Eliza Sinclair, Isabella Tod, Maria Cumming, Anna Wellard, Eliza McClure, Jane McIlwaine, Margaret Porter, Anna Murphy.

[50] Ibid., 3 Nov. 1873.

[51] Ibid., 21 Jan. 1874.

[52] Ibid., 8 Apr. 1874.

[53] Ibid., 29 Sept. 1882.

[54] Jordan, *Margaret Byers*, p. 16.

[55] MBBLI, 17 June 1873.

[56] Ibid., 25 June 1878.

[57] Ibid., 25 July 1878.

[58] Ibid., 3 Oct. 1879.

[59] Ibid.

[60] *Northern Whig*, 1 Jan. 1879.

[61] MBBLI, 19 Sept. 1868.

[62] Ibid., 15 Apr. 1868.

[63] Ibid., 19 Sept. 1868.

[64] Ibid., 29 Sept. 1868.

[65] Ibid., 26 Sept. 1868.

[66] Ibid., 10 Oct. 1868.

[67] Ibid., 8 Oct. 1872.

[68] Ibid., 22 Nov. 1873. It was proposed to increase charges for the hire of the museum from 3s. 6d. to 10s., which would have placed a heavy financial burden on the Ladies' Institute.

[69] Ibid., 7 Mar. 1874.

[70] Education remained the focus for the Ladies' Institute, as unlike Queen's Institute in Dublin, the Belfast Ladies' Institute did not help their students to find employment through a register. However, the

organisation did make some informal moves to facilitate women's employment opportunities. In Feb. 1878, Sir Dominic Corrigan wrote to the institute to draw attention to the suitability of women for the profession of pharmaceutical chemists, as the Irish Pharmaceutical Society had removed legal restrictions preventing women from entering this profession. The Ladies' Institute agreed to bring this subject to the attention of as many teachers and parents as possible. Ibid., 5 Feb. 1878.

[71] Ibid., 5 Sept. 1878. No details were given of 'other subjects' which the organisation taught.

[72] Ibid., 31 Mar. 1883.

[73] Mrs. Duffin, Miss Bruce and Mrs. Porter.

[74] MBBLI, 2 Apr. 1897. This was first meeting of the institute recorded since 31 Mar. 1883.

[75] Ibid., 8 Jan. 1872.

[76] Ibid., 25 June 1874. The minute book of the institute records on 5 June 1874, that Isabella Tod had been to London to organise this meeting.

[77] Ibid., 20 May 1880.

[78] Ibid., 30 May 1882.

PART II
POLITICS

NORTHERN VOICES: ULSTERWOMEN IN THE YOUNG IRELAND MOVEMENT

BRIGITTE ANTON

I

There were also "of honourable women not a few." But, accepting the sentiment of Pericles – that it is best for a woman "not to be talked about for good or evil among men" – I abstain from mentioning the names of these latter.[1]

'Young Ireland' was the nick-name given to the group of nationalists centred around *The Nation* newspaper, who in 1846 split from Daniel O'Connell's Repeal movement, formed the Irish Confederates in 1847, and attempted a rebellion in 1848 which utterly failed. Their newspaper was based in Dublin, but Young Irelanders came from all parts of Ireland, and a considerable number of their leaders came from northern counties, for instance Charles Gavan Duffy (Monaghan) and John Mitchel (Londonderry)[2]. Northern women who were involved were, in particular, the members of two families: the Mitchel women – John Mitchel's wife Jenny, his mother and sisters; and the Hughes sisters – Margaret Hughes Callan and Susan Hughes, who became Charles Gavan Duffy's second wife. Additionally, there was Elizabeth Willoughby Treacy, better known in Young Ireland circles as 'Finola' who was a frequent contributor to *The*

Nation. Together with other Irish women[3] they were the major female Young Ireland activists.

In this article, I want to determine whether or not these northern Young Irishwomen had a different input into the Young Ireland movement than both their male northern, and other female counterparts. Were they in any way characterised by their upbringing and environment? What were the reasons for their interest in nationalism? To aid this examination, it is necessary to look at female involvement in the Young Irelanders in general, and also to discuss Young Ireland's view of the north, before looking at the individual lives of these women.

II

Had we a Council of Women that I could select our cause were soon to triumph. John Martin to 'Eva', *1848*[4]

Women in general played an important part in the Young Ireland movement, although their input is often not acknowledged. Young Ireland women were popular contributors of prose, poetry and letters to editorials in *The Nation, The United Irishman, The Irish Felon* and *The Irish Tribune.* They were also an important support group who attended meetings of the Repeal Association, cheered speakers and watched court cases. When Young Ireland formed the Irish Confederation, women joined as members. However, the majority of women remained in the background and did not take part in the committee meetings of the Irish Confederation. Nevertheless, there were women who influenced the decision-making process through their informal contacts within the small circle of Young Ireland leaders, especially as wives (Jenny Mitchel), relatives (Margaret Callan) and close friends ('Speranza'). Revolutionary developments in Europe attracted the attention of the Irish Confederation in 1848 when many of its members talked about the possibility of an Irish revolution. When male Young Irelanders were arrested for seditious articles, female work became essential, particularly to maintain communication between the members. Female sympathisers living in outlying districts travelled to Dublin to help.[5]

In general, it is very hard to trace Young Ireland women, because the focus was always on men.[6] However some information does exist. The poetesses left plenty of material to investigate, and there was also a long debate in *The Nation* in 1847 about the role of women, which was intensified in 1848.[7]

In Young Ireland's view women had an essential part to play in the national struggle. However, since many Young Irelanders were romantic nationalists, they had very idealistic notions about women's contribution to the nationalist cause. Women were not supposed to be leaders, but were considered as very important auxiliaries in spreading the nationalist message through the education of children, conversation, and through their writings. Women found this ideology attractive because it gave them a sense of belonging and identified them as part of a national struggle where their work was appreciated. These women cannot be seen as feminists because their nationalism took priority over issues such as political equality. Nevertheless, in 1848, a considerable number of women demanded a more active role, and some wanted to participate in the actual revolution.[8] This received support from some male Young Irelanders[9], who thought that a national revolution would need the participation of both sexes. However, since the uprising never occurred on a large scale, their claim to allow women to take part was never tested.[10]

III

Come – pledge again thy heart and hand –
One grasp that ne'er shall sever;
Our watchword be – "our native land"–
Our motto – "Love for ever".
And let the Orange lily be
Thy *badge, my patriot brother –*
The everlasting Green for me;
And we for one another.[11]

The Young Irelanders were eager to win Protestant support for the Repeal cause. They were also aware of the religious tensions in Ulster, and *Nation* articles frequently addressed northern Protestants. However, they did not see the north as an isolated problem, but put it in the context of the general alienation of Protestants from Irish nationalism. Although they tried to make a strong distinction between Orangeism – 'a misled ideology' – and Protestants in general, they did not always succeed and sometimes used these terms indiscriminately. They believed that Protestants (north and south) would eventually support an independent parliament when they realised that they would benefit from it. This was the idea of 'nationalist conversion', which meant that Protestants would start to love Ireland as their own country. This belief also derived from the experience of Protestant Young Irelanders. For instance Anglicans like Thomas Davis, William Smith O'Brien and Jane Francesca Elgee, and Unitarians like John and Jenny Mitchel had become strong nationalists and believed it was possible for other Protestants to follow the nationalist path.[12] Consequently, Young Ireland was strongly secular and demanded unity of class and creed. However, Catholics from the north, such as Charles Gavan Duffy from Monaghan remembered from their childhood years how deep religious divisions were.[13] Duffy and others were more critical of the idealist view that northern Protestants would join the nationalist movement. However, many Young Irelanders argued that once Protestants realised that consecutive British governments had played Catholics and Protestants against each other, and that Britain had used them for its political purposes, they would support the nationalist cause. Young Ireland felt they could convince Protestants that they were too strong a minority to be oppressed by Catholics in an independent Irish parliament. The Young Irelanders praised northern Protestants for their thrift, industry, discipline, power, strength of character and courage. They also referred to their good spirit of co-operation, their strict adherence to principle and their free-thinking. However, on the other hand they described them as deceived by England, and contradicted their own view of an independent spirit in Ulster. There were signs that Protestants on the whole respected Young Ireland more than than O'Connell. They were seen as more honest, straightforward and secular.[14]

Young Irelanders used examples of history to show that unity of creed was possible.[15] However, stronger emphasis was put on economic arguments to win Protestants over. Since Young Ireland did not see any economic benefits in the Act of Union, they challenged the unionist view that Ireland had benefited economically from the Union. Although many Young Irelanders knew that the industrialised northern counties were different from the rest of Ireland, they did not realise how strongly unionists were attached to the Union in economic terms. They stressed that there would be no reversal of the seventeenth-century plantations, and stated that the Protestants in Ireland had a right to their holdings, because they had lived in the country for so long. They also praised the so-called Ulster custom[16] as a way forward for Ireland. Unfortunately, their radical policy of 1847–48 repelled, in particular, protestant landlords who feared for their property, in spite of Young Ireland assurances to the contrary.

Since Young Ireland found it hard to relate to the lower classes in general, they did not understand the fears of the Protestant working classes. They hoped that the Protestant upper and middle classes would persuade their lower-class compatriots. However, in 1848 John Mitchel abandoned the appeals aimed at the Protestant ascendancy, and directed proclamations in his *United Irishman* newspaper to 'the Farmers, Labourers and Artisans of the North of Ireland.' He argued that England had plundered both Catholic and Protestant farmers in Ireland, and asked them to join the nationalist movement to stop this exploitation.[17]

All these appeals could not overcome the divisions in the north. Repeal agitation had sparked a rise in Orangeism making O'Connell reluctant to hold monster meetings in Ulster. The Young Irelanders were very interested in the north and campaigned there. As in the rest of Ireland, the Irish Confederation also organised in the northern counties. The northern Young Irelanders came mainly from respectable families, and the arrest of John Mitchel and John Martin in 1848 caused great surprise and hostility among their northern neighbours.[18] Ulsterwomen in the Young Irelanders shared the mainstream Young Ireland thought on the north, but also had their own ideas and input.

IV

John Mitchel, came from a supportive and very close-knit family of eight: the Rev. John Mitchel, Mrs. Mary Mitchel, four daughters and two sons.[19] All had strong, independent personalities and the women never shrank away from danger. This attitude possibly originated with the Mitchel parents[20] and from their upbringing. In their home, all the Mitchels were involved in discussions about books, politics and religion.

Mrs. Mary Mitchel had always worked in her husband's parish, and was a remarkable person. When Rev. John Mitchel died in 1840, she successfully ran the Mitchel household together with her daughters.[21] She was described as:

> . . . very intelligent, her conversation was full of intelligence, wit, and fire. A very forceful character. There was a clearness, an energy, and a decisiveness about her modes of thought and action, which powerfully impressed and fascinated those who had the advantage of her friendship. . . . She had an excellent understanding and apti- tude for business and management, but was withal of a quick, impa- tient turn, and liked off-hand, practical solutions. In many ways John resembled her . . . his purely intellectual characteristics . . . were those of his mother.[22]

Whenever John and Jenny needed assistance because of their involvement in the Young Ireland movement, the Mitchel women rallied around them. In her support of John and Jenny, Mrs. Mary Mitchel travelled a great deal. Thus, she moved to Dublin, and after John was transported, she decided to emigrate to the United States. Hearing about her resolution, John wrote to his sister Matilda:

> So my dear Matilda we are *all* to be extirpated from Ireland, root and branch except yourself. I am surprised indeed a little at my mother's resolving to emigrate, and with a family not of sons, but of daughters . . . it would certainly be a vast advantage if of the whole muster there were more men and fewer women and children.[23]

She lived in America for several years, and then went to live in London, before moving back to Newry, where she died in 1865.

John's sister Matilda was closest to him in age, and closest in confidence. John wrote most frequently to her and trusted her implicitly.[24] She appears to have been an intelligent woman who shared her brother's passion for books. He wrote to her in 1849:

You have been reading Lamartine's Girondists. Don't put implicit confidence in that sweet and tender man's views of men and things. He calls himself a 'poet' and feels bound to look at every thing through a poetic medium . . . A far more accurate estimate of that clique of gentlemen and ladies is to be found in Carlyle's great book.[25]

Although both his sisters, Mary and Henrietta, frequently stayed in John and Jenny's home in Dublin during the Young Ireland period, and joined in their Young Ireland work, it was only Henrietta who remained closely involved in politics. Jenny Mitchel was the most active in the Young Irelanders, but the moral and physical support of all the Mitchel women was very significant.

V

My Dear Sir – Will you do me the kindness to present my tribute of 10/- to the personal necessities of that outraged and heroic lady, Mrs. Mitchel? She is the widow of Ireland; and it is fitting that, so long as she shall mourn in national widowhood among us, on each felon anniversary of the 20th May, the nation shall acquit itself towards her of the dues which the last act of English perfidity has charged upon Irish gratitude . . .[26] (letter to *The Nation,* June 1848)

Jane Verner[27] was born in the Newry area around 1820. By the age of sixteen she had eloped twice with John Mitchel, before eventually marrying him on 3 February 1837. The couple moved in with his family in Newry. Jenny was made very welcome and was soon considered part of the house-hold. In 1840, John and Jenny moved to Banbridge, where John practised as a county attorney. Strong willed, independent, but gentle, Jenny was more a partner to John than being solely a subservient wife. However, life with a quick-tempered, restless and spontaneous person such as John could not have been easy. In exile, he admitted in a letter to his sister Matilda:

While I was at home I was very reckless and had a buoyant self-confidence that no matter what difficulties might arise I would overcome them, and on the whole *get along* well enough. But now, when I can do absolutely nothing, when I can neither serve my family *nor hurt them* I am full of nervous anxiety until I hear everything that befalls them . . .[28]

Once John and Jenny Mitchel became interested in the ideas expressed in *The Nation*, and in the Young Ireland group, politics began to dominate their lives. When Duffy offered John Mitchel the post of assistant editor of *The Nation* in 1845, Jenny was opposed to the idea of John changing his profession. However, once the family had moved to Dublin, Jenny became a full participant in all political activities. Indeed, the Mitchel home became a centre for Young Ireland activities, both in terms of work and for socialising.[29] Since John was occupied with *The Nation*, he relied heavily on Jenny's organisational skills to manage family affairs on her own. In their home 'simplicity and frugality combined with neatness and elegance were the leading features'.[30] They had to live on a tight budget but Jenny was able to stretch their meagre income and thus ensure they could fulfil their social obligations to entertain.[31] The suppers which she hosted for Young Ireland activists can be compared to European-style *salons*, where the ladies presided when politics were discussed. Mrs. Mary Mitchel and her daughters were frequent visitors[32], before she, Henrietta, Mary, and William moved permanently to Dublin at the end of 1846[33]. All the Mitchels gave John their full support. For instance, Jenny and the Mitchel sisters went to meetings of the Repeal Association in Conciliation Hall, where together with the other women present they were seated in the galleries. Since women were also invited to the banquets of the '82 Club, an elitist group modelled on the Irish Volunteers of 1782, in the Rotunda, it is likely that some of the Mitchel women were in attendance.

To assist John with his work, Jenny read newspapers and kept files of clippings for future reference. When John Mitchel seceded from the Irish Confederation and *The Nation*, subsequently establishing the *United Irishman* in 1848, he depended on his family for support. All the Mitchel women were writing anonymous articles and letters, editing contributions, reading newspapers and undertaking all necessary work to guarantee the continuance of the journal. Like John, Jenny was radical in her ideas, and believed in the success of a revolution in Ireland. Her husband included women in his revolutionary plans, and even assigned them a role in combat.[34] The strong position of women in his family must have influenced his views on women in the nationalist movement. When John was arrested and sentenced to transportation in May 1848 for writing seditious articles, Jenny was sure that his friends would prevent the sentence being carried out. She tried to rally opposition to John's arrest and subsequent transportation, but failed in the attempt. Many nationalists saw her as the embodiment of oppressed Ireland. A special committee was set up for the collection of funds for Jenny Mitchel and her children. After the following advertisement appeared in *The Nation*, donations and letters of support flooded in:

A tribute from Ireland to the bereaved wife and family of John Mitchel, convicted of felony for the brave assertion of his convictions respecting the true interests of his native country.[35]

Jenny was extremely disappointed when John was convicted of sedition and transported without any resistance. However, her involvement in the Young Ireland movement continued, for instance, she helped Thomas Devin Reilly escape to America.[36] Jenny wanted to leave Ireland as quickly as possible to join her husband. She was the only woman who followed a Young Irelander into the Penal Colonies[37]. Additionally, she was disillusioned about the failed Young Ireland rebellion, and the bleak political and social circumstances in Ireland.[38] The Mitchel family also encountered certain difficulties after John's transportation. In an undated letter Jenny mentions that her correspondence was inter-fered with.[39] As John's final destination remained uncertain he worried a great deal about Jenny's desire to follow him, believing she might travel in vain. Besides, he felt she was not physically fit for a three month voyage.[40] He frequently wrote to his sister Matilda and repeatedly stated that Jenny should not travel:

> . . . you must tell Jenny (if she be still in Ireland) that she is on no account to come to Bermuda on the chance of seeing me. Under present circumstances she would only be placing both herself and me in a very unpleasant position by doing this. . . . On this point I am quite peremptory and would be very angry if she disobeyed me.[41]

Once John's place of abode was decided on, Jenny and her family followed him to Van Diemen's Land (Tasmania). When John resolved to escape to America, Jenny helped him, while at the same time organising her own departure.[42] In America, she again worked with John on his various newspa-pers, and remained interested in the Irish nationalist cause[43]. However, both John and Jenny felt an emptiness in their lives once they realised that their cause had failed. Young Ireland activities had been the centre of their lives, and nothing could replace the excitement of the 'Young Ireland years'.[44]

Being a Unitarian herself, Jenny was very tolerant and allowed two of her daughters to become Catholics.[45] When Jenny visited Ireland in 1862–63, she decided to bring back goods to the blockaded states[46], and she and her daughters, Minnie and Isabelle, travelled back on a blockade-breaker, which ran aground and caught fire. Left stranded on a sandy island near the cost of North Carolina, they made their way back to their home to Richmond only with great difficulty and hardship.[47] In 1875, John was asked to stand as a home rule candidate for Tipperary, although he was very critical of the home rule movement. He travelled to Ireland for the elections. Jenny was eager to accompany him, but for once John decided against it and took his only surviving son James with him instead. John was successfully elected, but died shortly afterwards.[48] Jenny Mitchel did not actively campaign for Irish nationalism after her husband's death, but remained interested in Irish politics until her own death on 31 December 1899.

VI

Unlike Jenny Mitchel, Henrietta Mitchel Martin, John's youngest sister, was publicly involved in the home rule movement. However, she began her nationalist career among the Young Irelanders. Frequently visiting John and Jenny in Dublin before moving there permanently, Henrietta helped the couple in their Young Ireland activities, and attended Repeal meetings before the split in 1846. She was also engaged in organising and writing articles for the *United Irishman*. After the disastrous rebellion of 1848, she remained a strong Young Ireland supporter, and continued to adhere to their ideas.

To the surprise of many friends and relatives, she married John Mitchel's best friend and fellow Young Irelander John Martin on 26 November 1868.[49] It was seemingly a happy marriage; she accompanied her husband to America and shared his political views.[50] A very energetic woman, she encouraged the quiet, amicable, but erratic and peculiar Martin to get involved with politics again, and to take part in the home rule movement.[51] Consequently, John Martin became home rule member of parliament for Meath from 1871–75, and secretary of the Irish Home Rule League from 1874–75. Henrietta also remained fiercely loyal to her brother, and was involved in his election campaign in 1875.[52] Unlike John, she did not see her support for home rule as a breach with the Young Ireland tradition. She perceived the fight for home rule rather as a continuance of the Young Ireland struggle for an independent national parliament.

After her husband's death in 1875[53], she stated in a letter to George Mahon:

. . . I never held him back from anything; never tried, I liked to see him in the House of Commons and at assemblies of his own countrymen and to hear their applause when he spoke, and if I could do nothing else I could sympathise warmly in all that interested him so that I think that his 6 years and 5 months of married life were pleasant on the whole.[54]

A strong nationalist, she was aware of the importance of Protestant representation in the home rule party:

I wish there were more in the movement. The new member for Meath (in John Martin's place) is a Protestant and is thought a great deal of. I am glad it is a man whom John Martin liked and trusted. I wish you were in this country and made some constituency in the North elect you a Protestant Nationalist. Indeed, the only thing I care about is to see some of the events coming round that those men gave themselves and their fortunes up for.[55]

However, she took a break from nationalist politics, when in the spring of 1876, a friend asked her if she would assist a Unitarian minister with his work in Milan. Although she felt she had no vocation, she wanted to leave Ireland, since she felt extremely exhausted and depressed after the death of both her husband and her brother. She came back to Ireland in May or June 1877[56], and she continued working in John Martin's name for the home rule movement. She supported the political line adopted by Charles Stewart Parnell and after the split in the home rule movement she remained a staunch Parnellite.[57] Travelling extensively to rally support for the nationalist cause, her name appeared frequently in connection with nationalist meetings, for instance in 1903 she went to the Irish League Convention in Boston (USA) where she met John Redmond, John Dillon and Michael Davitt.[58] However, it is interesting to note that all her activities were dedicated to her dead husband and *his* cause and were not done in her own right. She never claimed to work for herself. This attitude reflects her own romantic nationalism. Henrietta Mitchel Martin died on 11 July 1913 in her house in Dublin, and is buried in Newry.[59]

VII

Margaret Hughes was born around 1817, and her sister Susan, the fifth daughter of the large Newry Catholic family, was born on 19 August 1826.[60] Their grandmother had been a strong Irish nationalist and it is likely that their interest in nationalism derived from their family.[61] When their father, Philip Hughes, a merchant, died, Margaret and her mother

opened a boarding school in Blackrock, Dublin in 1835.
Later, Susan and other sisters worked in this school, which
advertised in the *The Nation*. Susan also gave piano lessons in
1846.[62] By this time, Margaret was already married to Dr. John
B. Callan, a physician, who also advertised in *The Nation* for
his selection of mineral waters.[63] Whereas Margaret Callan
got involved in Young Ireland and worked in *The Nation*
office, it is not recorded what specific work Susan carried on
in the movement. Like most women at that time, Margaret
was not in the forefront of public attention, despite putting
much effort into the Young Ireland movement. Of the occa-
sional articles she wrote in *The Nation*, only two are known to
be definitely written by her, as most articles were published
anonymously. Those attributable to her, 'A Day at Versailles'
and 'A Day in Paris', appeared in 1843, and were travel
reports. Claiming to be in France at that time, she used her
own experience to educate the Irish about different countries
and to show them what they could learn from other nations.
Similar to many travel reports in *The Nation*, they were
intended to heighten people's national consciousness, and to
illustrate how other nations loved their country. She wrote:

I have found much in the amusements of the people, and in the way
in which public monuments are thrown open to them, that would
be worthy our imitation, and which we might, to a certain degree,
adopt. The English, it is true, have left us no *national* monuments,
but we can create them . . . *Now, why should we not have a national
monument, where the deeds done by our countrymen should be preserved to
instruct this and future generations?*[64]

When reporting a visit to the Conservatoire in Paris, she
stressed the benefits of a national government which was able
to support a good national education scheme and offered
opportunities for individuals to improve their social situation. Events where foreigners showed solidarity with the Irish
were also emphasised in these articles. Thus, when Margaret
met a Frenchman on a bus in Paris, the following occurred:

After a few remarks on the beauty of the scenery, my *vis-a-vis* asked
if Madame were not *Anglaise?* – and when I made my invariable

reply – '*Non, Monsieur, je suis Irlandaise,*' he brightened up, compre-
hending at once the distinction I wished to convey, 'Ah! your's is the
country of O'Connell – is it not?, I see Madame is proud of her com-
patriot, and she is right. His is the greatest name of our age – "*le plus
beau nom du siecle*".' He spoke with enthusiasm of our struggle for
liberty, on which the eyes of his country were riveted, and of the
earnest sympathy and assistance (if need were) of the French
people.[65]

These travel reports were probably the first female writings of
length published in *The Nation* and were no doubt based on
actual first hand accounts.[66] From these articles a picture of
Margaret Callan as a very educated and sophisticated woman
emerges.

Under the pseudonym 'Thornton MacMahon', she went
on to edit *The Casket of Irish Pearls,* a collection of works of
Irish writers, for the Library of Ireland in 1846.[67] In her
introduction, she stated how important it was that the Irish
people read works by their own writers and not only by
English authors, who were often prejudiced against Ireland.
By learning about Irish history, culture and literature, young
people would develop pride in their country and gain self-
respect as Irish people. Like all Young Irelanders, she also
pleaded with her readers to overcome disunity. For her, as an
Ulsterwoman, this was extremely important:

Forswear for ever divisions of sects and parties, and become in heart
and soul "united Irishmen." Thus will you render harmless the arms
our enemies have heretofore so skillfully turned against us, and
frustrate that policy of disunion, which they have so long and so
justly reckoned upon. Had our fathers listened, in their day, to this
holy preaching of mutual love and mutual charity, instead of to the
promptings of an insane bigotry, stimulated by artful foes, how
changed a destiny might not they have left to us, their children.[68]

Discussing the historical writings in this book, she
explained what she saw as the intention of successive British
governments in Ireland. She blamed England for religious
divisions in Ireland. Thus the Penal Laws[69] were designed to
create disunion amongst the Irish people. However, she was

quick to cite examples in Irish history when all creeds came together and overcame divisions:

This distinction of a favored caste, so flattering to the religious prejudices of the Protestants, who were the most influential and educated of the nation, and should thence have been the legitimate leaders of the people, did its mission of disunion, and separated effectually the two creeds.

Secure in the policy of religious discord, we have the government forcing on the people certain brass halfpence, a scheme at which so much of Swift's matchless ridicule was levelled. This is memorable not so much for its intrinsic importance as that it proved the first rallying point where Catholic, Protestant, and Presbyterian combined against their rulers; and the result of that short-lived union was a triumph for the nation.

A mortal fear shook the English councils, lest that this passing intimacy should kindle into friendship, and so melt away the prejudices which they had so carefully nurtured.[70]

Thus she argued that England could only rule Ireland when the country was divided. Once the Irish people united, they could achieve self-government but this, she believed, required proper education. Explaining that the ideas of Drennan and Pollock[71], although addressed to northern Presbyterians, were misunderstood by most people through ignorance, she reasoned that national education would overcome prejudice:

Bigotry, and its nursing mother, Ignorance, still hold possession of the strongholds of the North, and no power, excepting education, can ever dislodge them. The pen, and not the sword, is the weapon to wield against prejudice.[72]

She seems to have been a moral force nationalist, and in 1848 she followed Duffy's moderate ideas rather than Mitchel's radicalism.[73]

Callan had little to say about women. Not only was her book dedicated to 'The young men of Ireland, her hope in the coming years', it only contained the work of three female writers, Mrs. Tighe, Lady Morgan, and Miss Edgeworth[74], but she also expressed a low opinion of charitable aristocratic ladies:

Who has not heard of schemes for the improvement of our peasantry in their habits of farming, cleanliness, &c., which have miserably failed? Sometimes the cause is easily traceable, as when a proselytizing landlord offered a new-fangled faith hand in hand with increased comforts; or that the Utopian community, which My Lady A, or the Hon. Mrs. B, planned and set a-going, occupied her mind only for a brief season, until that caprice was discarded for some other more novel mode of diverting *ennui*.[75]

She felt that these wealthy women did charitable work only because they were bored, and not because they had a deep interest in their tenants. She believed that the root of all evil lay in the lack of understanding between landlords and tenants. In her opinion, nationalism could overcome tensions between social classes because the desire to improve the social and economic situation of the native country would encourage co-operation of all classes. She suggested that the Irish rely on their own strength, skills and unity, and through good national education and self-reliance the miserable situation of the people would be relieved.[76] Margaret Callan saw nationalism as a unifying ideology, which would unite classes and creeds. She held beliefs that were central to Young Ireland ideology.

Margaret's sister Susan had met Charles Gavan Duffy in Young Ireland circles and eventually married him on 8 February 1847.[77] Consequently, she focused her attention on her home. Although she had been an excellent pianist, who had studied under Chopin and Liszt, she gave up her piano because Duffy did not like it. She also gave up her work in the school.[78] However, she continued playing a supportive role to her husband and the nationalist movement.[79] It is not known whether she wrote any political works.

During the revolutionary times of 1848, Margaret's work in the Young Ireland movement became more important. When Charles Gavan Duffy and other leading members of the Young Irelanders were arrested, Margaret and 'Speranza' worked to continue the publication of *The Nation*.

Whereas Margaret worked in the editor's room, 'Speranza' wrote most of the articles. Duffy remembers their work gratefully:

> Before the number issued the police were sent to seize and carry off the type, the manuscripts, and the proofs. When they took possession of the establishment they found a lady in the editor's room, and the journal ready to be issued. The manuscript of the number on which they had laid their hands consisted in a large degree of articles in two handwritings, both of them plainly feminine.
> The courageous woman found in control of the *Nation* office was Margaret Callan, my sister-in-law; the author of "Jacta Alea Est" was Speranza, the present Lady Wilde. Two women of genius.[80]

Margaret also seems to have passed the Young Ireland spirit on to her pupils: two of her former students offered to act as messengers for the Irish Confederate leaders when all communications had broken down during the revolutionary activities in 1848. Believing the mission too dangerous for young women, Duffy refused to send them to the disturbed counties.[81] After the failed rebellion, Margaret and Susan remained in contact with many Young Irelanders, even when their families emigrated to Australia in 1855–56.[82] In September 1878, Susan Duffy died of tuberculosis after a long illness.[83] Margaret died in Melbourne about 1883.[84]

VIII

> *Little ye dreamed that a woman's love*
> *Could rend the tyrant's chain:*
> I *dare to die for my fatherland,*
> *If a victim must be slain.*[85]

Elizabeth Willoughby Treacy was born in Ballymena. She came from a Protestant landowning family.[86] Whereas her two sisters married between 1848 and 1859, Elizabeth remained single for a long time and lived with her mother in Brigadie House, Ballymena.[87] Although counted by O'Sullivan in his book on the Young Ireland movement amongst the six most important female Young Irelanders[88], she did not contribute regularly to *The Nation* before 1848. Only from the 1850s, did she regularly write patriotic verse in the new *Nation*[89] under the pseudonym 'Finola'.[90] It seems that 'Finola' was not in personal contact with the Young Irelanders in Dublin, nor was she acquainted with the other northern women involved in the movement.[91]

In 1858, she wrote to William Smith O'Brien and claimed to be a distant kinswoman of his.[92] She told him that the patriotic feeling in Ulster was still alive, and that

. . . our people still indulge in the hope of Ireland's nationality being restored . . . the time is at hand to organise a spirited national party that would be all powerful in the event of England's difficulty with France.

She urged Smith O'Brien to form an Irish party, and to visit her if he would be in the north. Although a Protestant, she supported 'the desire of the Northern Catholics to see Ireland raised from her degraded state.'[93]

'Finola's' poetry was not warlike in nature, as was 'Eva's' or 'Speranza's' . Although strongly expressing her nationalist beliefs, she put more emphasis on people's social circumstances and their poverty than on blood and violence. Since social problems took priority, her poems were often very sad, but tender, depicting the effects of social decline. She described the life of impoverished people in workhouses or in low paid jobs, whose happy memories of the past were their only remaining possessions.[94] Her heroes were the socially disadvantaged industrial workers, impoverished women, poor children, victims of evictions and emigration. Her work reflected the poverty experienced in the northern counties from the 1850s. 'Finola' also employed powerful symbols. Many of her images were connected with natural catastrophes and their consequences, such as storms, tides or shipwrecks, which she used to express the ups and downs of life and the nation's societal problems. Women and girls were a particular feature of 'Finola's' poems, and their difficult destiny and suffering is portrayed in great detail. For instance, in 'Only a Factory Child' she describes the freedom a factory girl feels when she finishes her work. Nature here serves as an escape from hardship:

Only a factory child,
From her daily toil set free,
To bask for a few brief hours
In the light of liberty.

A child with the brow of age,
Decrepit, and sad, and worn:
A waif from the city's streets,
Unfriended and forlorn.

She had dreamed of the far-off sea,
The wild waves murmuring strain –
The crash of the spectral wheels
Still throbbing through her brain.

A few brief joyous hours
Away from the dismal street;
Through the shadowy lane she hastes
With childhood's willing feet.[95]

'Finola' did not idealise or romanticise poverty and her female heroines were not the passive, beautiful, poor women of romantic fantasy, but rather strong, stubborn and tough characters. In 'Rosaleen', her heroine personified Ireland in a very unusual way. Whereas the Young Irelander James Clarence Mangan idealised Ireland as a passive and defenceless woman in his poem 'Roisin Dubh'[96], 'Finola's' 'Rosaleen' did not sigh and weep, nor wait to be rescued, but verbally challenged her oppressors:

Rosaleen listened, struck dumb with scorn;
Only a flash of the downcast eye,
Only the gust of a stifled sigh,
A tremulous flutter of pulsing heart,
A clench of the hand and a sudden start –
Told how the blow was borne.

Dare you asperse my maiden fame
Because that I differ from lying wrong,
And side with the weak, and repulse the strong?
Though I may fail to avert the blow,
Pitying love can I still bestow,
Heedless of praise or blame.

Little you reck of the warring strife,
The passionate conflict that knows no rest,
Yearning to succor a land oppressed?–
Is it not womanly, holy and pure?
Dearer the faith that you bid me abjure
Than the perilous gift of life.[97]

The important question in 'Finola's' poem – why it was not considered womanly to fight for an oppressed country, had been previously asked by 'Mary' and 'Eva' in 1848.[98] Throughout 'Finola's' verse the women are very powerful.[99] The Young Ireland women wanted to contribute to the national struggle, and felt they constituted an integral part of the nationalist movement. This did not necessarily mean that they demanded equal power.

'Finola' also included criminals amongst the underprivileged and showed understanding for their situation. In 'The Convict's Flower' she asks:

Who may tell the dark temptations ere their footsteps turned astray,
With no light to guide them onward, with no hand to point the way?
Ye who call their sentence justice – ah, 'tis easy to condemn –
Boasting vainly of your virtue – have you e'er been tried like them?[100]

This attitude stood in stark contrast to the moralising opinions of some Young Irelanders, who looked down on lower-class criminals and condemned them for their deeds.[101]

'Finola's' poems also expressed the desire to unite people and to overcome social injustice. Therefore, her collection of poems entitled *Never forsake the ship and other poems*, published in 1874, was dedicated to 'All Creeds and Classes'. She felt solidarity with 'the people' and unlike many Young Irelanders, who meant only the middle classes when talking about 'the people', she included the lower classes. In 'Proudly We Stand in the People's Ranks', she demands equal rights for all:

> *Proudly we stand in the people's ranks, to war with the people's wrong –*
> *Though not always the race be to the swift, the battle to the strong;*
> *We dare to preach forth the branded creed of equal rights to all –*
> *On the evil and just will the fruitful rain and the cheering sunbeams fall.*
>
> *Our weapons – true thought and fearless speech – with these we will overthrow*
> *Each low device and base pretence, each aim of the crafty foe;*
> *We laugh at their hollow sophistry, their station, rank, and caste,*
> *Their senseless barricade of words our arms will soon lay waste.*

She believed in moral force, not physical force, to overcome inequality.[102] In the same poem, she also combined religious faith and social issues, and claimed that true religion did not breed inequality:

> *Rend the tyrant chains that custom forged, and recant the impious creed*
> *That a separate law for rich and poor by GOD's wisdom was decreed.*
>
> *Remember who sat at the publican's feast! – was there peer or noble there?*
> *What jewelled garter, or diamond star, did those guests, so honoured, wear?*[103]

Her opposition to religious hypocrisy also appears in her poem 'Laborare est Orare', where she attacks people who pretend to be pious, but do nothing to help others in distress:

> *Laborare est orare! struggling ever for the right,*
> *Bearing one another's burthens [sic], pressing nearer to the light –*
> *This a worship unrestricted by the forms of class or creed,*
> *This a doctrine, pure and simple, that the feeblest mind can read.*[104]

Since 'Finola' lived in the north longer than many other female Young Irelanders, she was in closest contact with the social developments there[105], and thus stressed the importance of the growing working class. Like Henrietta Mitchel Martin, she also focused on the recruitment of Protestants into the home rule movement, which became more difficult with the rise of organised unionism.[106] 'Finola' reflected a different kind of 'northern' identity in her poems, often neglected in historiography. She was both a Protestant and a nationalist, as well as sympathetic to social issues and the industrial workers.[107] Being interested in the Fenian movement, she campaigned for the release of Fenian prisoners, and wrote a letter to Gladstone on the subject.[108] Later, when she became involved with the Land League and the home rule movement, 'Finola' addressed meetings in Ireland and England on these issues. On 12 September 1883 she addressed a meeting organised by the Belfast branch of the Irish National League[109] under the chairmanship of Joseph Biggar[110], in St. Mary's Hall, Belfast, on 'Ireland as it is – North and South'. There she stressed the importance of the land question. Condemning the present land tenure as adverse to every just principle, she demanded that land should be inherited by all. She urged the Irish people to support home rule.[111] In her speech her strong religious beliefs are self-evident:

If the earth was the Lord's and the fullness thereof, had not all a right to share our Father's gifts? There was no law of primogeniture with God, no law of succession or entail. The Divine law ordained that the husbandman should first enjoy the fruits of his labour, whilst an edict of man allowed a landlord to usurp it. Thanks to that chivalrous Irishman, Charles Stewart Parnell . . . that wrong had been partly redressed. The lecturer then referred to the coercion laws, and urged her audience to resolve to be true to their pledge that under no circumstances would they take land from which a tenant had been evicted . . . Referring to Irish landlords and the ancient Irish elk, she hoped that in future the one species would be as extinct as the other. She advised all present to lead pure and holy lives, and strive to the best of their ability to rise their fallen Ireland.[112]

Her preoccupation with social issues derived from her strong faith. Her ideal of a just society was firmly based on her belief in a just God, who had created equality.

In 1871 she married Ralph Varian, who had been actively involved in the Young Ireland movement through the Cork Citizens Confederate Club. After her wedding, she moved to Blackrock, Co. Cork, and was very happy with her 'loving husband'.[113] Nevertheless, she did not lose contact with her home, travelling frequently to the north. The death of her husband[114] and ensuing financial difficulties caused her enormous distress. Used to wealth, she was now thrown into abject poverty and had to write begging letters to prominent political and literary nationalists trying to sell her poems. In these letters, written in 1893, she claimed to be recovering from an illness and being on the verge of starvation and eviction. She dreaded going to the poor-house. However, she remained a nationalist and hoped that the Irish people would not have forgotten 'Finola' who had always worked on their behalf.[115] These letters are painful reading. Her nationalism was the only thing left for her. The loneliness and the fear of being forgotten by her audience was harder to bear than poverty. That is why she signed with 'Finola' as well as with her full name, so that people would remember her. She received some help, but died in St. Patrick's Hospital, Cork, in 1896, aged 75.[116]

IX

The northern women in the Young Ireland movement came from very different religious and social backgrounds, and their lives developed in different directions after the Young Ireland movement dispersed. They certainly did not form a distinct group amongst the female Young Ireland activists. Since many of them moved to Dublin, and later emigrated from Ireland, they never focused on a specific 'northern agenda' in their writings. However, all northern Young Irelanders were influenced by their upbringing in a geographical area that was characterised by religious divisions. Therefore, all were concerned with the situation in the north. Young Ireland, with its emphasis on unity of all Irish people, appealed to them. Northern nationalists were also able to contribute their experience and beliefs to this ideology. Only two of the women, Henrietta Mitchel Martin and 'Finola', expressed a northern agenda of sorts. This is especially evident when these two women became directly involved in the home rule movement, where Henrietta Mitchel Martin attempted to convert northern Protestants to nationalism, and 'Finola' campaigned to improve the situation of the industrial workers.

The activities of the northern women in the Young Ireland movement varied; Jenny Mitchel, Henrietta Mitchel Martin and Margaret Hughes wrote articles for the Young Ireland newspapers, and also participated in the management and organisation of these newspapers. As wives of Young Irelanders, Susan Hughes and Jenny Mitchel gave their husbands valuable support. Jenny Mitchel became a public figure and consequently rallied support for the nationalist cause. Henrietta Mitchel Martin became a public figure later in life when she supported her husband and home rule. 'Finola' was a poetess who later spoke on behalf of home rule.

However, there was a difference in their political beliefs. Jenny Mitchel was a radical and shared her husband's beliefs in physical force, 'Finola' was a moral force nationalist with stronger views on social issues. Nevertheless, most of these women maintained contact with each other, except 'Finola' who was not personally known to them.

Why were these northern women so important for the Young Ireland movement? As northern nationalists, they were living examples of Young Ireland's claim that their ideology embraced all classes and creeds of people. As women, they illustrated the importance of women in Young Ireland, and the nationalist, movement in general, and their activities show the diversity of female involvement. None of these women became nationalist leaders, which would not have been possible at this time. However, they were all strong, independent characters who were not satisfied with the social constraints placed on them. They deviated from women's traditional role and also from class restrictions. Generally, an association with the Young Ireland group was not seen as acceptable behaviour for upper and middle-class women, especially after Young Ireland split from the Repeal Association in 1846 when Young Irelanders were perceived as extremely dangerous radicals. However, these women had the courage to get involved in a movement which was often opposed to the beliefs they were brought up with. As a Protestant gentlewoman, 'Finola' acted against the political beliefs of her class and her community.[117] Others, like the Mitchel and Hughes women, had supportive family networks with some kind of nationalist tradition. This probably influenced their politics, and certainly facilitated their decision to take part in the Young Ireland movement.

Nationalism gave the Young Ireland women a voice to express their beliefs and hopes. The emphasis on education and writing in the Young Ireland movement allowed women to participate, and to influence a considerable number of people through the organisation's newspapers and other publications. Young Ireland's ideology was romantic and theoretical but it had an important impact on perceptions and ideas. The northern women contributed to this ideology in their own way. Although these women were not 'feminists', and women's issues were not at the forefront of their agenda, their example encouraged other women to get involved in politics.[118]

These Ulster women might not have been representative of northern women, but they certainly brought to the Young Ireland movement an independence, coupled with stubbornness, strength, a readiness for action and for practical work, which Young Irelanders perceived as characteristic of northern people. The northern women therefore made the movement much more representative of Irish society as a whole.

---

[1] William Dillon, *Life of John Mitchel* (London, 1888), p. 124.

[2] Other northerners were John Martin (Co. Down), John O'Hagan (Newry), and Francis Davis – the 'Belfast Man'. Thomas D'Arcy McGee, although born in Co. Louth, came from an Ulster family.

[3] Ellen Downing from Cork ('Mary'), Mary Kelly from Headford, Co. Galway ('Eva of *The Nation*'), Jane Francesca Elgee, later Lady Wilde, from Wexford ('Speranza'), Olivia Knight from Castlebar, Co. Mayo

('Thomasine'), and Adelaide Hart and her sister from Dublin ('Two Irish Girls').

[4] John Martin to 'Eva', Dublin, National Library of Ireland (hereafter NLI), Ms. 10.520/ Micr. Pos. 8428, 31 Aug. 1848.

[5] For instance, 'Eva' came from Headford to Dublin when Young Irelanders were arrested, and John Mitchel's mother and sisters were often in Dublin.

[6] Occasionally, public attention was drawn to female activists as when Jenny Mitchel organised support for her imprisoned husband and during the trial of Duffy in 1848 when rumours spread that many of the 'highly seditious' newspaper articles were written by women (in particular by 'Speranza'). Dublin society considered this to be rather shocking.

[7] The discussion about women in *The Nation* between Apr. and June 1847 included many articles and letters. For instance, 'A Constant Reader', 'Female education', vol. 5, no. 237, 24 Apr. 1847, p. 459, cols. 2–4; Ralph Varian, 'The formation of a Ladies Irish National Association', vol. 5, no 244, 5 June 1847, p. 554, cols. 3–4. In 1848, more articles and letters on women appeared, such as: 'Eva', 'To the women of Ireland', vol. 6, no. 286, 25 Mar. 1848, p. 200, cols. 1–2; and letter of 'Catherine' in 'Answers to Correspondents', vol. 6, no. 288, 8 Apr. 1848, p. 233, col. 3.

[8] Both 'Eva' and 'Mary' advocated the participation of women in combat. See 'Eva', 'To the women of Ireland', *The Nation*, vol. 6, no. 286, 25 Mar. 1848, p. 200, cols. 1–2; and 'Mary', 'To the women of Ireland', *United Irishman*, 13 May 1848, quoted in T. F. O'Sullivan, *The Young Irelanders* (2nd ed., Tralee, 1945), pp 487–8.

[9] For instance, John Mitchel and Thomas Devin Reilly. Charles Gavan Duffy was opposed to it. In March 1848, Mitchel and Reilly advocated in the *United Irishman* the participation of women in the manufacture of weapons and their participation in street-fighting. However, the women would not take part in the actual fighting, but could aid the battle by throwing bricks from their windows. See Rebecca O'Conner, *Jenny Mitchel, Young Irelander* (Dublin, 1988), pp 67f.

[10] For more information, see my article 'Women of the *Nation*' in *History Ireland*, vol. 1, no. 3 (Autumn 1993), pp 34–7.

[11] J. D. Fraser, 'Song for July 12th, 1843', in *The spirit of the nation; or ballads and songs by the writers of 'The Nation'* (58th ed., Dublin, 1928), pp 36f.

[12] For instance, John Mitchel wrote to John Martin on 23 June 1844 about a repeal meeting in Tullylish: 'although Tullylish is the very stronghold of Orangeism in this neighbourhood, there was not the slightest manifestation of ill-will towards those who attended the meeting, either in going to it or returning. I think I see a growing interest about repeal amongst Protestants.' Cited in Dillon, *Life*, vol. 1, p. 54.

[13] See Charles Gavan Duffy, *My life in two hemispheres*, (2 vols., Shannon, 1969), 1, p. 13. He describes the religious tensions in Monaghan, and the privileged position of Protestants.

[14] In 1846, when conservative newspapers and the Orange journal *The Warder* praised the Young Irelanders for their stance against O'Connell, repealers were attacking them for being soft on unionism.

[15] They also hoped that the memory of Grattan's parliament could unite both Catholics and Protestants. Of course, their view of Grattan's parliament was idealised, but its myth had some attraction to Protestants. Young Ireland also attempted to show their desire for unity in their ballads.

[16] Ulster custom was the recognition of a tenant's saleable interest in his holdings. He could sell the occupancy of his holding to the highest bidder with the approval of his landlord. This allowed the tenant to secure compensation for any improvements. In the 1850s, the demand for this custom, also known as 'free sale', grew in the other provinces. Ulster custom was granted legal recognition under the Land Act of 1881.

[17] His main argument was that the tenants were losing hold of the soil and would consequently become impoverished labourers. He pleaded with them that social problems were more important than religious differences. See P. S. O'Hegarty, *John Mitchel* (Dublin and London, 1917), p. 92.

[18] See, for instance, Memorandum Book of the Shanks family, Public Records Office of Northern Ireland (hereafter PRONI), T. 2809/1, p. 50.

[19] The Rev. John Mitchel and Mary Haslett married in 1811. Their children were: John (b. 1815), Matilda (b. 1817), Mary Jane, Margaret, Henrietta (youngest girl), William (youngest child, born 1828). Matilda married Mr. Dixon (also spelt Dickson by some authors) and moved to Londonderry. Both Margaret, who had married Hill Irvine and also lived in Londonderry, and Matilda and their families later returned to live in the Dromolane area near Newry. Mary Jane Mitchel appears never to have married. See Dillon, *Life*, vol. 2, p. 285.

[20] For instance, the Reverend John Mitchel was highly esteemed by his parishioners and was not afraid to voice controversial opinions. In 1829, he and other congregations split from the Presbyterian Synod of Ulster and became Unitarians.

[21] The youngest son, William, was only twelve when his father died.

[22] Dillon, *Life*, vol. 1, p. 7.

[23] John Mitchel to Matilda Dixon, Bermuda, PRONI, D. 1078/M/3A-B, 4 Oct. 1848.

[24] However, she was not involved in any Young Ireland activities.

[25] John Mitchel to Matilda Dixon, Bermuda, PRONI, D. 1078/M/4A-B, 5 Mar. 1849.

[26] *The Nation*, vol. 6, no. 297, 10 June 1848, p. 378, col. 4.

[27] Jenny Mitchel's maiden name.

[28] John Mitchel to Matilda Dixon, Bermuda, PRONI, D. 1078/M/3A-B, 4 Oct. 1848.

[29] Additionally, at this time, Jenny was looking after a growing family.

[30] Dillon, *Life*, vol. 1, p. 122.

[31] Ibid., p. 123.

[32] Henrietta stayed with the Mitchels during the winter of 1845–46, and Mary and Margaret came to Dublin in the summer of 1846.

[33] Dillon, *Life*, vol. 1, pp 123, 160. When Thomas Carlyle visited the Mitchel home in the autumn of 1846, he was impressed by both Mrs. Mary Mitchel and Jenny Mitchel. Ibid., p. 127.

[34] O'Conner, *Jenny Mitchel*, p. 67.

[35] *The Nation*, vol. 6, no. 299, 24 June 1848, p. 416, col. 2.

[36] In the autumn of 1848, Jenny aided Thomas Devin Reilly's escape from Warrenpoint to New York, where he arrived in Nov. 1848. He escaped dressed as a poor peasant from the north of Ireland. It is not known how Jenny exactly helped him, but it is likely that she provided shelter, clothes and transport. See O'Conner, *Jenny Mitchel*, p. 118 and O'Sullivan, *Young Irelanders*, p. 305.

[37] Lucy O'Brien intended to move to the Penal Colonies with her children, but her husband William Smith O'Brien did not want his children to be brought up outside Ireland.

[38] By 1849, most Young Irelanders were either arrested, transported or had escaped to America and Europe. Thus, hopes of political change collapsed. Repeal agitation had completely broken down, and although revived in 1849, the Repeal Association finally disbanded in July 1850. The country was devastated by Famine and a cholera epidemic in Dublin.

[39] Jenny Mitchel to Mr. Reilly (Devin Reilly's brother), PRONI, MIC. 426/2/8, n.d.

[40] John Mitchel to Matilda Dixon, Bermuda, PRONI, D. 1078/M/4A-B, 5 Mar. 1849.

[41] Ibid., PRONI, D. 1078/M/3A-B, 4 Oct. 1848.

[42] John Mitchel described the stance his wife took on his escape: 'my wife does not shrink from all this risk and inconvenience . . . instead of dissuading, urges me strongly on the enterprise.' See John Mitchel, *Jail Journal* (Shannon, 1982), p. 304.

[43] For instance, they campaigned on behalf of the Fenian prisoners after the failed uprising of 1867.

[44] O'Connor, *Jenny Mitchel*, p. 113.

[45] One of them, Henrietta, died young in a French convent. The Mitchels also lost two sons fighting on the Confederate side in the American Civil War. John Mitchel strongly supported the southern states in the Civil War, and would have fought as well, if he had been in better health. He believed the south had the right to secede from the Union. Jenny also supported the southern states.

[46] In the American Civil War (1861–65), the Union attempted to stop the Confederacy's commerce with Europe, thereby blockading the southern coasts. Many naval and commercial ships tried to break this blockade.

[47] Dillon, *Life*, vol. 2, pp 187–190. The Mitchels never had a permanent home in America. They lived successively in New York, Knoxville (East Tennessee), Washington, Richmond, Paris (John Mitchel worked in Paris from 1865–66 as financial agent for the Fenian movement, while the family continued to live in Richmond), New York and Brooklyn.

[48] The election took place on 11 Mar. 1875. John Mitchel died on 20 Mar. 1875.

[49] They both were middle-aged and had known each other all their lives.

[50] They went to America in the autumn of 1869 and stayed mainly at the Mitchel's home in Brooklyn until Apr. 1870.

[51] O'Connor describes him as cranky; he always questioned orders. Judging from his diary and his letters, he seems to have been very particular, especially about his health. However, it seems he was a very generous and caring person who was well-liked by his tenants. O'Conner, *Jenny Mitchel*, p. 158.

[52] O'Sullivan, *Young Irelanders*, p. 172.

[53] John Martin died on 29 Mar. 1875, shortly after John Mitchel's burial.

[54] Henrietta Mitchel Martin to George C. Mahon, NLI, Ms. 22.226, 29 Feb. (1876).

[55] Ibid., 16 Sept. (1875). The new MP for Meath was Charles Stewart Parnell.

[56] In a letter, she stated the dread she felt upon returning to Ireland, because she knew she would feel the loss of her husband more forcibly. Part of this was no doubt due to her homelessness. A nephew of Martin's had inherited his estate and the Mitchel home in Dromolane had been sold. As a result she went to live with her unmarried sister Mary. The time spent in Milan helped her to cope with her grief, and the loss of her home. Ibid.

[57] Charles Stewart Parnell (1846–91): chairman of the Irish Parliamentary Party (hereafter IPP), who led the home rule campaign. The IPP split after Parnell was cited as co-respondent in the O'Shea divorce case in 1889, leaving Parnell with a small minority in 1890.

[58] O'Conner, *Jenny Mitchel*, p. 396. See also 'Nation Moans – Charles Gavan's Funeral Tomorrow' in *The Globe*, (Boston, MA), NLI, Ms. 8006/3, Charles Gavan Duffy – miscellaneous, 7 Mar. 1903.

[59] Taken from an anonymous manuscript entitled *The Women of Young Ireland*, 58 pp, written sometime after the 1930s (NLI, Ms.10, 906), p. 10.

[60] Newry Catholic Church Records, PRONI, MIC ID 26, 19 Aug. 1826. These records only date to 1818, and therefore the date of Margaret's

birth cannot be established. The family had six daughters and five sons.

61 Their mother was Susanna Gavan from Monaghan, and was a sister of Charles Gavan Duffy's mother. Their grandmother Judith Gavan was described by Duffy as a fierce nationalist and opponent to the Act of Union. According to Duffy, her husband who supported the Union, because he believed it would bring Catholic Emancipation, collected petitions in its favour. However 'Judith flew into a rage at the proposal to give up Ireland for a bribe, and flung the petition into the fire. The flame she kindled that day has illuminated her memory for more than three generations among a numerous progeny who are proud to bear her name.' Margaret's and Susan's cousin Charles Gavan Duffy was one of the Young Ireland leaders, and their brother Terence MacMahon Hughes (1812-49) also wrote many articles in *The Nation*. Duffy, *Life*, vol. 1, p. 3.

62 See *The Nation*, vol. 4, no. 170, 10 Jan. 1846, p. 209, col. 3.

63 Susan must have lived in the same house as the couple, because the address given in *The Nation* advertisements is the same as that of John B. Callan recorded in directories and advertisements. Their mother lived in Whitehall, Blackrock. See *Thom's Irish Almanac and Official Directory for the Year 1846* (Dublin, 1846), p. 269, and *The Nation*, vol. 5, no. 227, 13 Feb. 1847, p. 302: Marriage announcement of Susan Hughes and Charles Gavan Duffy.

64 'A Day at Versailles', *The Nation*, vol. 1, no. 42, 29 July 1843, p. 666.

65 Ibid.

66 Of the Young Irelanders, for instance, Adelaide Hart, travelled through Europe in 1842, and William Smith O'Brien in 1843.

67 The Library of Ireland was a series of works on Irish history and literature written or edited by the Young Irelanders.

68 Thornton MacMahon (ed.), *The casket of Irish pearls. A selection of prose and verse from the best Irish writers* (Dublin, 1846), p. xiii.

69 Penal Laws were severely discriminatory legislation excluding Catholics from all public life, passed between the end of the seventeenth and beginning of the eighteenth centuries.

70 MacMahon, *Casket*, p. xx. Jonathan Swift (1667–1745): Dean of St. Patrick's Cathedral, Dublin, from 1713; satirist and author of political pamphlets attacking British government policy in Ireland; author of *Gulliver's Travels* (1726) and *Drapier's Letters* (1724).

71 William Drennan (1754–1820): Belfast Presbyterian, influential poet and pamphleteer of the United Irishmen. Joseph Pollock: Ulster Presbyterian, barrister and radical pamphleteer, organised the United Irish Society in the north, wrote in the *Northern Star* under the pseudonym 'Owen Roe O'Neill'.

72 MacMahon, *Casket*, p.xiv.

73 Duffy and Mitchel split over the use of physical force in 1847–48. While Duffy was hesitant about an Irish revolution until mid-1848, Mitchel

became more revolutionary towards the end of 1847, when he demanded the arming of the people, and called for passive resistance to poor rates and rents. On top of Duffy's dislike of Mitchel's support for slavery there was a personality clash between these two men.

[74] Mrs. Mary Tighe (1772–1810): romantic poet; author of *Psyche* (1805). Lady Sydney Morgan (1777–1859): poet and novelist; author of over 70 works including *France* (1817). Maria Edgeworth (1767–1849): novelist; author of *Castle Rackrent* (1800).

[75] MacMahon, *Casket*, p. xiv.

[76] Ibid., pp xv–xvi.

[77] Susan bore Charles Gavan Duffy eleven children, of whom three boys and three girls survived. One of Margaret's daughters later married a son of Duffy.

[78] This might have been the reason why the thirty bed school was put up for sale in Apr. 1847. It had been running successfully for twelve years, but 'the present proprietors desired to retire.' See advertisement in *The Nation*, vol. 5, no. 236, Apr. 1847, p. 433, col. 1.

[79] Cyril Pearl, *The three lives of Gavan Duffy* (New South Wales, 1979), p. 69.

[80] Duffy, *Four years*, p. 681.

[81] *The Women of Young Ireland*, pp 32–34, and Duffy, *Two hemispheres*, vol. 1, p. 290.

[82] See also 'More about Mary of the *Nation*', *Irish Monthly*, vol. 36 (1908), pp 69f.

[83] Pearl, *Three lives of Gavan Duffy*, pp 211, 232f.

[84] *Irish Press Supplement*, 12 Sept. 1945.

[85] 'Finola', 'A Tale of the Past', in *Never forsake the ship, and other poems* (Dublin, 1874), pp 82–87, stanza 25.

[86] In *Slater's Directory for 1846*, Anne Tracy [sic], Brigadie, is listed under Nobility, Gentry and Clergy in Ballymena.

[87] Her mother Anne Treacy had been married twice, firstly to John Love who died in 1812, and then to John Treacy of Brigadie House, Ballymena in 1816. When he died in 1843, his four surviving children, William Augustus, Elizabeth Willoughby, Anne Beccles and Catherine Hyndman were all over twenty one, and received two-thirds of his personal property. See Appointment of New Trustees and Assignment of Trust Estate, PRONI, T. 662/234A, 1859, and Release of 3rd parties in respect of Trust Estate, 1873, PRONI, D.366/960, 1873.

[88] The other five were Ellen Downing ('Mary'), Mary Kelly ('Eva'), Jane Francesca Elgee ('Speranza'), Olivia Knight ('Thomasine') and Marie Thompson ('Ethne').

[89] After it was banned in July 1848, *The Nation* began publishing again in Sept. 1849. Charles Gavan Duffy remained its editor until 1855, when he emigrated to Australia. *The Nation* continued publication well into the 1890s.

90 For instance 'Watch and Wait' and 'Never Forsake The Ship'. A similar pseudonym, namely 'Fionnuala' had been used by Mary Kelly before she discovered that there was another female writer with such a name. Mary Kelly never knew Elizabeth Treacy. 'Finola' might have become acquainted with some of the Young Irelanders after 1848. See autobiographical sketch by 'Eva', NLI, Ms. 10.521, p. 4.

91 Letter by R.D. Williams to 'Eva', NLI, Ms. 10.520, n.d. This states that Jenny Mitchel did send her regards to 'Mary' and 'Eva', so obviously they knew each other.

92 Their fathers were related.

93 Elizabeth Willoughby Treacy to Smith O'Brien, NLI, Ms. 446, Item 3059, Smith O'Brien papers, 21 Aug. 1858.

94 For example in 'In the Workhouse' or 'The Artificial Flower Maker', in 'Finola', *Never forsake*, pp 47–9, 54–8.

95 Ibid., pp 32–4.

96 This famous nationalist poem was first published in *The Nation*, and can be found in nearly every nationalist song book.

97 'Finola', *Never forsake*, pp 4–7.

98 For instance 'Eva', 'To the women of Ireland', *The Nation*, vol. 6, no. 286, 25 Mar. 1848, p. 200, cols. 1–2; and 'Mary', 'To the women of Ireland', *United Irishman*, 13 May 1848, quoted in T. F. O'Sullivan, *The Young Irelanders* (2nd ed., Tralee, 1945), pp 487–8.

99 For instance, in 'A Tale of the Past', she tells a story of a brave woman who freed her lover from jail and thus saved his life. This is intended to illustrate the initiative and strength of women in the national struggle. See 'Finola', *Never forsake*, pp 82–7.

100 Ibid., pp 40–3.

101 For instance, John Mitchel explicitly describes how he desperately distanced himself from lower-class convicts. See Mitchel, *Jail Journal*, pp 66f, 123–25, 285–87.

102 However, it is not known how she reacted to the 1848 rising.

103 'Finola', *Never forsake*, pp 43–5.

104 Ibid., pp 26–8. The Latin phrase translates as 'to work is to pray'.

105 After the Famine, Ulster experienced increasing urbanisation and industrialisation, as well as rising migration to Belfast.

106 The introduction of the first home rule bill in 1886 caused unionists to organise the opposition to home rule. In the twentieth century, unionism was mainly concentrated on a parliamentary level, but included a strong populist appeal.

107 In this she followed the tradition of the United Irishmen, although she was not a revolutionary.

108 O'Sullivan, *Young Irelanders*, p. 129. He does not date this letter.

109 The Irish National League, inaugurated by Parnell in Oct. 1882, replaced the Land League and was the constituency organisation of the IPP. After the split of the IPP, membership of the league decreased.

110 Joseph Biggar (1828–90): Belfast Presbyterian; in 1877 converted to

Catholicism; nationalist politician and specialist in the technique of parliamentary 'obstruction' in the house of commons; member of the Irish Republican Brotherhood.

[111] O'Sullivan, *Young Irelanders*, p. 129.

[112] 'Lecture on Ireland', *Northern Whig*, 13 Sept. 1883, p. 5, col. 1. At 'Finola's' lecture, a Mr. Duddy referred to the services rendered by the female Young Irelanders to the cause of Irish nationalism, stating that women had rights which should be recognised by legislation.

[113] See letter by Treacy to an unknown person of literary standing, NLI, Ms 11.449/1, 3 Sept. 1893. Ralph Varian also edited her second volume of poems in 1874. The first volume had already been published by Anderson in Belfast in 1851.

[114] The date is unknown.

[115] See letter by Treacy to an unknown person of literary standing, NLI, Ms 11.449/1, 3 Sept. 1893 and 7 Sept. 1893.

[116] *The women of Young Ireland*, p. 21 and O'Sullivan, *Young Irelanders*, p. 129.

[117] However, it is not known what the Treacy family thought about 'Finola's' politics.

[118] In letters to *The Nation*, women declared that they saw the poetesses as role models. The *Galway Vindicator* states, 'Animated by the example of those patriotic ladies, whose inspiriting [sic] poetry has given a zest to the more serious pursuit of independence, the ladies of Loughrea, adopting 'Eva' as their 'Prophetess and Guide', have most zealously engaged in this cause [collecting money for Mrs. Mitchel], and under their auspices the most happy results may be hoped for.' Quoted in *The Nation*, vol. 6, no. 297, 10 June 1848, p. 380, col. 4.

'THE FEMALE OF THE SPECIES IS MORE DEADLIER THAN THE MALE'? THE ULSTER WOMEN'S UNIONIST COUNCIL, 1911–40[1]

DIANE URQUHART

I

The 'part women had played in helping the men in recent troublous times would, when the history of those times came to be written, compare favourably with the part played by the women of old'.[2]

This was the conviction of Lady Cecil Craig in 1927. Although the history of this period has been written and rewritten, the resolute and assiduous excitations of the Ulster Women's Unionist Council[3], and that of their female predecessors, have been largely neglected by the historical establishment.[4] Fernand Braudel's terminology of 'submerged history'[5] can be effectively applied to the study of women, who, until recently, have been denied an historical role. However, by placing women at the centre of historical inquiry a serious and stimulating challenge is posed to what has previously been determined as historically significant. To take the traditional periodisation of Irish history from the late nineteenth century as an example, historical attention has largely focused on the diametrically opposed doctrines of unionism and nationalism. However, even here, in the study of politics,

that most male defined of societal landscapes, re-interpre-
tation is necessary to include women's participation.[6] Much
research into Irish women's historical role must be forthcoming before any theoretical framework can be definitely
applied, but the study of women should transcend the gap-
filling process and the recreation of notable or oppressed
lives. In the study of women in politics it is, however, difficult
to avoid 'a male-defined conceptual framework'.[7] Certainly a
wide definition of 'politics' should be adopted, as looking
solely to the formal power structures of government institutions excludes not only the majority of women, but also men.
Politically active women, like men, have always constituted a
minority of their sex, but what should be assessed are what
prompted women's participation and what was their political
agenda. It would be fallacious to discount the history of an
organisation like the UWUC solely because they were largely
under male control and defined their own existence with
reference to their male counterparts. Instead of critiquing
the 'compensatory' nature of political women, it would be
more constructive to ultimately aim for an analysis of the
inter-relation between the public, political and private arenas
of female experience, as women 'have always been part of history, experiencing its impacts and contributing to its movement.'[8]

Formed on 23 January 1911[9] with the incipient intent of
supporting male unionists' opposition to home rule for
Ireland, the UWUC proved to be sufficiently pliant to initiate
extensive war work, during 1914–18 and to inflect their interests post-war to encompass a myriad of areas; social, economic and political. Essentially the women's council was a
conservative organisation with few pretensions of influencing
policy and with no ambition to shake the status quo. The
organisation believed that theirs was a 'steady, silent movement'[10], but this should not place it within the ranks of the
historically insignificant.

In the period 1890–1914, British women became involved
in party political work, not for feminist reasons, but for pragmatic ones. The Corrupt and Illegal Practices Act of 1883,
which forbade the payment of political canvassers, and the

extension of the electoral franchise in 1884, encouraged party organisers to reconsider their electoral strategies. The emergence of women's political associations from the late nineteenth century[11] should therefore be identified with this background of deviating party systems, and the genesis of an organisational network which harnessed the energies of party workers, who increasingly were female. Intrinsically women became a source of voluntary and unpaid political labour. After 1900 women became more politically prominent, volunteering in their thousands within a relatively short period of time.[12] Although women were excluded from the main political parties until the extension of the franchise to their sex in 1918, women's auxiliary associations made their contribution an integral factor in the political process before this date. The UWUC can be placed within this context. In the north of Ireland women had been sporadically involved in the nineteenth century protests against the implementation of home rule[13] in 1886[14] and in 1893.[15] The institution of a formal body of women unionists was induced by a heightened sense of crisis following the removal of the house of lords power of veto by the Parliament Act of 1911.[16]

The UWUC was governed by an executive committee headed by a president and initially one vice-president.[17] Also on the executive were the council's office bearers and representatives of affiliated local women's unionist associations. Both the council and its executive met regularly to discuss policy, progress and problems.

II

The inaugural meeting of the organisation was held in Belfast in January 1911, initiating:

> . . . the beginning of real and solid work and a thorough organising of the women of Ulster . . . to begin work at once, to canvass voters, to trace removals, and to endeavour to bring every single voter to the poll during elections, so that every seat in Ulster shall be won for the Union . . . the women of Ulster will be in no way behind the men in striving for so noble a cause.[18]

The UWUC co-operated with the men's Ulster Unionist Council[19] in promoting religious, economic, constitutional and imperial arguments against home rule. The women were sufficiently politically astute to realise that their 'Council should urge the Ulster case against Home Rule mainly on social and economic grounds, by which the charge of Ulster bigotry will be avoided'.[20] For example, Lady Cecil Craig assessed the economic fallacies of home rule, when addressing the annual meeting of the East Down Women's Unionist Association in 1914:

Apart from their own destation at the Bill in Ulster, it was a bad Bill for the rest of Ireland, the finance being absolutely unsound . . . There was, moreover, no desire for it in the South and West except amongst the political agitators, and ignorant peasants, who had been told that when they got Home Rule Ireland would flow with milk and honey, and be a kind of Utopia, such a thing as paying rent being unknown.[21]

The organisation also highlighted a 'women's dimension' to home rule. In 1911 they voiced their opposition to any home rule bill for Ireland:

. . . as they know that the civil and religious liberty of the women of Ireland and the security of their homes can only be guaranteed under the Legislative Union of Great Britain and Ireland.[22]

Indeed, the home, the traditional sphere where a woman's influence was socially acceptable, featured prominently in the iconography of women's unionism. Moreover, women's political action was portrayed as an extension of their maternal and protective responsibilities:

If our homes are not sacred from the priest under the existing laws, what can we expect from a priest-governed Ireland . . . let each woman in Ulster do a woman's part to stem the tide of Home Rule . . . the Union . . . meant everything to them – their civil and religious liberty, their homes and children . . . once the Union was severed there could be no outlook in Ulster but strife and bitterness. . . . Home was a woman's first consideration . . . in the event of

Home Rule being granted, the sanctity and happiness of home life in Ulster would be permanently destroyed.[23]

The council accentuated the point that women and their dependants would ultimately suffer most under home rule, 'for when bad times came and work was scarce women and children were more severely affected than the men.'[24]

The UWUC rapidly developed into a strong, dynamic and democratic body. The membership figures bear witness to the fact that the council was not only popular, but was needed to co-ordinate the activities of unionist women. During the first month of the council's existence over 4,000 women had joined the West Belfast branch and by March 1911 women's unionist associations affiliated to the council had been formed throughout Belfast, Londonderry, Antrim, Armagh, Tyrone, Fermanagh and Monaghan.[25] Within a year of its establishment the minutes of the organisation record membership of 40,000–50,000. No further overall membership figures are available in the council's records, but newspaper coverage dating from 1913 quotes figures of between 115,000–200,000.[26] Membership of the council was mainly upper and middle-class, especially amongst its leaders. Analysis of presidents clearly reveal the UWUC's social composition: 2nd Duchess of Abercorn was president 1911–13, succeeded by 6th Marchioness of Londonderry 1913-19, 3rd Duchess of Abercorn 1919–21, and Lady Cecil Craig (later Viscountess Craigavon) 1923–42. Similarly in the period 1911–39 only one of ten vice-presidents was untitled. In Ulster, the rest of Ireland and throughout Britain, women of these classes possessed the time and economic freedom to participate in public life. However, within the council there were no membership restrictions on the basis of social classification. Undoubtedly some working-class women were involved, for instance, it has been alleged that 80 per cent of the West Belfast association of the council were mill workers and shop girls.[27]

The council's appointment of a male organising secretary[28] in 1911 provides the only indicator of any sense of insecurity with regards to their single sex composition. The organisation seemingly experienced no initial learning phase when they were unsure of policy or direction, as four months after the establishment of the council six of its members were in England canvassing electoral support for a unionist candidate and by May 1911 the council's executive sent women speakers around Ireland studying the Irish question at first hand. In their canvassing work the council co-operated with women's unionist associations in England and Scotland, the Primrose League and the Women's Amalgamated Tariff Reform Association. Addressing the political meetings of these organisations, the UWUC focused solely on the Union, as all other questions were believed to be of secondary importance. The constitution of the council clearly revealed their political priorities:

The sole object of the Council shall be to secure the maintenance in its integrity of the Legislative Union between Great Britain and Ireland, and for this purpose to resist all proposals, of whatever kind they may be, which have for their object the establishment of any form of an Irish Parliament. It is a fundamental principle of the Council that no other subject other than the above shall be dealt with . . . it being understood that all other questions, in which individual members may be specially interested, shall be subordinate to the single issue of maintenance of the Legislative Union.[29]

All unionist activities were expedited to face the third, and most severe, home rule crisis of 1912–14.[30] As Sir Edward Carson wrote to Theresa Londonderry in March 1912:

This is very private. I have made up my mind to recommend very drastic action in Ulster during this year . . . There is growing feeling we do not mean business and I certainly think this is the critical year and I am prepared for any risks.[31]

There was extensive press coverage of public demonstrations organised by the women's council, indeed it appears that the organisation was valued for its publicity value. L. Cope Cornford, the editor of various unionist publications, also contacted Theresa Londonderry:

The press as a whole reported the Ulster Women's Unionist Council well. It is essential that the interest should be maintained . . . and I foresee a difficulty here. If the Women's Council could issue another manifesto, and take some action, it would help from the spectacular point of view.[32]

The sense of urgency and impending crisis amongst unionists helped the UWUC gain momentum. Analysis of attendance figures at female unionist meetings emphasises the high level of enthusiasm unionism could rouse. For example, 10,000 women attended a council demonstration in October 1912. In 1913 they organised a meeting to welcome Edward Carson on his first visit to West Belfast. This was reckoned to be 'the largest assemblage of women which ever took place in Ireland, the attendance being estimated at over 25,000.'[33] In addition to mass demonstrations, unionist women also held many drawing-room meetings. For instance, addressing such a meeting in February 1914, Lady Theresa Londonderry urged women:

. . . to march with their menfolk in all that they did to oppose Home Rule. A great poet had told them that "the female of the species is more deadlier than the male" . . . there was nothing that the women of Ulster would not do or sacrifice in their determination to maintain the Union. The most dangerous feature of the situation was the extraordinary apathy of the people in England towards the Home Rule question . . . [so] spread the light among the unheeding and the indifferent, and . . . educate the millions who had little chance to go in search of information and knowledge.[34]

Attempting to overcome this apathy, the council was involved in comprehensive petitioning. In January 1912 they launched a women's petition against the *Ne Temere* papal decree.[35] Within a month this petition measured a mile in length[36] and it eventually had 104,301 signatories when presented to parliament by Sir John Lonsdale on 11 June 1912.[37] The petition's introduction outlined women unionists' objections to the decree, and to home rule:

Serious dangers would arise to our social and domestic liberties from instructing legislative functions to a body of which a large per-

manent majority would be under ecclesiastical control . . . No legislative safeguards would avail to protect us against such dangers, as
the Catholic Church refused to recognise the binding effects of any
agreements which curtail her prerogatives and claims of uncon-
trolled jurisdiction in the provinces of education, and the marriage
laws . . . in an Irish Parliament the natural instincts of humanity
would be of no avail against the dictates of the Roman Church . . .
The dominating power of ecclesiastics over education in Ireland,
which is already excessive, would be largely increased . . . There
would be no prospect of beneficial legislation to ameliorate the
conditions of life of unprotected women engaged in industrial work
as the Irish Nationalist members of Parliament steadfastly oppose
such legislation. No valid reason has been advanced for depriving
Irish women of the rights or privileges which they now enjoy.[38]

In May 1912 the women's council collected over 100,000
women's signatures in another petition against the implementation of home rule, which was also forwarded to the
commons.

Unionist leaders were conscious of the importance of
maintaining unity and discipline within their ranks to present
a favourable public image of Ulster unionism to the English
electorate. Consistent attempts were made to demonstrate
that unionists were a respectable community with valid reasons for resisting home rule. Illustrative of this was a scheme
for the establishment of an Ulster covenant, exemplifying
unionist solidarity, self-discipline and determination. As
women were barred from signing the male unionists'
covenant, the UWUC organised their own declaration with
the primary aim of associating unionist women with 'the
men of Ulster in their uncompromising opposition to the
Home Rule Bill'.[39] 28 September 1912 was proclaimed Ulster
Day for the collection of signatures for both the declaration
and covenant. The fact that 218,206[40] men signed the
covenant, compared to 234,046[41] female signatures on the
declaration construes the comparative strength of women's
unionism.

The council was also accountable for sending thousands of
leaflets and newspapers relating unionist anti-home rule con-
tentions to Britain, America and the Dominions. The UWUC

aimed to enlighten Britain's populace, not only of the impact
home rule would have on Ulster, but also to publicise, what
unionists believed to be, the 'true' character of Irish nationalists, who:

. . . were not the kind of half angels which Mr. Redmond had
described . . . The Nationalists painted the future of Ireland in glow-
ing colours, but the Protestants of the country did not come into
the picture[,] . . . it was a masterpiece of impressionist painting, as
the further one stood away from it the better it looked.[42]

The didactic element of the women's work was extensive
and unrelenting. Working through their philosophy of
'Prevention is better than cure'[43] the council established a literary sub-committee to co-ordinate their huge propagandist
workload.[44] By September 1913 10,000 leaflets and newspapers were being sent weekly to Britain under the auspices of
the women's council[45] and between 1 June 1913 and 13
March 1914 literature was forwarded to 14,902 electors in 65
constituencies.[46] Moreover, local associations of the council
were coupled with English women's unionist organisations,
and by 1912, twenty-one of their thirty-two branches, representing 66 per cent of the UWUC, were involved in this
work.[47] Many women unionists were sent from Ulster to work
in England and Scotland[48] and by March 1913 nineteen
women were permanently based in Britain working as unionist missionaries.[49] Indeed by the end of this year, 'it was reckoned that not less than 100,000 electors heard the Unionist
case from the lips of earnest Ulsterwomen'.[50] Workers from
the council were often specifically requested by other political organisations which suggests that they were considered
effective propagandists. They were certainly not diffident, as
in 1912 the council averred that their speakers were 'most
anxious to address Radical Audiences rather than meetings
of convinced Unionists'.[51]

The council's activities were not limited to demonstrating
and propaganda. In co-operation with the UUC, unionist
women made a major fund-raising contribution to the
Carson Fund, which was established in 1912 to finance anti-

home rule propaganda. The organisation also worked with the Ulster Volunteer Force[52] which was formed to convince British opinion of unionists' determination not to accept home rule in any guise. This military body of men was backed by an equally disciplined female force of volunteers, whose activities the women's unionist council helped administer. The UWUC successfully drafted a scheme for the training and organisation of the UVF Nursing, Driving and Signalling Corps, held first-aid classes, fund-raised and secured equipment and supplies for medical units which were set up throughout Ulster in preparation for civil war with Britain.

Although unionists attempted to focus solely on home rule, the issue of women's suffrage infringed on their concerns during the third home rule crisis. Consistently the UWUC:

> . . . kept the one question of the Union before them pre-eminently. On other questions – [like] women's suffrage . . . they might have and hold different opinions – but on the one question of the Union they had no room for differences – the Union was their one rallying point, and held them together with a force that no varying opinion on lesser subjects would interfere with.[53]

However, it seems that the existence of the council had a positive, though indirect and unintentional, impact on the question of women's enfranchisement. By bringing women into the political arena and initiating extensive political work, the women's council provided a visible illustration of how women could be civically responsible. There were suffragists within the ranks of the women's council[54], but unionists who also campaigned for the vote increasingly had to develop different political facades and prioritise their own political convictions. However, the women's council was unable to totally evade this issue, as suffragette militancy focusing on unionist owned property began in Ulster in 1913. This was prompted by unionist plans for the establishment of a provisional government in Ulster, which included the co-option of women onto various government boards and informally promised votes for women on the basis of the existing municipal register. These plans never came to fruition. Carson, a known

opponent of women's suffrage, responded to severe dissen-
sion amongst his party by attempting to distance himself from
this pledge. The women's council were also concerned about
the politically divisive nature of suffrage. In September 1913
Lady Dufferin wrote to Lady Theresa Londonderry with
regards to the unionist decision to include women in
provisional government:

There is a great deal of feeling . . . and the suffragettes are tri-
umphant, others write to suggest that we "veto" the resolution, so I
came to the conclusion that it would be best to ignore the suffrage
part of the letter . . . our association stands for *one* political question
only – that on Home Rule we are united; on every other question we are probably divided, and therefore it is all important
that we should refrain from any expression of opinion on other
policies . . . I *know* that if any opening had been given for a
discussion . . . there would have been unpleasantness.[55]

Their reluctance to discuss the question of women's
enfranchisement continued, as in March 1914, the council's
president, Theresa Londonderry requested that the organisation 'took no action . . . in connection with the recent deputation of Suffragettes to Sir Edward Carson, as it was
considered advisable not to re-open the matter'.[56] The
women's council made no further comment on suffrage, con-
centrating instead on their consequential political work. By
July 1914 unionists increasingly saw civil war as their only
remaining option. The women's council, although clearly
appalled by this prospect, were determined to continue supporting male unionists:

. . . we now must be prepared for the worst . . . to stand with our men
to the last . . . To us women the very thought of strife, accompanied
by bloodshed, is an unspeakable horror. In such times it is the
women who suffer most . . . [but] we women of Ulster are resolved
not to be a hindrance but a help to the men . . . we must give them
our sympathy, our encouragement, our approval, our admiration.[57]

However, the situation was dramatically altered by the outbreak of the First World War in August 1914, which led to a

cessation of suffragette militancy and of unionist plans for
civil war, as the scene of conflict moved from Ulster to the
wider expanse of Europe.

III

The whole unionist political campaign was officially suspended for the duration of the war.[58] However, when circum-
stance rendered inaction dangerous to the unionist cause,
the women's council did embark on political work. The
organisational machinery of the UWUC remained operative,
although their priorities altered. With the outbreak of war
the council initially believed that it was their 'duty to see that
the families and dependents [of men in military service] are
cared for, and that any want and suffering which may result
shall be minimised as much as possible.'[59] To fulfil this aim
the women's council became engaged in extensive charity
work, co-operating with organisations like the Soldiers' and
Sailors' Families Association.

Just three months after the outbreak of war, unionist
women discussed 'equipping the Ulster Division with comforts, and offering the sum of £100 towards the purchase of a
Machine Gun, or failing that, an Ambulance'.[60] Clearly paci-
fist sentiments had no place within their wartime rhetoric.
Indeed it seems plausible that the purchase of a gun provided
a way for women to become indirectly involved in the male
preserve of fighting, rather than contribute in a traditional,
caring manner befitting their sex. The council eventually
opted for the purchase of an ambulance which was used in
France during the war.[61]

In August 1914 the women's council inaugurated the
Ulster Women's Gift Fund for soldiers, which by 1918 had
raised in excess of £100,000. Unionist headquarters in Belfast
were converted into premises where the women's council
sorted, packaged and dispatched food and comforts and
assembled military dressings for not only Irish regiments, but
for other army and naval units and for hospitals. In 1916 this
work was augmented, as a fund to provide similar comforts
for prisoners of war was initiated by the council. Visits to families of men serving in the forces were organised and the

council made arrangements to care for those who were discharged from the forces as medically unfit. The UVF hospitals in Belfast and France received the special attention of the council, and they totally financed the running of the French UVF hospital, 1914–16[62], explicating that although war was being fought on an international scale, Ulster still remained the focus for the women's council.

Unionist women were also involved in recruiting Voluntary Aid Detachments and soldiers for both the Ulster and imperial forces. The council fund-raised for the UVF Patriotic Fund. However, they only agreed to undertake this work after firm assurances had been received that a fair representation of women would serve on this funding committee, emphasising that although feminism within the ranks of women's unionism was usually superseded by political concerns, there was some comprehension of the importance of asserting women's rights.[63] The UWUC also protested against the exclusion of Ireland from the Compulsory Military Service Acts of 1916 and 1918. In 1916 they declared:

We the members of the Ulster Women's Unionist Council representing a quarter of a million loyal women of Ulster desire to express our deep dissatisfaction at the exclusion of Ireland from the Compulsory Service Act. We protest against the refusal of the Government to join our people with their fellow citizens of Great Britain in a common bond of service to the Empire.[64]

Although formal unionist political work was suspended, the council's concern and sense of insecurity with their own domestic situation was evident. Remaining at home in Ulster, it was apparent the women had difficulty overlooking the uncertainty of their own position, and continued to question how the post-war situation would affect them. In 1916 the council even altered their constitution to meet changed conditions after the war. Increasingly the UWUC undertook political work through its individual members, rather than through their organisational network.[65] For instance, in 1917 the council 'urged that members . . . should in their private capacity try to reach as many Colonial Soldiers as possible, and instruct them in the Home Rule question'.[66] Similarly, the council were worried by the outcome of a post-war general election. As a result they worked continually to keep electoral registers up to date. This electoral work became increasingly important after the granting of the franchise to women aged over thirty in February 1918 and the Redistribution of Seats (Ireland) Act of the same year which rendered it necessary to re-organise several existing WUAs, and to establish new associations in newly created electoral areas. This was political work that the council refused to disregard and by June 1918 they were planning a scheme to ensure that all women who were entitled to vote were on the electoral register.[67] In May 1918, the UWUC reaffirmed that their premier political objective was to be 'occupied entirely in helping to defeat the latest Home Rule Measure and that before everything else.'[68] As war weariness grew and the political situation altered, the UWUC became increasingly discontent with unionist leaders, who openly discouraged the women's council from widespread political work.[69] Their dissidence with the constraints imposed upon their organisation was vociferously expressed in June 1918. Demanding a definition of their status with regards to the Unionist Party, the UWUC articulated:

During the last four years of war, our opinion on any one political matter has never been asked. We ourselves have been mute, under what we consider has been a very insidious and slow disintegration of our power . . . Our advice was never asked when the Covenant was broken. No intimation was given [to] us about the suggested Federal Scheme. All the same, we have held fast to our Unionist opinions, and our voice has been heard and acted upon although perhaps the "Ulster Unionist Council" may have thought us an entirely negligible quantity . . . [we] have no desire to emphasise any difference between the men and women of Ulster. We should be comrades in arms in defence of a common cause . . . what is the position of the Ulster Women's Unionist Council? It has none – we are nothing . . . is it right or just that we should be in this position[,] that we should remain in this position – are we wise to re-organise and spend the large sum of money involved and trouble ourselves and expend our health and strength if we have no recognition? . . .

We cannot give up the reins and remain the leading *Women's Association in Ulster* . . . [we] realise many anxieties, difficulties, and dangers that have to be faced by the Men with regard to the Vote for Women, and its possibility on future elections. But . . . we have not been treated as comrades . . . We must have more power for immediate action . . . we have mediated and thought to do [what] will be of supreme importance in keeping our people together, in educating women's opinion and to bring the war to a final and satisfactory conclusion . . . let us stand out now for the rights and liberties of the Ulster Women's Unionist Council. Let us fight under the motto of our old banner "Union is Strength".[70]

This proved to be a catalyst for change. Unionist leaders gave the women's council permission to re-organise and to continue as a separate organisation. Moreover in 1918, women were granted twelve representatives on the UUC and a joint committee of the men's and women's councils was established to co-ordinate consultation and co-operation between the two organisations.

IV

In the post-war period the political work of the women's council was fully revived, and they expanded their areas of interest. Preceding the establishment of the Northern Ireland parliament, unionists accepted six county exclusion for Ulster and not nine counties as originally intended. Partition had vexed the UWUC even during the war. For instance, Lady Dufferin expressed the organisation's anxieties, writing to Lady Theresa Londonderry in July 1916:

Our women are naturally much upset by the turn things have taken, and are longing to be up and doing[,] of course we all feel heartbroken over the proposed partition of Ulster, and are still hoping some better solution of our difficulties may come out of the melting pot.[71]

Edith Mercier Clements conveyed similar sentiments to the council's president:

We must very diplomatically hold together our warm supporters in the three counties, many of them are at present too sad to even want to attend our committees and we must show them that they mean more to us than ever before because of their inestimable and incomparable self-sacrifice. You can hardly form any idea of how many women are irreconcilable and never would have consented to anything which meant the breaking of the Covenant . . . [72]

Sentiments expressed by Lady Cecil Craig in April 1919 summarise the unionist women's view of partition, as they, 'all agreed that they would rather remain under the Union, but if that was not possible they had to do the best they could.'[73]

Partition was debated at a UWUC meeting in March 1920, where the 'majority of the meeting was of the opinion that Ulster should remain intact and abide by the covenant'.[74] The council sent delegates to the UUC meeting held to decide policy on the geographical definition of Ulster but the women's council imposed no restrictions on their representatives, leaving them 'free to vote as their consciences direct them'.[75] Ultimately the UWUC sanctioned six county exclusion, although there was some internal criticism and resignations did occur within their ranks.[76]

The establishment of a 'form of Government which was entirely unasked for and undesired by the majority of the people of Ulster'[77] ensured the continuance of unionist women's work:

The future holds much uncertainty for the loyal population of the Six Counties . . . our watchword is still "UNION", the struggle against the enemies of the Empire and of Ulster is not at an end, it is merely transferred to a new field. Ulster stands alone as never before, and every Loyal Ulsterwoman must give of her best; must realise her responsibilities, and by working and voting must help to hold fast that Civil and Religious liberty which has been handed down to us as a sacred trust.[78]

Even in 1927 the UWUC still emphasised the importance of resisting any false sense of political security and of maintaining their organisation:

. . . at the highest state of perfection . . . if a time of crisis should again arise the loyal women of Ulster must be well prepared, and with this end in view should see that the necessary machinery is kept in smooth working order . . . [79]

Parallel to their internal political insecurity, was the unknown corollary of women's enfranchisement. The UWUC's response to the partial enfranchisement of women in 1918 was complex, and illuminates much, both of their own inter-war policy and the attitude of the UUC towards women in politics. The UWUC worked to ensure that every unionist woman who was entitled to vote was on the electoral register, in Ulster and in England.[80] The Duchess of Abercorn, addressing a women's unionist demonstration in Belfast in May 1921, conveyed:

They had never clamoured for the vote, but now it had been given to them she was confident they intended to use it to the safety, honour, and welfare of their Church, their country, their homes, and their children by helping to put a strong loyal Government in power . . . Remember, therefore, that no personal feeling or personal inconvenience must prevent them from voting for the official candidate, no matter what might be the claims of children, home, or business . . . [81]

However, the organisation's integral conservatism, coupled with the prevalent insecurity amongst unionists concerning the establishment of a separate legislature for Northern Ireland, seem to have dissuaded the UWUC from patronising female parliamentary candidates. In 1921 they expressed the opinion:

. . . that the time was not ripe for this, and the essential thing in the first Parliament was to preserve the safety of the Unionist cause, that too much organisation and construction work would be necessary for which perhaps women had not the necessary experience, and except in the case of outstanding qualifications, men candidates were preferable.[82]

Moreover, male unionist leaders, prompted by self-interest and concern over the impact of female enfranchisement, encouraged women to use their vote for the benefit of unionism. James Craig impelled women:

. . . having got the vote it was up to them to use their influence in every possible direction for the uplighting of the masses . . . looking after their welfare, and taking that keen interest in those vast fields which lay before them all in making the world a better place for both men and women to live in. That was a task which was just as much a woman's, if not much more, than a man's.[83]

Addressing the annual meeting of the women's council in February 1921, Sir Edward Carson also emphasised:

As to the responsibilities now laid upon women by the franchise he urged upon them the necessity of using the vote. He advised them in choosing candidates to choose the man who they thought would best represent their views.[84]

Again, Craig forwarded similar convictions:

A strenuous campaign lay before them, the success of which would largely depend upon the women of Ulster, and before any woman put herself forward for Parliament she should fully consider the matter. Patience . . . should be the watchword of the moment.[85]

Indeed, following unionists' electoral victory of 1921, Craig, paying tribute to his supporters, categorically stated, 'I am proudest of men to-day.'[86] The council essentially sacrificed 'feminist' beliefs for the ultimate benefit of Ulster. However, given the wealth of political and organisational experience UWUC members had attained, their lack of confidence in women's capabilities indicates their own fundamental conservatism and the impact of male value systems, which reduced women to secondary status. Therefore, throughout the 1920s, the women's council worked comprehensively to maximise the possibility of unionist candidates being elected, without ever actually encouraging women unionists to come forward and stand for parliamentary election.[87]

The council's disposition towards women standing for election to less powerful bodies than the Ulster and imperial parliaments was more progressive. For example, by March 1919 they openly encouraged all their branches to identify suitable female candidates for urban district and county councils.[88] From March 1920 women unionist candidates standing in the poor law elections for the Board of Guardians received official and, more importantly, financial support from the council and by 1930 they declared 'Poor Law work is women's work'.[89] The UWUC also induced women's political participation, as during the inter-war years they funded scholarships to train unionist women in politics, economics and citizenship, and employed female trainee political organisers in their headquarters.[90] Following the further extension of the franchise to all aged over twenty-one in 1928, the UWUC considered it imperative that women unionists continued to be fully organised to facilitate an expression of their rights. However, no overt encouragement was ever given to women standing for parliamentary election in the period 1918–40.

During the inter-war years there was no cessation of the council's political work. To take 1930 as an example, over 7,000 propaganda leaflets were sent under their auspices, their speakers addressed over 160 meetings, and three new associations and twenty-nine new branches of the council were formed. Educational propaganda remained a core component of their work. In 1934 they reported a

. . . steady advance being made along the lines of political education, the goal being that every woman elector should be given an opportunity of studying Unionist aims and ideals [so] the Unionist women of Ulster realise their political responsibilities and their power as citizens.[91]

The organisation also expanded its objectives, making unionism as a political creed appear relevant to Ulster's inter-war position. This enabled the women's organisation to maintain members and continue its public activity, campaigning against Sinn Féin propaganda in Britain, America and the Dominions, opposing socialism[92] and the escalation of sectarian violence in Ulster.[93] They also answered press statements affording what unionists considered to be false information on the Irish question.[94] Unionist women also promoted the purchase of empire produced goods, and the enforcement of licensing legislation. Demonstrating and petitioning remained an intrinsic feature of their work[95] and clubs for girls were established to recruit the support of future women voters to unionism. Public speaking competitions and classes were held, and a speakers' class for men was organised.

In the inter-war period there was also evidence of increasing levels of co-operation between the UWUC and their male counterparts, perhaps because of women's enfranchisement; from 1924 to 1926 both councils appointed female and male travelling organisers. On several occasions the UUC provided free literature for the women's council, and the two bodies of popular unionism co-operated in establishing branches of the Junior Imperial League in Ulster to educate young unionists and jointly fund-raised to provide Carson's memorial stone in Belfast cathedral.

It has been claimed that the women's council was a non-sectarian body[96], but their bestowal of official representation to women's Loyal Orange Lodges in 1920 reflects an overlap of personnel between these two organisations, tending to refute this contention. In addition the UWUC produced and distributed 10,000 leaflets on the eviction of Protestants from Catholic areas of Belfast and in 1932 they discussed:

> . . . whether any steps could be taken to prevent the penetration of Roman Catholics in certain parts of the Province, and if anything could be done to prevent Disloyalists buying property over the heads of Protestants, [UWUC members] in their individual capacity should do whatever lay in their power to check this failing.[97]

V

War may have forced a reconsideration of women's capabilities, but it failed to permanently alter the entrenched belief that women were responsible for the home life of the nation. Increasingly:

> . . . housewifery was described as though it were a science requiring intelligence and dedication . . . [women] were supposed to take pride and pleasure in a spotless and modern home, and to take seriously the trade of housewifery . . . [98]

The council was not immune from this ideological climate. For example their concerns over security were tainted by domestic and maternalistic ideals:

To the women security meant even more than it did to the men. If they had secure and happy homes in which to rear their children they would bring up a race of men who would rally to the air of their country in its hour of danger . . . It was the men who won the war but it was the women who would win the peace.[99]

These sentiments were clearly expressed in the papers that the UWUC produced inter-war. Their first paper, entitled *Ulsterwoman, a journal for Union and progress*, was published from July 1919 until August 1920, whilst its successor, *Northern Ireland, home and politics, a journal for women*, was produced from October 1925 until June 1927. The council's president at this time, the 3rd Duchess of Abercorn, stated that the aim of the *Ulsterwoman* was:

. . . to bring before the Ulsterwomen the chief questions of the day . . . in a form that will not make too great a demand on busy women's time . . . Ulsterwomen have always interested themselves in politics. We can do more now, and we must . . . be able to give a reason for our convictions, and an answer to those who would try to refute them . . . every woman who has our cause at heart, who is anxious for improvement in the lives of the worker in town or country, in the housing question . . . in education . . . and in the countless reconstruction schemes . . . will take advantage of the opportunity this Journal will afford . . . to show we are as competent to take our share in the difficult problems of Peace, as women proved themselves capable in the last four terrible years of war.[100]

Although Carson wrote an article in the first edition of this journal paying tribute to the work of female unionists, his tone of condescension was apparent, as he gave his 'heartiest wishes . . . to this little journal'.[101] *Ulsterwoman*'s contents were somewhat contradictory. As articles discussing women's position in trade unions appear alongside others enshrining the inter-war ideal of a woman's place being firmly in the home, with domestic management, gardening and other areas being seen as suitable for women's attention.

Northern Ireland, home and politics, a journal for women[102], was revealing even in its title, putting home before politics as befitting the general inter-war trend to keep women within the domestic sphere. The paper commented on Ulster affairs like the boundary question, along with articles on wider issues like unemployment, women's pensions, the empire, socialism, as well as areas seen as 'traditionally' female in interest. In a report from a unionist and conservative women's conference the opinion of female unionists was suitably circumspect:

. . . there was little or no so-called 'feminism' in their discussions, but just a wholesome desire to find out what was best for the nation as a whole, which is a far worthier attitude . . . The Foreign Secretary paid the women Unionists the compliment of addressing them exactly as though they were MEN.[103]

Women's social responsibilities were also discussed. For example, in April 1927 Dehra Chichester, one of the first women MPs in Northern Ireland, wrote an article reassuring women that participation in government was not incompatible with women's designated social role:

. . . women's advent into these branches of public life do not, necessarily, entail any departure from the confines of the home . . . it is possible for her to combine her public with her private duties . . . Local Government work . . . is absolutely interwoven with the root and fibre of home life.[104]

One of the most overtly feminist articles on women's position was published anonymously in August 1926:

Undoubtedly women's influence in State affairs has been great from the earliest times . . . It is only about fifteen years ago that the sex began to knock more insistently at the doors which men had held closed against it, and to demand admission. A stern negative was persistently returned . . . Then came the war. And immediately the closed doors fell down . . . like the walls of Jericho . . . the Ulster Women's Unionist Council can, if it so chooses, shape the political destinies of Northern Ireland.[105]

In spite of this uncharacteristic feminism, the UWUC's conception of the womanly ideal largely persisted throughout the inter-war period. Even though the organisation knew from their own experience that women could organise into a proficient political force, they did not want to assert their political rights too firmly, fearing loss of favour with male unionists. Therefore, the *Ulsterwoman* was careful:

... not to suggest that the men have failed in their efforts on behalf of the Union, but that there is a phase of the question which they do not touch, and aspects of it that appeal more to women than to men. They realise that time and legislation have recognised that women have a place and sphere in the public life of the country, and the members of the Council feel that the time has come when they should try to do their part independently ... They realise that there are great social and moral issues involved, questions of housing and home ... the family ... social life ... which ... depend upon the Union, and in which they desire to interest their fellow-women ... there are home, social, and domestic issues involved which none but women can fully understand. To them the question of class ... is secondary to the much greater issues of home and happiness, of freedom to live our own life and the right to live it under conditions which will make for the greatest happiness.[106]

The council's ambiguous position and evident fusion of conservatism and feminism fit the general inter-war experience of British women. It seemed the vote and extensive war work had a minimal impact on women's social status and position, but had significantly increased their expectations. For many women the inter-war period was a confusing time with little feminist activity. Women were treated as a form of surplus population, largely forced out of the workplace and back into the home. Women's reluctance to stand for parliamentary election was not restricted to Ulster[107] and the inter-war experience of the UWUC largely conforms to the British precedent. However, through an expansion of their activities beyond the nucleus of the Union, the council succeeded in sustaining interest, support and members, whilst preserving their unionist principles. To summarise, the council took one feminist step forward, and two conservative steps back, producing a representative, though complex, inter-war depiction of many female attitudes in Ulster.

VI

The UWUC deferred politics throughout the Second World War to concentrate on war work. This suspension was more determined than it had been two decades previously, when the perception of political crisis had lingered over their war efforts. However, as in the previous conflict, women's war work afforded no guarantee of change. Indeed Edith Londonderry commented in her autobiography, 'It is not unjust to say that women as a whole had a very poor time in these . . . years'.[108] The Second World War produced an even stronger ideology of maternalism, fuelled by pronatalist interests and eugenic concerns about the quality and quantity of the race absent in its predecessor. Only a slight blurring of sexual divisions occurred, leaving attitudes largely unchanged. Although the period 1911 to 1940 saw dramatic legislative and socio-economic changes come into being in Britain, and by the late 1930s women possessed full property, political and judicial rights, there was no progressive erosion of what were deemed to be feminine and masculine spheres. In 1909 it was believed that women's political enfranchisement would be:

. . . a revolution of such boundless significance [it] cannot be attempted without the greatest peril to England . . . woman suffrage must . . . finally lead to its logical result – that is, the complete political equality of men and women . . . a revolution which will work the political and social and moral renovation of England.[109]

The reality proved very different. Neither in Britain nor in Ireland did women emerge as a political force representative of their numerical superiority in the population.

However, the UWUC instilled many women with a sense of freedom and independence which was forbidden to them in other spheres. This was especially significant for their middle-class members, who were more firmly entrenched in the domestic world than their upper or working-class sisters.

Although the council must be viewed as a women's organisation largely under male control, the UWUC contributed to the strength of popular unionism. Further, the women's council proved to be more flexible in the inter-war years than many of its counterparts, continuing to introduce women to unionism and to political activity.[110]

Essentially, the history of the UWUC reveals that Ulster unionism constituted more than a male policy of resistance which adapted to governing Northern Ireland from 1921. The organisation received mention in contemporary accounts, which indicates their significance. For example, Roland McNeill, author of the 1922 publication, *Ulster's Stand for Union*, appropriated unionist women as being, 'no idle sightseers . . . but a genuine political force'[111] who were:

. . . scarcely less active than the men in the matter of organisation. They took as a rule a keener interest in political matters – meaning thereby the one absorbing question of the Union – than their sex in other parts of the United Kingdom. When critical times for the Union arrived there was . . . no apathy to be overcome by the Protestant women in Ulster . . . [who] very quickly became a most effective organisation with that of the men.[112]

The women's council developed from a political auxiliary force resisting home rule out of a deep seated sense of duty, to become a significant force within unionism. When the concerns of the women's council and their achievements are considered, 'unionism' is exposed as a wider political belief which cuts across the gender divide. Even if numerical strength is the only determinant applied, the organisation, as a body of thousands, demands historical recognition. Dedicated unionist women escaped from the confines of the domestic sphere onto Ulster's political terrain, making a valuable contribution to decades of consequential and, too often underrated, political work for the cause of unionism.

[1] I am grateful to the Deputy Keeper of the Public Record Office of Northern Ireland and to the following individuals for permission to publish: the papers of Lady Craigavon, acknowledgements to Viscount

Craigavon; papers of Theresa, 6th Marchioness of Londonderry, acknowledgements to Lady Mairi Bury and the Marquess of Londonderry; papers of Edith, 7th Marchioness of Londonderry, acknowledgements to Lady Mairi Bury; papers of the Ulster Women's Unionist Council, acknowledgements to the Ulster Women's Unionist Council. I am also grateful to Dr. Mary O'Dowd for reading and commenting on earlier drafts of this article, which is based on my unpub. M.A. diss.(1991), The Queen's University of Belfast.

[2] Diary of Lady Cecil Craig, Public Record Office of Northern Ireland (hereafter PRONI), D. 1415/B/38/163-277, 21 Jan. 1927.

[3] Hereafter UWUC. I use the term 'unionist' in accordance with the definition: 'an advocate or supporter or believer in union . . . an opponent of Irish Home Rule'. Chambers Twentieth Century Dictionary (Edinburgh, 1988), p. 1427.

[4] See T. A. Jackson, *The Ulster party. Irish unionists in the house of commons 1884-1911* (Oxford, 1989). Jackson does not mention the UWUC. J. F. Harbinson, *The Ulster Unionist Party, its development and organisation, 1882–1973* (Belfast, 1973). Harbinson mentions the women's unionist council but groups the association under the collective title of 'The Minor Affiliated Organisations', p. 61. P. Buckland, *Irish unionism. Ulster unionism and the origins of Northern Ireland, 1886–1972* (Dublin, 1973), vol. 2. Buckland fails to get the organisation's name correct, referring to it as the 'Ulster Unionist Women's Council', p. 75.

[5] Robert Wutherow, *Cultural analysis* (London, 1984), p. 136.

[6] See Joan Wallach Scott's persuasive argument in *Gender and the politics of history* (New York, 1988), S. Jay Kleinberg, (ed.), *Retrieving women's history. Changing perceptions on the role of women in politics and society* (Oxford, 1988) and Gerda Lerner, *The majority finds its past: placing women in history* (Oxford, 1979).

[7] Maria Luddy and Cliona Murphy, (eds.), *Women surviving* (Swords, 1989), p. 3.

[8] Marilyn J. Boxer and Jean H. Quataert, (eds.), *Connecting spheres* (New York and Oxford, 1987), pp xvi-xvii.

[9] The council was established following a proposal by Edith Mercier Clements, which was seconded by Lady Cecil Craig. Lady Craig was a vice-president of the UWUC 1912–23 and 1942–60, and its president 1923–42. Edith Mercier Clements was one of the council's most ardent workers, she held the positions of assistant honorary treasurer 1911–20 and of vice-chairman in 1920.

[10] *Belfast News-Letter*, 19 Jan. 1912.

[11] The Conservative women's organisation, the Primrose League was established in 1883, the Women's Liberal Federation dates from 1886 and the Women's Labour League was operative from 1906. For further information see Jane Rendall, *Equal or different. Women's politics, 1800–1914* (Oxford, 1987).

[12] For example, the Primrose League was the largest and most widespread

organisation of its time, having half a million members by 1887. Fig. Martin Pugh, *The tories and the people, 1880–1935* (Oxford, 1985), p. 25.

[13] Information on the specifics of women's involvement is scant, but they appear to have been actively involved in unionist mass demonstrations.

[14] The first home rule bill was introduced by W. E. Gladstone in Apr. 1886. This legislation proposed the establishment of an Irish legislature with restricted functions, but was defeated in the house of commons in June 1886.

[15] This bill was introduced by Gladstone in Jan. 1893 and only passed its third reading in the commons with the repeated use of closure. It was subsequently rejected by the house of lords in Sept. 1893.

[16] This was introduced by the Liberal government of H. H. Asquith and removed the house of lords' ability to defeat a bill outright, replacing this with a power to veto for two years. From a unionist perspective this meant that the future passage of any home rule bill could only be delayed.

[17] The number of vice-presidents gradually increased to five.

[18] *Belfast News-Letter*, 24 Jan. 1911.

[19] Hereafter UUC.

[20] UWUC executive committee minutes (hereafter ECM), PRONI, D.1098/1/1, 30 Jan. 1911.

[21] *Belfast News-Letter*, 17 Jan. 1914   .

[22] Ibid., 16 June 1911.

[23] Minute book of Lurgan Women's Unionist Association (hereafter WUA), PRONI, D.3790/4, 13 May 1911.

[24] Minute book of Dunmurry and District branch of Lisburn WUA, PRONI, D.1460/11, 31 Jan. 1912.

[25] The establishment of local branches of the council were not always welcomed. For example catholic shop owners in Portaferry, Co. Down, threatened boycott in response to a branch of the women's council being formed in their vicinity in 1914. However, a successful branch was set up in spite of this. Mrs. Kerr to Lady Theresa Londonderry, PRONI, D.2846/1/8/1-78, 1914.

[26] *Belfast News-Letter*, 22 Sept. 1913, *Darlington and Stockton Times*, 22 Nov. 1913. Although a margin of exaggeration is to be expected, it seems likely that previous assessments of the UWUC's membership have been very conservative.

[27] Roland McNeill, *Ulster's stand for union* (London, 1922), p. 38.

[28] John M. Hamill was organising secretary of the women's council, 1911–29. He was the only male member of the council in the period 1911–40, and all successors to this office were female.

[29] Constitution included in UWUC minutes (hereafter min.), PRONI, D.1098/1/3.

[30] To summarise, in Apr. 1912 the third home rule bill was introduced in the house of commons by Asquith. It was fervently opposed by unionists and conservatives, and did not pass its third reading until Jan. 1913. It

was subsequently defeated in the house of lords, which delayed its implementation for two years. The bill was signed into law by King George V on 18 Sept. 1914, however, in agreement with Ulster Unionist Party and the Irish Parliamentary Party, it was suspended for the duration of the first world war, leaving the question of Ulster's exclusion from home rule unanswered. The home rule bill was repealed by the Government of Ireland Act of 1920, which attempted a compromise by granting a large measure of independence to the south of Ireland and established a separate state of Northern Ireland within the six north-eastern counties.

[31] Sir Edward Carson to Theresa Londonderry, PRONI, D.2846/1/1/86, 27 Mar. 1912. Theresa Londonderry was vice-president of the UWUC, 1911-13 and its president, 1913–19.

[32] L. Cope Cornford to Theresa Londonderry, PRONI, D.2846/1/7/19, 24 Jan. 1912.

[33] UWUC 1913 annual report, PRONI, D.2688/1/3.

[34] *Evening Standard*, 24 Feb. 1914.

[35] Unionist alarm was magnified by the McCann case in Belfast in 1912, which was widely reported in the press, whereby a Catholic man was allegedly encouraged by his priest to take his children and desert his Presbyterian wife. Unionists interpreted this as a practical illustration of the effect of the decree, and of the type of leglislation that could be expected from an Irish home rule parliament.

[36] UWUC min., PRONI, D.1098/1/1, 30 Apr. 1912. The women's council sought to attain the co-operation of women from Dublin in the collection of signatures for this petition, however no indication is given of the success this endeavour.

[37] Nancy Kinghan, *United we stood. The story of the Ulster Women's Unionist Council, 1911–74* (Belfast, 1974), p. 20.

[38] UWUC ECM, PRONI, D.1098/1/1, 27–29 Mar. 1912.

[39] Ibid., 16 Jan. 1913.

[40] A. T. Q. Stewart, *The Ulster crisis. Resistance to home rule, 1912–14* (London, 1967), fig., p. 65.

[41] UWUC ECM, PRONI, D.1098/1/1, 16 Jan. 1913.

[42] Dunmurry and District branch of Lisburn WUA, PRONI, D.1460/11, 31 Jan. 1912.

[43] McNeill, *Ulster's*, p. 166.

[44] This sub-committee was responsible for issuing leaflets and newspapers and for organising women unionist speakers.

[45] *Belfast News-Letter*, 22 Sept. 1913.

[46] UWUC ECM, PRONI, D.1098/1/2, 14 May 1914.

[47] Dunmurry and District branch of Lisburn WUA, PRONI, D.1460/11, 1913.

[48] The majority of these workers were unmarried. This was not surprising given the nature of this work, which involved weeks, and sometimes months, away from home. Between Jan. and Apr. 1913, 23 women workers were sent to England and Scotland under the auspices of the

council, and between Apr. and May of the following year this number increased to 53. Analysis of a list of workers dating from June 1914 reveals that 68 per cent were unmarried.

49 *Northern Whig*, 29 Mar. 1913.

50 UWUC ECM, PRONI, D.1098/1/1, 17 Feb. 1914.

51 UWUC active workers' min., PRONI, D.2688/1/3, 15 Nov. 1912.

52 Hereafter UVF.

53 *Belfast News-Letter*, 12 Jan. 1912.

54 For example, Lady Edith Londonderry, vice-president of the UWUC 1919-59, was a vocal supporter of the non-militant campaign for women's enfranchisement and published several articles on suffrage.

55 Lady Hariot Dufferin to Lady Theresa Londonderry, PRONI, D.2846/1/8/23, 16 Sept. 1913. Lady Dufferin was a vice-president of the council, 1921–36.

56 UWUC advisory committee min., PRONI, D.2688/1/6, 10 Mar. 1914.

57 *Northern Whig*, 15 July 1914.

58 Ironically preparations the unionists had made to resist home rule by military force were quickly adapted to meet the wider imperial, instead of the Ulster, crisis, as UVF Nursing and Driving Corps were utilised during the war.

59 UWUC min., PRONI, D.1098/1/3, 18 Aug. 1914.

60 UWUC advisory committee min., PRONI, D.1098/1/5, 3 Nov. 1914.

61 Unfortunately there are no records of how the women's council reached this decision.

62 Located in Pau, Cabinet du Maire, France, the UWUC financially supported the hospital until the end of 1916 when the French authorities decided to move the hospital nearer the war front and provide the necessary finance for its operation.

63 UWUC advisory committee min., PRONI, D.2688/1/5, 2 May 1916. This fund provided financial aid for those injured, widowed and orphaned during the war.

64 UWUC ECM, PRONI, D.1098/1/2, 8 Feb. 1916.

65 Unionist leaders seemed not to object to the women's council working in this somewhat private capacity. Indeed, Richard Dawson Bates wrote to Lady Theresa Londonderry on 3 Jan. 1917 to encourage work of this kind: 'the fact that they [UWUC members] are doing war work, they should not lose sight of the main object of the association, namely, the defeat of Home Rule.' PRONI, D.2846/1/8/65.

66 UWUC advisory committee min., PRONI, D.2688/1/7, 2 Jan. 1917.

67 Ibid., 4 June 1918.

68 Ibid., 7 May 1918.

69 For example, in Apr. 1917 the women's council was anxious to organise a public demonstration of women to reaffirm their opposition to any political compromise on home rule, but Carson discouraged this. Similarly in Oct. 1917 lectures and study circles for women were cancelled.

70 UWUC min., PRONI, D.2688/1/7, 4 June 1918.

71 Lady Hariot Dufferin to Lady Theresa Londonderry, PRONI, D.2846/1/8/38, 6 July 1916.

72 Edith Mercier Clements to Lady Theresa Londonderry, PRONI, D.2846/1/8/43, 19 July 1916.

73 *Northern Whig*, 7 Apr. 1919.

74 UWUC min., PRONI, D.1098/1/3, 9 Mar. 1920.

75 Ibid.

76 Especially from women unionists in the three 'excluded' counties of Monaghan, Cavan and Donegal.

77 UWUC 1920 annual report, PRONI, D.2688/1/9.

78 Ibid.

79 UWUC ECM, PRONI, D.1098/1/2, 21 Jan. 1927.

80 Local WUAs were given responsibility for their own area and the council provided district government electoral registers from 1918. Branches of the UWUC were also assigned an English constituency to keep the electoral register up to date and forward unionist literature to. This was an attempt to maximise unionist candidates' chances of electoral success. From 1920 the council paid for the services of a special female inspector of the electoral register and in 1921 they held classes on proportional representation at their headquarters. In 1929 they also partially financed the publication of an election leaflet for women.

81 *Northern Whig*, 20 May 1921.

82 UWUC ECM, PRONI, D.1098/1/2, 25 Jan. 1921.

83 *Northern Whig*, 7 Apr. 1919.

84 Ibid., 7 Feb. 1921.

85 Ibid.

86 *Ulster Gazette*, 4 June 1921.

87 However, when two UWUC members, Mrs. Dehra Chichester and Mrs. Julia McMordie, were elected to the first Northern Ireland parliament in May 1921 the council were congratulative.

88 UWUC ECM, PRONI, D.1098/1/2, 18 Mar. 1919.

89 UWUC min., PRONI, D.1098/1/3, 6 May 1930.

90 It should be emphasised that the women's council represented these activities as beneficial to the unionist, as opposed to the women's, cause.

91 UWUC 1934 annual report, PRONI, D.2688/1/9.

92 Unionist concern surrounding the rise of socialism was linked to a fear of this vote being dominated by nationalists, especially in areas like Belfast and Londonderry, consequently depriving unionism of working-class support. The UWUC called upon its members to 'strive in every way possible to expose the fallacies and dangers of its doctrine'. UWUC ECM, PRONI, D.1098/1/2, 17 Jan. 1928.

93 For example, in 1922 the council recorded their 'horror at the outrages which have been perpetrated in Belfast and Ulster'. They subsequently made several donations to the Loyalist Relief Fund, which was estab-

lished to provide financial aid for the victims of sectarian violence. Ibid.,
4 Apr. 1922.

[94] A special sub-committee of the UWUC was established specifically for
this purpose in Nov. 1920.

[95] For example, in 1930 their petition against the Blasphemy Law
Amendment Bill was forwarded to both the Ulster and imperial parliaments.

[96] See Kinghan, *United*. It is claimed throughout this work that the UWUC
aimed to protect the wellbeing of Ulster's populace, regardless of class
or religious difference. Kinghan was organising secretary of UWUC,
1938–71.

[97] UWUC min., PRONI, D.1098/1/3, 26 Jan. 1932. Sectarian sentiments
do not dominate the council's records from this period, but need consideration within an overall history of the organisation.

[98] Gail Braybon, *Women in the first world war. The British experience* (London,
1981), p. 221.

[99] *Northern Whig*, 20 May 1921.

[100] *Ulsterwoman, a journal for Union and progress*, 12 July 1919. This is the only
edition of the paper which is available.

[101] Ibid.

[102] This paper was issued in bulk by unionist headquarters in London, with
local women's unionist associations contributing their own sections.

[103] *Northern Ireland, home and politics, a journal for women*, July 1926.

[104] Ibid., Apr. 1927.

[105] Ibid., Aug. 1926.

[106] *Ulsterwoman*, 12 July 1919.

[107] For example, between 1918 and 1931 only 3.9 per cent of all British
Labour candidates, 3.1 per cent of all Liberal and 1.5 per cent of all
Conservative candidates were women. Figs., Brian Harrison, *Separate
spheres. The opposition to women's suffrage in Britain* (London, 1974), p. 234.

[108] Edith, Marchioness of Londonderry, *Retrospect* (London, 1938), p. 140.

[109] Albert V. Dicey, *Letters to a friend on votes for women* (London, 1909),
pp 10–11.

[110] This was a marked contrast to the experiences of many other women's
organisations inter-war. For example, suffrage societies, in Britain and
Ireland, largely failed to adapt and survive following women's
enfrachisement, while associations like the Primrose League became
increasingly absorbed into mainstream political parties after 1918.

[111] McNeill, *Ulster's*, p. 113.

[112] Ibid., p. 37.

PART III
RELIGION

THE 'WORLD TURNED UPSIDE DOWN': WOMEN IN THE ULSTER REVIVAL OF 1859

JANICE HOLMES

I

The Ulster revival of 1859 was a sudden and powerful explosion of intense religious excitement which took place primarily within the Protestant communities of Antrim and Down and to a lesser extent in Londonderry, Tyrone and Armagh. Although the Established Church, Methodists, and Baptists did support and participate in the revival effort, the majority of those actively involved were Presbyterians, simply because they formed such a large proportion of the Protestant population. In the largely Catholic counties of Donegal, Cavan and Monaghan the revival, predictably, had proportionately less success.

Essentially, a revival is an extraordinary increase in interest in religion which manifests itself in a large number of conversions over a short period of time and is characterised by the occurrence of pentecostal phenomena, a high level of lay participation and the temporary moral transformation of society. This is certainly what happened in Ulster. Over the course of the summer, various types of religious meetings were held at frequent intervals and in numerous locations. Individuals were exhorted to 'turn away from their sins in repentance and to Christ in faith', a process of sudden change which involved intense feelings of agony, guilt and eventual relief.[1] The emotional intensity of these crowded

meetings caused many people, and especially women, to give
in to their spiritual anguish in physical ways – from moaning
and hysterical sobbing to fits and shaking and even more
ecstatic phenomena such as visions, clairvoyance, trances and
the appearance of stigmata-like markings. The resulting
chaos and confusion gave the laity an opportunity to exercise
their leadership abilities – conducting prayer meetings, assisting with conversions and preaching publicly. Religious leaders focused on the revival's more pragmatic goals of church
growth and reinvigorated denominations. The inevitable
result was a moral transformation of society as the new converts, infused with an aggressive religiosity, shunned previous
social vices such as crime, drunkenness, prostitution, family
strife, laziness, vulgarity and sabbath-breaking.

II

Despite an ongoing historiographical interest in the revival
there has been no serious discussion of the role women
played.[2] Women, however, featured prominently in the many
pamphlets, newspapers, letters and denominational reports
that were published in 1859 and 1860. Much of what these
women said and felt was filtered through the medium of a
male reporter or clergyman. Although this presents certain
difficulties of interpretation, it is still possible to get a sense of
what women believed and what motivated them to embrace
religious activity. The conclusion that stands out above the
rest is the simplest. Women were drawn to religious behaviour for practical, down-to-earth reasons. According to the
1851 census of Ireland, the population of Ulster was
2,011,880, 51.5 per cent of them female.[3] By 1861 that proportion rose slightly to 52 per cent, while the overall population of the province declined. In contrast to the national
trend, the population of Belfast was rapidly increasing, from
103,295 in 1851 to 121,602 a decade later, an increase of 15
per cent.[4] In the city the proportion of women comprised 53
per cent in 1851 and 54 per cent in 1861, perhaps in response
to the increasing number of jobs available for women in the
linen industry.[5]
Of the women involved in the revival, it appears that a

majority of them were from the lower classes. In the country
they were farmer's or labourer's wives, daughters and servants while in the city they were mill workers or occupied in
some other branch of the textile industry, be it weaving, shirt-
making or sewed-muslin work. Other occupations included
shopkeepers, washerwomen, street-sellers, domestic servants
and prostitutes. Middle-class women attended revival meetings as well, but were usually described in relation to their
closest male relative. Despite claims that the revival reached
all classes of the population, it was really labouring women
who were most heavily involved.

   Much of life in nineteenth-century Ireland was ordered
around the concept of 'separate spheres'. Activities, responsibilities, duties and behaviour could be labelled as belonging
either to the 'female' or 'male' sphere.[6] Religious activity was
undoubtedly part of the former, as women were expected to
exercise moral influence upon society and their families.
Women were seen as especially receptive to religious experience and considered responsible for the maintenance of a
religious atmosphere in domestic life. The Wesleyan
Methodist Conference, in its annual address to its members
in 1859, stressed how important this role was:

In all this much depends upon mothers and upon elder sisters, they
are generally in the family; their principles and manner, their counsel and spirit, mould and fashion domestic life, and greatly aid in
the formation of habits and character. To you, dear sisters, we say,
be thoroughly devoted to God; use all your influence and spend all
your life for the eternal welfare of those whom you dearly love.[7]

The Ulster revival provides an ideal context in which to examine the roles society expected women to fulfill, and the conflicting demands those roles presented. On the one hand,
women were perceived to be compassionate, virtuous and
especially sensitive to religious sentiment. As such they were
to set an example for men, who were considered easily susceptible to moral corruption. On the other hand, women
were also felt to be nervous, excitable, weak and therefore
particularly prone to fits, visions, physical manifestations and
other examples of religious unorthodoxy.

Male contemporaries and revival supporters felt the process of conviction and conversion experienced during the revival (with or without the physical manifestations) either heightened the virtuous stereotype of women or revealed it for the first time. Consequently, contemporaries believed conversion made female mannerisms delightful to watch and their countenances glow with spiritual light. This almost other-worldly gracefulness was matched by an extraordinary ability to pray. According to Rev. Samuel J. Moore, women prayed with a 'sweet, reverential familiarity, a poetry, a suitableness, a sublimity altogether inconceivable.'[8] When Rev. J. H. Moore tried to pray with a female convert he was forced to stop because her prayer was so much more eloquent than his.[9] Society already viewed women as virtuous and religious. The revival heightened these qualities to a supernatural level. For those women outside the ideal feminine stereotype, such as working women and prostitutes, the revival restored them to respectability. Even if they had been previously coarse and immodest, the process of conversion could miraculously bless them with a graceful deportment and an exceptional ability to pray. 'Every movement, every gesture of the person, the countenance, the head, the hands, is the very perfection of gracefulness, though the party be utterly uneducated, and naturally most uncouth and awkward.'[10]

Prostitutes, however, presented the most blatant violation of this feminine ideal, and were viewed as the worst example of a depraved society by the religious community. The very nature of their profession had deprived them of their natural feminine virtue and dignity and they had 'sunk to the lowest level of degradation which any human creature can occupy.'[11] As a result, the conversion of prostitutes functioned as a powerful endorsement of the feminine ideal and was an image which revival writers used frequently. The *Londonderry Guardian,* for example, claimed that by means of the various revival meetings held throughout the city, eight prostitutes had been 'won to the paths of virtue and religion ... showing that good has been produced even among the most abandoned class of the community.'[12] The conversion of prostitutes was also touted as proof that the revival really was a work of God, for only by such supernatural means, it was implied, could this transformation have occurred. One former prostitute was quoted as saying:

For eleven years I was a prostitute on the streets of Portadown, and no beast ever lived such a miserable and filthy life as I did. Now, glory be to God, Jesus has found me and brought me to himself, and I'll gladly work my fingers to the bone for the poorest crust rather than ever leave him again.[13]

Even women normally considered outside the established feminine ideal, through the medium of conversion and revival, could aspire to the grace, virtue and holiness deemed essential to the female role in society. Contemporaries saw the revival as restoring women to their proper nature, making working women respectable, not by human efforts, but by the work of Divine grace. For those women who were already respectable, the revival helped to emphasise the stereotype that saw their female religious practice and moral influence as a duty.

In contradiction to this idealisation, a writer for the *Northern Standard* expressed his surprise that no emotion had been shown at a revival meeting at the Presbyterian church in Monaghan, 'not even after nearly two hours preaching, no not even among the exciteable part of the congregation the female sex.'[14] If anyone was going to succumb to revival excitement, popular opinion felt it would be women. Critics of the revival constantly reported that the stuffy meetings in crowded churches which went on until the early hours of the morning, provided manifold opportunities for promiscuous behaviour. They described revival meetings as 'disgraceful exhibitions, rendering women forgetful of the modesty which belongs to their sex, and men of the reason for which they ought to be distinguished.'[15] The worst criticism was reserved for the physical manifestations themselves partly because they occurred more readily and more frequently among women. One of the first cases ever recorded took place in a Presbyterian church in the Ballymena area. During the course of the meeting a middle-aged married woman from Laymore, Kilconriola, Co. Antrim appeared to be greatly affected by the proceedings:

She appeared to be greatly excited, and feverish; her pulse was quick, there was a hectic tinge upon the cheeks, her eyes were partially closed and bloodshot, and her face was streaming with perspiration. Her appetite was entirely gone, and for the space of fifty-six hours she was unable to taste anything but water. After the first four hours of racking pain, and incessant cries for mercy, she became more composed, but remained prostrate for nearly three days in the condition which we have described.[16]

Such behaviour became a common experience for many women throughout the province. Women rarely expressed any fear or dread of these spiritual marathons, in fact, they were often eagerly desired as proof of conversion. However, the clergy strongly condemned this attitude and criticised the manifestations as a 'bodily disease' that 'if tampered with and encouraged, become a positive outrage on woman's nature, and almost necessarily lead to frightful consequences.'[17] Just what those consequences were was left to the imagination. Women were considered more susceptible to physical manifestations because they were naturally weak and excitable. The fact that women may have used these experiences for other reasons did not occur to them.

The debate over the propriety of physical manifestations raged over and above the potential ruination of female virtue. Critics also feared for the mental stability of the populace, claiming the revival had made people insane.[18] There were claims that the revival had actually increased drunkenness and crime.[19] Clergymen worried that the proliferation of lay preaching and other lay-led initiatives would pose a threat to clerical influence within the existing structure of society. Supporters of the revival and its detractors were united in their confusion surrounding the physical excitement. Such phenomena were outside their experience and their ignorance was reflected in their contradictory responses. Clergymen who supported the revival and were concerned about its reputation attributed the ecstatic behaviour to the Holy Spirit. Through this divine influence, women were transformed into virtuous, compassionate and pious individuals. For others, women who showed signs of physical excitement gave them a reason to criticise the revival, blaming such behaviour on the weak and excitable feminine nature. As a result of conflicting male views about the origins of revival and its impact on the feminine stereotype, women had the potential to be elevated to a higher religious plane by the revival, or to be 'de-natured' by its tendency to excess.

III

These observations, for the most part, reflect male perceptions of the female sphere. They also reflect male attitudes to female religious experience and not what women themselves thought, felt or believed. Defining the latter is extremely problematic, mainly because of the paucity of source material.[20] It is possible, by using accounts of female conversions reported in local newspapers and pamphlets, to gain a sense of how women viewed their own religious experience.

Conversion was the central defining feature of the revival. The first step involved a deep conviction of sin and the realisation that the individual was not worthy of Christ and would go to hell. Frequently, women were depicted as verbally expressing their despair in words like, 'Oh I am lost, I am lost! I am a God-forsaken sinner! Hell is gaping for me! My wickedness is too great for pardon! I cannot pray – I have never prayed; I am lost – I am lost!'[21] Women commonly visualised this mental struggle with sin as a supernatural battle between Jesus and Satan. As Satan sought to drag them from the narrow path they were on, Jesus would come, break the devil's grasp and set them firmly on the rock within sight of heaven.[22] Women had no trouble believing in the ability of the spiritual realm to influence events in their natural world. This conviction of sin made hell seem like the only option and created an incredible despair and agony that often was expressed in verbal cries, groans and even physical self-abuse. Almost as a last hope, Jesus was petitioned to save the woman – from Satan, from hell and from herself. Once she reached a certain point, Jesus did save. He calmed her fears, removed her doubts and gave her the assurance that he had pardoned all her sins. As a saviour, women most commonly portrayed Jesus as a beautiful being, often wearing 'a crown of dazzling brightness' with an 'undescribable' look on his face.[23] He also became the object of an affection that, although sentimentalised, had distinct sexual overtones. One woman claimed that 'even maternal love paled in comparison to her love for Jesus.'[24]

Assurance of salvation was one doctrine that women especially related to. Agnes J. was a factory worker who had been under conviction for nearly three weeks when:

. . . that assurance that 'God never commences his own work in a soul but he perfects it,' went like a dart to her heart. She was overpowered and fell. She said her heart felt as if it would burst; but now the load was gone, and sin was pardoned. She was full of gratitude – humbled in the dust for past sin and neglect of God, but, blessed be his name and His Holy Spirit, all was now changed. 'Never, oh! never,' she exclaimed, 'will I doubt; He will never let me go.'[25]

Accounts like this could be used to postulate lofty theories of economic change and insecurity as the cause of this desire for assurance. From all appearances there were no grand motivations, merely a desire to be accepted as an individual and liberated from the fear of rejection. Perhaps the changing economic situation could make the concept of assurance more desirable, but women may not have viewed it in those terms. In the Ulster revival, conversion, and the assurance it provided, was a concept which could be viewed from an internal spiritual perspective.

The way in which women got involved in the conversion process reveals a great deal about feminine religious practice. Most women were converted through some form of a 'female support group'. A good example of this operated in the Belfast linen industry. In the various weaving factories and spinning mills, women comprised almost the entire workforce. Mill-girls, the common term used to denote wet flax-spinners, had a reputation for being 'reckless and degraded' and for possessing an altogether low character.[26] They were also, of course, considered spiritually destitute. The negative reputation mill-girls had was partly a result of the nature of their work.[27] The prejudices other working people held against these women served to create a strong in-group solidarity amongst them which was revealed when the revival began to make its presence known. If one worker was 'struck', it was not unusual for her friends and co-workers to experience conviction as well. At Davison's spinning mill in Ballymena, it was reported that six or seven women were convicted of sin at the start of the day. Within one hour, between twenty and thirty women were prostrated and the mill had to shut down for lack of workers.[28]

Another common means of conversion was attendance at the various revival activities, including prayer meetings, Bible classes and open-air services. Here women were surrounded by friends and acquaintances of the same gender and if one woman was prostrated under the influence of Jesus, there were likely to be several of her friends praying and singing over her, encouraging her to achieve the promised assurance of salvation. This tendency for women to minister to each other was strengthened by the perceived impropriety of a man ministering to a woman's prostrations too intimately. Clerical restrictions on female teaching impelled women to form all-female Bible classes which proved influential arenas for conversion and subsequent support groups. For example, one girl, the daughter of a tradesman, had been saved at a meeting of Rev. Hugh Hanna's. A female friend had invited her to attend and once saved she started a Bible class for the girls on her street, where not only scripture memorisation but also penmanship, arithmetic and domestic skills were taught.[29]

Apart from these more formalised support groups the influence of family and friends were important connections encouraging women to convert. Women exhorted each other to attend meetings, and prayed for their unconverted relatives and neighbours. When they visited those under conviction they spoke reassuringly, quoted scripture, sang hymns or prayed.[30] Where ministers failed to provide comfort, women often could succeed. Rev. James Morgan of Fisherwick Presbyterian Church, Belfast, recalled his first revival conversion. She was a poor widow who had doubts about her spiritual condition and wanted him to pray for her and give her advice. 'I gave her the best counsel I could,' said Morgan. 'I dwelt especially on the truth, that the blood of Jesus Christ, God's Son, cleanseth us from all sin.' This seemed to quiet her fears somewhat, but it was not until she had gone to chat with his maidservants, whom she knew well, that she became 'filled with the joy and peace in believing.'[31] It is apparent that discussing her fears with friends of the same gender created an atmosphere more conducive to conversion than the doctrinal exhortations of her minister. Female support groups, be they formal or informal, served as powerful incentives for conversion.

IV

For many women, the standard conversion as outlined above was not the extent of their religious experience. Some women claimed to have visions, others were prostrated or fell into trances that lasted for days, while others professed the ability to be clairvoyant. Still others exhibited what they believed were marks which the Holy Spirit had miraculously placed on their bodies. Some visions were seen on a corporate level, within a specific congregation, and a few men came forward to claim they had received a direct revelation from God. For the most part, these so-called aberrations were an almost exclusively female phenomenon and were widely condemned, even by supporters of the revival. Women were held responsible for discrediting the movement on an international level. Determining the origin of such phenomena dominated the contemporary debate. Were these events evidence of a Divine presence or the work of the Devil? Although opinions differed on this theological issue, an examination of the visions women had reveals certain themes which illustrate how they viewed religion and why they chose to adopt a religious framework for their lives. For even if the clergy did not believe that these visions came from God, the women who experienced them did.

One such theme was the allusion to clothing in several of the women's visions. Church attendance was not only a reli-

gious duty, but also a social one, and therefore decent clothing was considered essential. If poor people did not have the
proper attire, they simply did not attend church. Even if the
clergy frowned upon this attitude, it was strongly reinforced
by the working people themselves. Rev. Edward Stopford tells
the story of one woman who had not been to church for nine
years, claiming as her excuse the lack of proper clothes.
Although she was newly converted she still refused to attend
public worship. When Stopford remonstrated with her and
encouraged her to attend, the woman replied, 'it would be
easy before Him, but it would be hard to do it before man,'
and flatly refused.[32] Cultural prohibitions and concern about
the opinions of others proved to be powerful forces discour-
aging working women from taking full advantage of the religious opportunities before them. Some ministers realised the
authority these social mores wielded and in an attempt to cir-
cumvent them held services in local shops or barns, to enable
the poor to feel more comfortable attending in their working
clothes.[33]

These cultural demands on appearance strongly impressed
women, who often dreamed of heaven as a place where they
would be able to wear beautiful clothes. The woman Rev.
Stopford referred to had just such a vision, in which she saw
heaven opening and Jesus coming towards her:

. . . and I see Him now, and He is beautiful; and, look! the angels
open out, and He comes forward, and He comes to me; and what
has He in His hand? Oh, it is a gown! and how beautiful it is! What
a beautiful gown! And it is a gown of glory. And it is for me. And,
look! He comes straight to me! What is He going to do now? He is
going to put it on me Himself. And now He puts it on . . . Where am
I now? What a beautiful seat! No, no, it's not a seat. I am sitting on
the throne of God, and Jesus sitting beside me![34]

For this woman the dress may have represented the wealth
she would never attain in this world. Her seat on the throne
with Christ beside her symbolised the social position she
lacked. 'Jane' from Belfast had a similar vision in which Jesus
approached her 'bringing in His hand *a suit* (which [she]
explained to be "a robe" – the robe of righteousness), which

He pointed at, to show it was for me; and He turned, and passed on, and left me.'[35] That the item was a 'gown of glory' or a 'robe of righteousness' suggested women's hopes for recognition and status. One element of these visions of clothing was the emphasis on the concepts of beauty, cleanliness, and purity. Jesus often was described as extraordinarily beautiful. Part of his beauty was his cleanliness, reflected in the use of the terms 'white', 'clean' or 'pure'. Jesus wore white robes, the path to heaven was white, as was the light which illuminated that place.[36] The conversion process itself was really a process of becoming clean in a spiritual sense. As one woman explained:

O blessed Jesus, come! Thou art my hope, my life, my all; wash me in Thy most precious blood; take away this filthy garment, and cover me with Thine own pure righteousness.[37]

If women's own existence was to be dirty, poor and downtrodden, religion could provide a vision of an alternative, even if only achievable in the next world.

Several women's visions exhibited a more literary tone. The woman referred to previously, from Laymore, who had one of the earliest visions maintained:

. . . that a Bible, traced in characters of light, was open before her; and that, although unable to read, a spiritual power had endowed her with capacity to comprehend the meaning of every word in it.[38]

Additionally, she was able to quote extensively from both the Old and New Testaments and to use them in connexion with the various prayers and hymns she constantly uttered. This ability faded as she was restored to good health. Women apparently were concerned about their illiteracy and general lack of education. If not in reality, at least in their visions they could aspire to literacy and the status it conferred. Sometimes this desire went beyond a dream as some women exhibited the ability to read even though illiterate. 'Mary' was illiterate yet while in a trance she held a New Testament and began to look for specific verses which she subsequently marked by folding over a corner of the page. When she came out of the trance she had no recollection of her actions, just a feeling of peace.[39]

This desire to read was part of a general longing for education – be it secular or spiritual. Sermons were often complex treatises on doctrinal issues, usually lasting over an hour. Women were more than just passive listeners. Grace Hunter, a Methodist from Downpatrick, Co. Down, is remembered for the intensity with which she listened to sermons, following the preacher's outline closely and taking copious notes. Sometimes she even confronted preachers on points of doctrine she felt were being neglected and encouraged them to speak on these subjects more often.[40] One woman, upon hearing the gospel for the first time, exclaimed to the minister, 'thank God . . . for that meeting, I never got such teaching before. I thought that while you were speaking to me that I could have risen through the ceiling with joy.'[41] What made religious instruction so popular was the fact that women could fulfill their desire for education within a religious context without fear of disapproval. They may even have been encouraged to pursue a godly interest as part of their duty as women. In this way it was possible for women to achieve a level of self-improvement while operating within the feminine stereotype.

The local church not only functioned as a legitimate sphere for female learning but also provided one of the few opportunities women had to obtain an informal education. Sunday sermons were the most obvious means, but other options included the various Bible classes, Sunday schools and day schools. The Sunday schools offered religious instruction, but also taught basic literacy. Their primary function was to teach children but the revival stimulated demand for adult classes, which subsequently were formed. Members of exclusively female classes often gave credit to their local church, who ran the schools, for teaching them how to read.[42] Berry Street Presbyterian Church, Belfast, had the most extensive Sunday school system, with over 1500 scholars on the rolls, many of them women. One school, located on Ewart's Row, educated many mill workers and their families.

One student recalled that they learnt to read, but only scripture or the Shorter Catechism, to write, and to calculate basic sums.[43] Methodists supplemented their Sunday schools with class meetings. Teachers were advised to bring their new students to their class meeting, to introduce them to the procedure and make them feel welcome. The class meeting functioned as a time of mutual encouragement and sharing faith experiences, rather than of actual 'learning', but the Methodists saw it as an important complement to the Sunday school.[44]

Working-class men and women eagerly sought education of any type and quality. For women, religion provided a legitimate forum for learning and the church placed that type of education within easy reach. The content of women's visions reveals this desire for education. Some women were apparently able to read under supernatural conditions, but lost this ability once the trance had ended or soon thereafter. This suggests that literate women (among the working classes at least) were considered an anomaly and acceptable only in extraordinary situations. That some schools allowed only scripture to be read suggests clergymen and other lay leaders, while permitting female education, hoped to confine it to a religious context.

Life in the mid-nineteenth century continued to be quite precarious. Cholera, factory accidents and shipwrecks occurred frequently enough to be a constant worry.[45] The visions women had during the revival indicate the proximity of death and how they attempted to deal with it. Although it was not a typical visionary experience, there were instances of women who, during their ecstatic trances, claimed to see or converse with loved ones who had died. One 8 year-old girl, described as shy, intelligent and well instructed in religion, had been prostrated while getting ready for school. She remained in a trance for about five hours at which point she sat up and claimed:

. . . she had been in the company of superhuman beings in a world of light and blessedness; and, to the utter amazement of her parents, she affirmed that she had there intuitively recognised her infant brother, who had died eleven months after his birth, and *five years before she was born.*[46]

Mary Sarah Buchanan was in the Kilwarlin Moravian Church on 11 September 1859 when she was struck with a vision and professed to see departed loved ones, including Rev. Zula, the former minister, and his wife.[47] Critics of the revival labelled these visions mere hallucinations; others went so far as to call them the Devil's work. Both blamed their occurrence on the assumed weak and nervous character of the women involved. The validity of these visions remained a sensitive issue. Looking beyond them there lies a picture of women and children struggling to cope with the nature of death in all its complexities. The revival was a time of emotional upheaval when people were encouraged to examine themselves, confess their sins and exhort others to do the same. As people expressed themselves in prayer meetings it was only natural that they would think of loved ones who had died. Visions of relatives and friends happy in heaven comforted those who remained and gave them hope that eventually they would be reunited, thus easing the pain of their present separation.

It is unfortunate that so little of the female religious experience during the revival has been recorded. From the little we know it becomes apparent that women adopted religious behaviour for a variety of reasons; through peer group pressure, for the fulfillment of material desires and as an opportunity for education. Some theories claim women were attracted to religion by psychological anxiety. If so, it was the constant proximity of death rather than any sort of industrial angst. Nowhere do women associate their conversions with an escape from the misery of industrialisation.[48] To view female religious behaviour as simply a reaction to economic stress is to ignore more important positive motivators which show women acting assertively and using the revival as a vehicle to achieve personal goals and aspirations.

Another variety of visions had apparently little to do with religion but were extremely unusual, sensational and attracted an enormous amount of attention.[49] Their presence suggests a time of emotional chaos, when traditional, conservative forms of religious behaviour were exchanged for the extraordinary, supernatural and miraculous. Five years earlier the clergy would have condemned such events outright. Even during the revival Anglican ministers represented a strong body of criticism. Evidence does suggest, however, that for the working classes these visions and miracles were considered credible and in fact were keenly desired. Clerical condemnation had little impact. People flocked to see those who had been 'stricken', as if they were circus sideshows, and attended meetings in the hopes that they too would 'get the revival'. They believed that to be truly saved, one had to be physically stricken. In that sense, women formed the vanguard of this movement with some of the most extravagant visions.

One of the visions' more popular forms was a type of clairvoyance in which women were able to predict when they would fall into a trance or lose their sense faculties. Mary Ann H. was an 18 year old girl who lived in Drummaul, Co. Antrim. She was a Presbyterian and regularly attended Sabbath school. On 30 June 1859 she was stricken down, whereupon she began to pray in a deeply earnest fashion for half an hour. When completed she rose, stating:

"I know I will be deprived of sight, speech, and hearing, till twelve o'clock tomorrow; but, Oh God, Thou wilt be with me! – Thou wilt never leave me! – Thou wilt pour Thy grace into my heart!" She then explained to her parents that she would have the power of speech only for a few minutes on Sunday at twelve o'clock. . . . Immediately after giving this intimation her eyes closed, her teeth went together with an audible snap, and she was found motionless![50]

Hearing of this extraordinary occurrence, hundreds of people crowded around her, convinced she was caught up in a form of spiritual vision. When she did awake those gathered were most interested in what she had seen, but Mary Ann rebuked them for their curiosity and told them nothing.

Other visions vividly portrayed heaven and hell and the spiritual battle that raged between Satan and Jesus. 'A— S—' described hell as 'a burning lake, and that as she was passing it by, the gates flew open, and she beheld burning mountains of fire – the road leading to it was very dark and slippery'.[51] Margaret Martin and Elizabeth Dumigan, both of Portadown, claimed to have been visited by evil angels dressed in black who tempted them to leave Christ and physically abused them. Elizabeth stated that she prayed until good angels dressed in white banished the evil angels and comforted her 'with the assurance of the Saviour's care and love'.[52] Some visions were more fanciful. Rose Ann Wilson of Christopher Street, Belfast, predicted she would fall into a trance on 24 August that would last for 36 hours. While she was stricken, a crowd gathered, waiting for her to awake. When she regained consciousness she remained deaf and dumb, but motioned for writing materials to communicate with those assembled around her. Her first question was, 'Did any of you see balls of fire in the air between four and five o'clock this morning?' They were amazed since no one had observed anything unusual and Rose Ann was supposedly unconscious. However, a gentleman from the London City Mission who was present verified her report, claiming to have seen ten such fire-balls, while Rose Ann claimed to have seen twenty four.[53]

The most extravagant cases of physical manifestations occurred in mid-September 1859 when a variety of newspapers reported women's claims that they had been marked by the Holy Spirit. Popularly known as the 'marks controversy', words such as 'God' and 'Jesus', letters and religious symbols, such as a cross, were imprinted on women's chests or upper arms, usually while in a trance.[54] These manifestations were universally condemned, even in newspapers which were on the whole quite open-minded about such events. Women believed the marks had been 'divinely imprinted' while the clergy claimed they had been painted on because some words were spelt incorrectly or could be rubbed off.[55] Newspapers were critical for different reasons, the first being that these women were charging admission to see the marks, and thus 'clairvoyant laziness became a better paying occupation than honest labour.'[56] Newspapers also pointed to what they felt to be the blatant Catholic overtones to this phenomenon. It was reported that the marks had a remarkable similarity to 'stigmata' and that good Protestant readers should leave superstition and idolatry to Catholics. Protestantism did not have to resort to these carnival acts, for it appealed to reason, understanding and 'truth in its naked simplicity.'[57] Only the *Ballymena Observer* was willing to admit that perhaps the women had been dupes – imprinted by others while unconscious and led to believe these marks were the calling cards of the Holy Spirit.[58]

It would be impossible to determine the validity of these visions or the purpose they served in the revival for certain. For those involved, reasons did not appear necessary. These extraordinary events were simply accepted as part of the revival atmosphere. Instead of viewing the revival as the source of these manifestations it is possible to see it as the means of removing some of the cultural prohibitions and restrictions on proper religious practice and thereby revealing popular attitudes to religion that were already in existence, but were exaggerated somewhat in this time of upheaval. More than anything else these visions reflect the capacity of women to believe in the direct interaction of the infinite with their finite lives. Women could exhibit the bruises from their encounters with evil angels, they felt Satan trying to push them from the narrow path, they could see supernatural lights in a darkened church, and fire-balls could appear out of heaven and hover over them. These experiences reflected a mixture of beliefs that included Christian concepts, as well as popular folklore and magic. For those involved it seemed logical to believe in both systems, although they may have appeared contradictory to the outsider. Attachment to popular superstition and folklore persisted despite the efforts of the clergy, who attempted to train their congregations in doctrine and rational Christianity. Recent theories have tried to show that increasing industrialisation and modernisation made it impossible for people to believe in a supernatural world existing above the natural

one. Revivalism was supposed to effect the transition to this
new rationalistic religion. Instead the revival in Ulster only
revealed the continued existence of superstition and supernatural beliefs among a large majority of the population,
including those city dwellers who were supposedly becoming
'rationalised'.[59]

For women in particular, these visions allowed them to
express themselves in ways that would not have been normally available. Spectacular visitations could increase the reputation women had among other working people. They were
certainly condemned by the clergy, but it is obvious from the
crowds surrounding the stricken cases that those so affected
were considered to be the recipients of special religious blessing. For example, Rose Ann Wilson was automatically
endowed with a certain status as a result of her vision. People
asked her to describe what she had seen while in heaven and
to predict the spread of the revival as well as requesting her
to lead the group in hymn-singing and prayer. As a result of
of her experience, which no one could challenge, Rose Ann
obtained a level of authority and leadership she never could
have achieved elsewhere. The revival presented both the
opportunity, and the context, for that experience by legiti-
mating it as a special blessing from God.

This deeply personal and mystical experience with God
also acted as a means of gender empowerment. Women
could go directly to God with their religious desires and no
longer had to be content with the mediation of men in their
lives. The clergy had always been the traditional interpreters
of God's will and power in society, via their sermons, church
discipline and communion examination. The ecstatic visions
totally bypassed this system, eliminating the clergy from any
sort of power they derived from their role as religious media-
tors. The clergy were rendered powerless in the face of these
visions. To claim they were false was not only to challenge the
character of the woman involved but to challenge the nature
of her experience, the legitimacy of the revival itself and its
claim to a Divine origin. To maintain some sort of leadership
role, clergymen were forced to accept these phenomena,
albeit reluctantly.

V

Women and their role in the revival were influenced by two contradictory forces: the liberating force of conversion that stressed a spiritual equality based on a shared religious experience, and the restrictive force of a society preoccupied with respectability and propriety. Conversion could happen to anyone, and from then on the dividing line between people was redrawn as 'saved' and 'unsaved'. Revival writers noted that one of the characteristics of conversion was the immediate desire of converts to tell others about the assurance they had found and to encourage their friends to make a similar choice. Thus there was a dramatic increase in the amount of lay involvement in the various meetings, from praying aloud to exhorting and even leading them without the presence of a minister. Women took advantage of the excitement and the apparent loosening of restrictions on their participation, to exercise a variety of leadership roles.

Unlike England, Ireland had only a limited tradition of female preaching. Alice Cambridge preached in Irish Methodist circles from 1780–1826, experiencing her greatest successes in Ulster.[60] Anne Lutton, another Methodist, preached at over 159 meetings in twenty seven places during the course of 1818–31, but her audiences were restricted to women in accordance with the 1803 ruling of the Methodist Conference. Men often tried to sneak in to her sermons by clustering around the church windows, hiding in the galleries or even dressing up in women's clothes.[61] Irish clergy, therefore, were not used to women in spiritual leadership roles. When the revival provided opportunities for women to preach and exhort in mixed company, ministers were some of their most vociferous opponents.

It is important to clarify the term 'preaching'. Olive Anderson defines it as 'the deliberate undertaking by women of evangelisation, spiritual instruction, of exhortation in mixed public assemblies held for that purpose, with no attempt to disguise the nature of their activities or their audience.'[62] With such a definition it is possible to state that little formalised female preaching took place in the Ulster revival. Miss McKinny of Fintona, Co. Tyrone, preached in

Londonderry's Corporation Hall on 6 October 1859. 'The novelty of having a female preacher attracted a large audience, the hall being filled to excess.'[63] Another woman, Miss Buck of Leicester, preached in the Victoria Hall, Belfast, on 9 October 1859 to help raise funds for schools in connection with Melbourne Street Primitive Methodist Church.[64] These references indicate that female preaching could have taken place on both a local and national level, but the small amount of evidence makes any generalised conclusion impossible. The most famous woman to preach in Ulster during the revival was the American Methodist, Mrs. Phoebe Palmer. She and her husband while on a tour of Britain, visited Belfast, Coleraine and Antrim to observe the progress of the revival.[65] During their stay they addressed several meetings. Dr. Palmer spoke first and was followed by his wife, Mrs. Palmer who

... came forward, and standing within the rails of the communion table, addressed the people in a very feeling manner upon the necessity of those who had not already done so, at once surrendering to Christ; and upon the Church she urged the necessity for immediate action. Her language was elegant, choice, and effective, and the address which the lady delivered occupied about half-an-hour.[66]

Any formalised preaching occurred only in connection with the Irish Methodist Church, but even this was rare. Of the two branches of Methodism that supported female preaching, the Bible Christians and the Primitive Methodists, only the latter – a mission church from England – was represented in Ireland.

The level of informal female involvement compensated for the absence of any formalised female leadership roles. A stricken woman commonly exhorted those gathered around her to repent, praying for them and quoting Scripture. The crowd could number from five to over a hundred, but the average seems to have been about thirty. The woman would then lead the group in the singing of hymns, prayer and scripture reading.[67] Women also acted as counsellors and visitors, helping their local pastor to minister to his congregation. For instance, the Misses Harley of Glasgow came over specifically to help the minister of Portrush comfort his female members.[68]

Female leadership during the revival most commonly took the form of sharing testimonies at meetings. During the course of a gathering at Berry Street Presbyterian Church, Belfast, the service had to be dismissed to allow ministers and friends to exhort and pray with the thirteen people who had been stricken. One spectator realised that none of the ministers was able to help, so he suggested that a woman, the first convert to recover, be taken to speak with those still struggling under conviction. The effect was 'instantaneous', as those stricken found peace.[69] Methodist class meetings were eminently suitable for this sharing of experience. They were instituted so that people could encourage one another. This function continued throughout the revival. In a more formal setting, two women were invited to address a meeting held in the Methodist chapel in Londonderry, not to expound scripture but to relate their testimonies.[70]

Public addresses involving women were rarely, if ever, set up with the intention of preaching a text. Many clergy were opposed to the idea of laymen exercising this role, and they were hardly expected to approve of women doing the same. Women's addresses, therefore, operated on an informal level. They exhorted at their own bedsides, and shared personal testimonies in their class meetings, at open-air and prayer meetings.

The impact of such leadership opportunities on many women is encapsulated in the story of 'R____'. Upon her conversion 'R____' went around the countryside exhorting people to repent, saying, 'The Lord . . . has sent me to bring you to Him. He is waiting for you. Arise and follow me.' People did follow her, until she had attracted a substantial crowd. Whilst walking, accompanied by her entourage, she met her minister, Rev. William Magill, who advised her to be quiet lest people would think she was mad. He records her reply:

She drew herself up in the most commanding manner, and measuring me from head to foot, exclaimed, 'I am astonished at you,

Mr. M.; did you not teach me in your Sunday-school and Bible class? Oh, I can teach the children now. I will bring them to Jesus. Must I not do the will of my heavenly Father? Oh, I have a Father *now*. . . . I cannot hold my peace. It is not I, but the Spirit of the Lord, that is speaking.'[71]

Magill was awed into silence at this 'young Deborah', fell in behind her and became one of her followers.

The nature of 'R___'s experience impelled her to speak out and exhort those around her. Like many female preachers in England, she claimed the authority of the Holy Spirit justified her actions, thus shielding her from criticism. This Divine sanction could then be 'blamed' for what appeared to be a violation of the feminine stereotype. The fact that a man, and a clergyman at that, followed her, lent further credence to her activities by implying the approval of a member of the establishment. The most significant aspect of her behaviour was that it was only temporary. According to Magill, after a few days she settled down as a consistent follower of Jesus, 'her work' completed. 'She roused the country, and then retired into private life, and in the quiet home of the family circle she and her sisters are adorning the doctrine of the gospel by a becoming walk and conversation.'[72] Only during revival excitement were her abilities required. Once the goal of a revived population had been achieved, women like 'R___' were expected to return to their positions as guardians of the home. In the long term, the revival did not permanently alter the moral and spiritual basis of society, and, as a result, was not a liberating force for women.

How did women react to female leadership roles? There is little evidence to answer this question. One woman, however, has left us with her feelings on the subject. Grace Hunter from Downpatrick described how she felt when she heard Mrs. Phoebe Palmer preach in Belfast. 'When the Dr. ceased, Mrs. P. addressed us. I cannot describe my feelings as she went on, for I was overwhelmed.' She returned the next night and described it as a 'time of power', attributing Mrs. Palmer with being a major influence on her life.[73] It is impossible to generalise about all women from this single account, but for

Grace Hunter, at least, seeing a woman in a position of spiritual leadership was a particularly significant event.

As the wave of religious enthusiasm which accompanied the Ulster revival temporarily broke down the traditional barriers to lay led religious activity, Irish women experienced increased opportunities to exercise their religious feelings in their own way. Women who had visions were considered spiritual experts and specially blessed by God. Women were allowed to speak in front of mixed audiences with little criticism – indeed, with outright acceptance from the majority of the laity. If expounding Scripture was still prohibited, they at least could share their conversion experience and encourage others to adopt a similar lifestyle. However, much of the excitement was soon to fade, and with it the mandate for women's leadership roles. Only when the world was 'turned upside down' were their activities considered acceptable. Once established norms reasserted themselves, women were forced back into their old positions, as the stereotype of women as spiritual and as submissive was only temporarily abandoned.

[1] David Bebbington, *Evangelicalism in modern Britain* (London, 1989), p. 5.

[2] For the main sources see Ian Paisley, *The Fifty-nine: an authentic history of the great Ulster awakening of 1859* (Belfast, 1958); J. T.Carson, *God's river in spate* (Belfast, 1958); A. R. Scott, 'The Ulster revival of 1859,' unpub. Ph.D. diss., Trinity College, Dublin (1962); Peter Brooke, *Ulster Presbyterianism* (Dublin, 1987). Myrtle Hill, 'Ulster awakened: the '59 revival reconsidered,' in *Journal of Ecclesiastical History* 41, no. 3 (July 1990), pp 443-62 and David Hempton and Myrtle Hill, *Evangelical protestantism in Ulster society, 1740–1890* (London, 1992) are the only accounts which consider the position of women.

[3] *The census of Ireland for the year 1851*, pt. 6: general report, p. 520, H.C. 1856 [Cd. 2134], xxxi, p. 664.

[4] *The census of Ireland for the year 1851*, pt. 1: Report on the area, population and number of houses by townlands and electoral divisions, p. 36, H.C. 1852–3, xcii, p. 42. *The census of Ireland for the year 1861*, pt. 1: Report on the area, population and number of houses by townlands and electoral divisions, p. 329, H.C. 1863 [Cd. 3204], lv, p. 335.

[5] Betty Messenger, *Picking up the linen threads* (Belfast, 1975).

[6] F.K. Prochaska, *Women and philanthropy in nineteenth century England* (Oxford, 1980), p. 3; Joan Burstyn, *Victorian education and the ideal of wom-*

    anhood (New Brunswick, NJ, 1984), pp 18-22; and Jane Rendall, (ed.), *Equal or different: women's politics 1800–1914* (Oxford, 1987), pp 9 and ff. As Rendall points out, it is important to distinguish between the separation of spheres promoted in the prescriptive literature and the reality of that separation. Although a pervasive ideal, research has shown how frequently women, both working and middle-class, challenged such divisions.

[7] 'Address of the conference to the members of the Methodist societies in Ireland', *Journals of the Methodist Conference* (1859), Public Record Office of Northern Ireland (hereafter PRONI), CR6/3A/3.

[8] Rev. Samuel J. Moore, *The great revival in Ireland: 1859* (London, [1902]), p. 39. Originally published in 1859.

[9] Rev. John Weir, *The Ulster awakening: its origin, progress and fruit* (London, 1859), p. 38.

[10] Rev. Samuel J. Moore, *The history and prominent characteristics of the present revival in Ballymena* (Belfast, 1859), p. 13.

[11] Rev. William Gibson, *The Year of Grace: a history of the Ulster revival of 1859*, 2nd edn., (Edinburgh, 1860), p. 108. Quoting Rev. William Johnston of Townsend Street Presbyterian Church, Belfast.

[12] *Londonderry Guardian*, 28 June 1859, p. 2. Hereafter *LG*.

[13] *Tyrone Constitution*, 16 Sept. 1859, p. 1.

[14] *Northern Standard*, 16 July 1859, in Lindsay Brown, 'The Presbyterians of Co. Monaghan,' pt. 1, *Clogher Record: the journal of the Clogher Historical Society* 8, no. 3 (1990), p. 39.

[15] Weir, *Ulster*, p. 165.

[16] Rev. George Salmon *A sermon preached in St. Stephen's Church, Dublin on Sunday July 3, 1859. With an appendix on the revival movement in the north of Ireland* (Dublin, 1859), p. 46.

[17] *Belfast Daily Mercury*, 27 Sept. 1859, p. 2.

[18] For an in-depth discussion of the psychological impact of the revival see James G. Donat, 'Medicine and religion: on the physical and mental disorders that accompanied the Ulster Revival of 1859', in W.F. Bynum, Roy Porter, and Michael Shepherd, (eds.), *The anatomy of madness*, vol. 3 (London and New York, 1988), pp 125–50.

[19] The most famous of these claims is Rev. Isaac Nelson, *The year of delusion: a review of 'The year of grace'* (Belfast, 1860).

[20] The deficiency is not in quantity but in quality. There are numerous recorded cases of female conversion experiences, and even more allusions to the actual numbers of women attending various revival functions. But very few actually let women speak for themselves and describe how they felt, apart from set phrases probably inserted by the author after the fact. Letters, diaries and journals that allow women to speak for themselves are practically nonexistent and male accounts of the revival predominate.

[21] *Ballymena Observer*, 25 June 1859, p. 1. Hereafter *BO*.

[22] *Portadown Weekly News*, 11 June 1859, p. 4; 23 July 1859, p. 2. Hereafter *PWN*.

[23] Ibid., 23 July 1859, p. 2. Cf 11 Sept. 1859, p. 4.

[24] *Newry Telegraph*, 18 Aug. 1859, p. 3.

[25] Weir, *Ulster*, p. 53.

[26] Mr. Robert Workman in *Newry Telegraph*, 16 June 1859, p. 2. Workman was a licencer in the Presbyterian church.

[27] The machines used in the process of wet flax-spinning splashed oil over the workers and caused a revolting smell. The use of water meant there were always puddles on the floor so many mill-girls left their shoes at home and went to work barefoot. The sight they presented as they left the mills only hardened attitudes against them. Although the time periods are different, Betty Messenger's analysis of women in the early twentieth-century linen industry reflects what conditions and attitudes must have been like in the 1850s and '60s.

[28] *BO*, 28 May 1859, p. 1; *Belfast News Letter*, 25 May 1859, p. 3 (hereafter *BNL*); Gibson, *Year*, p. 54.

[29] Gibson, *Year*, p. 103.

[30] *Coleraine Chronicle*, 4 June 1859, p. 5.

[31] Weir, *Ulster*, pp 11–12.

[32] Rev. Edward A. Stopford, *The work and the counterwork; or the religious revival in Belfast*, 4th ed., (Dublin, 1859), p. 53.

[33] Rev. R. T. Simpson, *Recollections of and reflections on the revival of 1859* (Dungannon, 1909), p. 25.

[34] Stopford, *Work*, p. 52.

[35] Ibid., p. 56.

[36] Gibson, *Year*, pp 170–1; *BNL*, 15 June 1859, p. 3.

[37] Ibid., p. 52.

[38] *BO*, 21 May 1859, p. 1; *Coleraine Chronicle*, 28 May 1859, p. 6; *BNL*, 24 May 1859, p. 3.

[39] Salmon, *Sermon*, pp 57–60.

[40] Rev. George Alley, (ed.), *Witnessing and working: memoir of Grace Hunter, Downpatrick, with excerpts from her journal* (Belfast, 1896), p. xii; cf. entry for 10 Oct. 1859.

[41] *PWN*, 17 Dec. 1859, p. 4, addressing Rev. Thomas Fletcher, Wesleyan Methodist missionary teacher, Antrim.

[42] Gibson, *Year*, p. 88.

[43] Ibid., p. 104. For other Sabbath schools see Gibson's Appendix E. Noteable ones include Banbridge; Fisherwick Place, Belfast; Ballycarry and First Ballymena.

[44] *Armagh Guardian*, 22 July 1859, p. 2.

[45] People vividly remembered the massive cholera epidemic of 1832, and even in 1859 newspapers reported localised outbursts of the disease with considerable unease. The wreck of the 'Royal Charter' in early November of 1859 killed 450 people and left only one survivor. See *PWN*, 5 Nov. 1859, p. 2.

[46] *BO*, 25 June 1859, p. 1.

[47] Diary of the minister of Kilwarlin Moravian Church, Kilwarlin, Co. Down, 1851–98. PRONI, MIC 1F/2A, 11 Sept. 1859.

[48] Studies of women in the early twentieth-century linen industry indicate that rather than dreading the mill, many women eagerly anticipated their employment there. See Messenger, *Picking*, p. 34.

[49] These visions represented only a small proportion of the total number of conversions that occurred throughout the revival. Their number may appear larger due to the disproportionate amount of coverage given in local newspapers.

[50] *BO*, 13 Aug. 1859, p. 1.

[51] *PWN*, 23 July 1859, p. 2.

[52] Ibid., 24 Sept. 1859, p. 2. Letter of Rev. D'Arcy Sinnamon, rector of Portadown.

[53] *BO*, 3 Sept. 1859, p. 1.

[54] *PWN*, 17 Sept. 1859, p. 2; *Londonderry Standard*, 15 Sept. 1859, p. 2; *LG*, 20 Sept. 1859, p. 2.

[55] Letter to John Megaw of Ballyboyland, Ballymoney, Co. Antrim, from J.B. Armour, Royal Belfast Academical Institution, Belfast. PRONI, D. 1792/A2/1, 14 Sept. 1859. Armour was studying to become a Presbyterian minister and went on to become a famous opponent of home rule.

[56] *Londonderry Standard*, 15 Sept. 1859, p. 2.

[57] *LG*, 20 Sept. 1859, p. 2.

[58] *BO*, 17 Sept. 1859, p. 1.

[59] I am referring here to the theories of David Miller and E. P. Thompson on revival participation. See David Miller, 'Presbyterianism and "modernisation" in Ulster,' *Past and Present* 80 (Aug. 1978), pp 66–90 and E. P. Thompson *The making of the English working class* (London, 1980), pp 385–404. Thompson claims that industrialisation forced a new type of work discipline onto people used to a more fluid work schedule. Methodism was responsible for the acceptance of this new ideology as it linked work discipline with Christian virtue.

[60] C. H. Crookshank, *Memorable women of Irish Methodism in the last century* (London, 1882), p. 200.

[61] The 1803 Methodist Conference forbade women to preach in front of mixed audiences, restricting them to females only, and even then, only if the female preacher had an 'extraordinary call'. See Miss Anne Lutton, *Memorials of a consecrated life* (London, 1882), pp 59–60.

[62] Olive Anderson, 'Women preachers in mid-Victorian Britain: some reflexions on feminism, popular religion and social change' in *Historical Journal* 12 (1969), p. 468.

[63] *Londonderry Journal*, 12 Oct. 1859, p. 2.

[64] *BNL*, 3 Oct. 1859, p. 2.

[65] Mrs. Phoebe Palmer, *Four years in the old world*, 10th ed., (Toronto, 1866), pp 45–83.

[66] *PWN*, 24 Sept. 1859, p. 2.

[67] Correspondence of the Workman Family, Belfast. Letter to Miss Sarah Davis, Sligo from Robert Workman, York St., Belfast, PRONI, D.3335/1/149, postmarked 8 July 1859.

[68] *LG*, 5 July 1859, p. 1.

[69] *BNL*, 15 June 1859, p. 3.

[70] *LG*, 14 June 1859, p. 2. These women were from Rasharkin, Co. Antrim, and appeared to be part of a group of converts travelling around the countryside, addressing meetings and spreading the news of revival.

[71] Gibson, *Year*, p. 134.

[72] Ibid.

[73] Alley, *Witnessing*, entries for 4 and 7 Aug. 1859.

'THE CURSED CUP HATH CAST HER DOWN': CONSTRUCTIONS OF FEMALE PIETY IN ULSTER EVANGELICAL TEMPERANCE LITERATURE, 1863–1914

ANDREA EBEL BROŻYNA

I

Yet, modest grace was once her crown,
And love a very queen confessed her;
The cursed cup hath cast her down,
Dishonoured, vanquished, and possessed her.

> 'On Seeing a Woman Drunk'[1]
> W. Maxwell, Belfast 1894

These sentiments might sound overwrought or unduly maudlin to us today, but to the readers of the *Irish Temperance League Journal* and *Everybody's Monthly*, they were part of a shared and well-understood image of Christian womanhood. Ulster temperance literature may appear melodramatic or even hysterical, yet the subject of alcohol and women was an emotionally trenchant one in late Victorian evangelical discourse.

What portrait of evangelical womanhood did Irish temperance literature create? This model of female piety is, fundamentally, a paradoxical one. Women were portrayed as having real moral power in their role as 'angel in the house'.

Through the strength of their 'moral suasion', women could determine the course of the nation, whether it would be 'on the side of righteousness' or 'fall into ungodliness'. Yet, women were portrayed as morally and physically weak. Their purity, innocence and virtue – their chief weapons in the war against 'the demon drink' – were fragile creations indeed.

A gender analysis will be employed in this paper in order to understand the construction of female piety and womanliness that evolved in Ulster temperance literature during this period. Marilyn Westerkamp has recently described this particular analytic tool in the following manner: '. . . gender analysis understands gender as a primary category for social and cultural historical interpretations under investigation and then explores social and ideological systems operating within that society in terms of gender as a signifier of power.'[2]

The 'silent influence' of women was deemed an awesome source of female power and responsibility, and the pages of temperance literature were overflowing with images of virtuous self-sacrificing women who through sheer dint of their holy example and gentle admonishments could save those cursed by 'drink'. Christian women could only have a significant influence for good, if they themselves were morally suited to the task. At the annual meeting of the Belfast Ladies' Temperance Union in May 1884 the Rev. J. Waddell had the following to say about female piety:

Women were especially fit to engage in a work like this, because they were possessed of a keen moral perception. They see the right at once and they did not allow their judgment to be warped with regard to consequences. Woman instinctively pronounces in favour of what was right and just and true . . . [at this point he received a Hear, Hear from his mixed audience][3]

The supposedly heightened moral sensitivity and natural piety of women was part of a transatlantic evangelical dialogue on women and Christianity that included Ireland. Male Irish temperance advocates frequently commended their diligent female workers by praising what they believed to be the innate spirituality and pious 'feeling' of their female adherents.

At the beginning of this period, while women's influence was mentioned in temperance literature and they attended temperance meetings, they did not have temperance organisations of their own. The most prominent temperance association to which women belonged was the Belfast Ladies' Temperance Union which began in 1862 and reorganised as the Women's Temperance Association in 1874. Both organisations had their headquarters in Belfast, and although there were affiliated branches throughout Ireland, they were concentrated predominantly in Ulster.

An article in the February 1881 edition of *ITLJ*, entitled 'Woman's Work' described the origins and activities of the Women's Temperance Union:

It was organised on 10th May 1874, and since then has been engaged in various branches of Temperance work and spread itself out in many different directions. Since 1874 forty-five branches of this Association have been established through the country districts; indeed, almost from one end of Ireland to the other branch associations have been formed, and keep up regular correspondence with the central association in Belfast.[4]

This article goes on to mention that Belfast committee members must have abstaining homes and be personal abstainers themselves.[5] Thus, at the highest organisational level, the personal influence of women over their children, servants, husbands and other members of their households was considered their most significant contribution to the temperance cause.

The female readers of temperance literature would hardly have been surprised when told that they had an enormous influence over the men and children in their care. Hackneyed notions of 'the power behind the throne' and that 'behind every great man there lies a great woman' had existed for centuries and were still in broad circulation during this period. The notion of children as *tabula rasa* upon which parental influence could be exerted without impediment was somewhat newer (having just recently replaced more calvinistic views on the morality of the young), but it was nonetheless potent.

In advice to children the central role of the mother became apparent. During times of trouble they were advised to remember her teachings, especially if she had 'passed beyond the veil'. In a story in the *Youth Temperance Banner* entitled 'Home and Mother' by Mrs. J. E. McConaughy, a young boy made his way home from a friend's house despite a threatening storm:

But the thought of "home and mother" cheered him on . . . but, more than all, the mother-love which watched and waited by the window-pane, would more than make amends for the dreary ride. And so the home was reached, and all his pleasant visions realised. Those two words, "home and mother", were Harry's watchwords all through the perilous road of boyhood and early manhood. They led him safely on through dangers far greater than those which beset him on that stormy night. When lads urged him to join their moonlight excursions, the thought of mother by the mellow lamp-light always caused him to give the decided "No." . . . O boys! cherish the home-love warm and strong in you hearts, and it will shelter you from a thousand storms of temptation. And oh! if you have a mother on the blessed shore, ponder her teachings well and often. She has left "a light in the window of heaven for you." Do not turn away from that blessed light to stumble and fall upon the dark mountains.[6]

The mother's pious teachings and moral purity make her a figurative 'beacon' by whose light those over whom she has influence, children in this example, can make their way through temptation to the safe ground of religious orthodoxy. The 'Juvenile Department' pages of temperance periodicals are replete with examples of this model of Christian motherhood. Mothers were depicted as a conduit of grace through which sin could be avoided and the sinner could be redeemed.

The following piece of advice, which was published in *The Puritan*, an American magazine, 40 years previously, and subsequently reprinted in the March 1881 issue of *ITLJ* was recommended by the editor because he thought that 'Hints to Females' contained 'excellent thoughts and precepts.' The anonymous author noted that:

A woman then should promote temperance by example . . . But it is on the children that a woman's influence will be most apparent. They are little images of plaster clay, put into her hands to be moulded into vessels of utility or ruin. . . . In a word, a mother should remember in training her children up to the practice of virtue, she has a double sting in her hand – the body and the mind, and if she is successful, she may be a blessing to future generations.[7]

This indicates the enduring nature of the mother as a powerful image in the construction of female piety. A mother's influence over her children was held to be second to none and one that would determine not only the future of her own offspring but also that of future generations.

A woman's moral influence over her own husband was a constantly repeated theme in the Irish temperance material. While clearly the temperance advocates, male and female, clerical and lay, all felt that this influence was a significant one, they were always careful to couch it in language that was acceptable to evangelical orthodoxy concerning the 'headship' of the husband. According to St. Paul, Christ was the head of the Church, and the Church his bride. In the same fashion, wives were to submit to the headship of their husbands. Despite this obstacle, the construction of female piety that we are examining, clearly gave wives the moral authority to redeem, retrieve and restore errant husbands. Women were not to 'usurp' male authority, but rather by moral suasion, restore their menfolk to righteousness. The following excerpts from a temperance poem by the Rev. E. E. Wilmot illustrate how this process was supposed to work. The poem started with a description of Johnny McCree's ideal marriage, which was going to ruin as Johnny 'liked something stronger that tea.' According to the third verse:

> *He'd a good little wife,*
> *As you saw in your life,*
> *And sober and tidy was she;*
> *She both washed and she charred,*
> *But t'was all labour marred,*
> *As he liked something stronger than tea.*

By the seventh verse Johnny was drinking away his wages and coming home in various stages of inebriation and causing his dear wife a great deal of grief:

> *When she'd got him to bed,*
> *Like a fool off his head,*
> *She wept, did poor Nancy McCree;*
> *But the big tears of grief,*
> *Gave her little relief,*
> *As he liked something stronger than tea.*

In her sorrow Nancy turned to God and lovingly prayed for her poor husband's redemption:

> *But like a kind prudent wife,*
> *She avoided all strife,*
> *Nor scolded her Johnny McCree;*
> *When he cursed her and swore,*
> *She more gently forbore,*
> *As he took something stronger than tea.*[8]

These tactics eventually proved successful and Johnny McCree became an abstainer and temperance advocate. He was now content with a cup of tea. However, it should be noted how explicitly it was stated that Mrs. McCree did not harass or criticise her husband about his behaviour. Instead, she used 'moral suasion'. Women were told by temperance writers that their gentle, self-sacrificing forbearance was essential to their success as agents of redemption. No usurpation of a husband's authority was allowed even though the righteousness of their anti-alcohol campaign afforded them the moral high ground. Gentle persuasion was to be used because it fitted evangelical gender norms and because it was said to work.

II

Male temperance authors readily admitted the ubiquitous authority of the women in their lives. Later, theories explaining their propensity to turn the tables of gender authority upside down in this way will be suggested, but for now let us examine what construction of female strength they were presenting. In an article in the first issue of the league's journal, entitled 'Words for Wives,' the editor, Mr. William Church, had the following advice to give his female readers:

I believe the influence of a wife, to be always, for good or bad, very decided. There is not a woman living, unless she has forfeited all claim to her husband's respect, but is making her mark day by day upon his character. We men are foolishly proud, and do not like to let the women see how they influence us, but we know that, outside of our business, and sometimes even in it, – all our doings are more or less controlled by our wives, and he is a knave who will not honestly own it. Is it a disgrace to a man that he is kept at home, away from bad company, away from doubtful pleasure and foolish expense, through his wife's influence? Some poor, cowardly souls think so, and utter senseless cries against her who, as a guardian angel, stands between these and their victim.[9]

Several decades of *ITLJ* did not uncover a single voice rising up to contradict this opinion. It appears to have been universally accepted in evangelical circles that women did wield a powerful influence over their husbands' lives. Needless to say, this power was not political or physical. Rather, it was entirely moral or spiritual. Whether this constitutes what modern feminists would consider *real* power is not an issue here. What is important for our purposes, is that the authors of this construction of evangelical Christian womanhood, both male and female, depicted women as having significant moral authority and moral power.

Frequently in temperance fiction, the vast majority of which was written by women, the heroine actually martyred herself to reach an unrepentant man. Heroines in these popular temperance tales were usually the wives, mothers, sisters or daughters of alcoholic men. Exactly what malady brings about the inevitable decline of the heroine's health the authors seem strangely reluctant to say. The presence of alcohol in the home or the decline into an inebriate state of the central male figure in these stories usually resulted in the woman's 'fading', 'sinking' or 'wasting' with incredible rapidity. Nonetheless their holy, patient and virtuous example, especially on their death-beds had the effect of shaming the male drunkard into repentance.

In the inappropriately titled 'A Narrow Escape', written by Mrs. Bewsher, a popular writer of temperance fiction, the heroine, Martha Newton, made just such a sacrifice. When Martha discovered that her husband had started to drink:

She tried to undo the mischief that bad company had wrought; [she] made her home as cheerful as possible, for she knew how quickly untidy homes sent men to fill the public-houses . . .

Obviously Martha knew her temperance literature, for a frequently repeated prescription for keeping men from 'drink' was the requirement that the household be a bright, clean, cheerful, and welcoming place. Contemporary temperance poems often focussed on the theme of 'women's rights', one of which was to 'brighten earthly homes with pleasant smiles and gentle tones.' This, however, was not enough for the Newton household. Mr. Newton's drinking worsened and Martha, was 'fast sinking . . . [because] of his behaviour to her.' The author did not specify whether his behaviour was physically abusive[10], but such conduct was a common cause of suffering and sometimes death for the spouses of alcoholics in Victorian times. To continue the narrative:

But death was coming nearer, nearer every moment to Martha. Yet *she* was not the one to be pitied. The drunkenness of her husband, the cruel usage, the penury, all had led her to look out of herself, and out of the world, for support.

Her heavy afflictions had led her to God, to prayer, the weapon of the Christian warrior on the battle-field of life. With her last breath she warned him once again not to give way to this besetting sin drink! "Better that you should know at once from one who has never deceived you what an awful thing drink is – drink has killed me through you!"

Fortunately for her husband, these were not Martha's final words. Rather, she told him of God's mercy and saving grace

and then went 'beyond the veil.' Not surprisingly,
'Remorseful anguish filled his soul; he saw his vileness;
he accused himself of being his wife's murderer'.[11]
Subsequently Mr. Newton begged for God's mercy and vowed
never to touch intoxicating spirits again. Even though Martha
died (there was no 'narrow escape' for her), her self-sacrifice
was, according to this model of Christian womanhood, worth
making. Martha transcended, through a personal relation-
ship with God, her suffering and misery. As Mrs. Bewsher
instructs us, it was her husband who should be pitied, as if he
had died unrepentant, he would have faced eternal damna-
tion. As a result of Martha's virtuous example, not to mention
the powerful agent of guilt at work here, Mr. Newton, provi-
dentially, had a 'Narrow Escape.' The reader was not meant
to feel real pity or outrage on Martha's behalf, she had
triumphed and fulfilled her role of Christian womanhood
to the utmost degree.

Not only adult women, but also female children were
deemed to have a peculiarly powerful influence over those
'caught in the grip of the demon liquor'. The following story,
entitled 'What Love Can Do', illustrates this point in a typi-
cally Victorian melodramatic way. The author, a temperance
worker began by saying, 'This short story has a beautiful
moral. One wonders at the fidelity of the dear child, even
more than the brutality of the father'. She recounted the tale
of little Millie, whose father was a 'drunkard':

I tried to take her home with me; she was a martyr to her faith, she
struggled from me, and returned to the now dark and silent cabin.
Things went on for weeks and months, but at length Lee [the
father] grew less violent, even in his drunken fits, to his self-deny-
ing child; and when he awoke from a slumber after a debauch, and
found her preparing breakfast for him, and singing a childish song,
he turned to her, and with a tone almost tender, said:
"Millie, what makes you stay with me?"
"Because you are my father, and I love you."
"You love me?" . . . "Millie, what makes you love me? I am a poor
drunkard. Everybody despises me; why don't you?"
"Dear father," said the girl, with swimming eyes, "Mother taught me
to love you, and every night she comes from heaven, and stands by

my little bed, and says, 'Millie, don't leave your father; he will get away from that rum-fiend some of these days, and how happy you will be.'"
The quiet, persistent love of this child was the redemption of this man.[12]

Thus, in combination, the persistent love of the female child and the love of a Christian mother from beyond the grave had an awesome redemptive power. These are but a few examples of the pervasive presence in temperance literature of the motif of the redemptive power of female piety. Women were also seen as uniquely suited for this restorative role because of their good-hearted and affectionate natures. It was thought that Christian women had an enormous capacity for compassion and love:

Oh, woman, whoever you may be, wherever you may be placed, remember your influence is great. One word "fitly spoken" may turn the footsteps of an erring one. By your exemplary life a brother may be saved from ruin. A look may melt a heart of stone . . . What would our world be were it not for the great fountain of affection placed in the heart of woman? Its constant ripplings have been flowing on from age to age. Silently, steadily, we see it raising the fallen, guiding the erring, protecting the weak, and its workings shall never cease till the last woman's heart shall have ceased to throb over the last object of pity. [13]

This passionate declaration of women's capacity for compassion was an affirmation of the moral power of women.

So strong was this perception of female moral power, that when clerics and temperance activists felt that women were not doing their utmost to further the anti-alcohol campaign, they held women responsible for its failure. In the following example, the belief in women's power and moral influence was again unequivocally stated, but it was also implied that by not doing all they could they were impeding the way of temperance. The female author of this piece in *The Irish Templar*, entitled 'Women's Rights', encouraged her readers by stating that:

Yes! women have rights, and rights that belong to themselves in an almost boundless degree. If they do not claim their rights and make the use of them that God intended they should make, the fault lies at their own door . . . We want the women of Ireland to see their duty in this matter . . . Oh! if we could rouse women to see and exercise their God-given rights at home, and not in apathy to say, "boys will be boys you know," but to remember the boys will soon be men, and with us rests the issue what kind of men they will be.[14]

The 'right' of women to influence their sons, meant that they were somehow responsible if their sons were intemperate - theirs was the power to determine the future. Pleas for women to do their part and wield their considerable moral influence for the temperance cause were not always this moderate. Editorials heaping scorn on women who did not lend their aid to the temperance crusade through personal abstinence and moral influence, fulfilled the dual function of further reinforcing the construction of the strength of female piety, while attempting to regulate and channel that power. The Rev. John Pyper, in an editorial article praising the good work of the Belfast Ladies' Temperance Union, made the following remarks:

Observation, however, convinces us that not only are thousands of influential women standing aloof from a cause which has special claims upon their sympathy . . . Now, no human agency has contributed so largely to the sum of domestic happiness, nothing has been so greatly blessed of God to the preservation and restoration of home-comfort; and yet the movement has few, if any, more serious hindrances in its way than the wives and daughters of Ireland. Happily, there are many honourable exceptions, and amongst these our glorious cause has no more devoted and earnest workers than the members of the "Belfast Ladies' Temperance Union."[15]

With moral power came responsibility and those who contributed to the construction of female moral authority did not hesitate to castigate women who they felt were not living up to their model of female piety.

III

This brings us to the reverse side of this paradoxical model. According to temperance writers, women may have had many strengths but their weaknesses were thought to be considerable. The purported physical weaknesses of women were inextricably linked with their moral failings and susceptibilities. In this construction, biology was destiny. From the same female temperance author who exhorted her sisters to further temperance activism we are given the following warning:

With the drunken woman the case is even worse – the very delicacy of her system, its special sensibility, is of itself enough to make her feel keenly the consequences of her sin . . . Man will do much to get drink . . . but we have never known a man to do what woman has done. She has parted with everything dear to woman . . . She has done things which for meanness could not be surpassed, and which for vileness no man could equal. And we believe the constitution of the female frame – its very delicacy and sensitiveness – accounts for this. Words . . . cannot describe the degradation of a female drunkard, it so shocks every feeling and is so utterly repugnant to every idea of what a woman ought to be . . . [16]

While intemperance was sinful for men, it was somehow *more* sinful or 'vile' for women. It was a complete negation of all that Christian women were meant to be. It struck at the very essence of evangelical womanhood. Yet, ominously, women in their weakness, were highly susceptible to it. They needed the care and protection of orthodox teaching, 'Christian' medical warnings, and godly legislation. A paper delivered by the Rev. William Caine, a former chaplain at the Manchester County Jail, to a Belfast meeting of the Economic Science and Statistics Section of the British Temperance Association, had this to say about women and alcohol:

Female drunkenness is increasing to a frightful extent – 60 per cent in four years – and their drinking leads to the commission of other crimes. We are told by Plutarch . . . that in the early ages of Rome women were strictly prohibited from tasting intoxicating wine; and other ancient writers tell us that they were punished with death for their crime, just as if they had committed adultery, "because the drinking of intoxicating liquor was regarded as the beginning of adultery." When will English legislators be as wise as Romulus and Numa so far as to prevent females from using these poisonous drinks? The fact I have just mentioned proves most clearly that the ancient Romans set a far higher value upon the innocence, and purity, and virtue of the female sex than modern professing Christians do . . . It appears almost incredible that men professing to be followers of Jesus Christ should allow women, who ought to be models of everything pure and holy and lovely, to sink to such a degraded condition . . . Let us imitate old Romulus and Numa and prohibit women from tasting this destructive poison, alcohol, which leads to such fatal results.[17]

Although the writer who filed the report on this meeting did not say so, it would not be surprising if the all male audience had responded with a hearty 'Hear, Hear' at this point in the proceedings, for this type of 'expert' opinion was prominent in the pages of the *ITLJ*. The Rev. Caine went on to describe the sex ratios of the prison population in Manchester, and, not surprisingly, they presented a shocking picture of female depravity. However, it was depravity of a uniquely sectarian nature. The Protestant inmates charged to Rev. Caine's care were, he stated, predominantly male. He sympathised with the sad plight of his Catholic fellow chaplain, the Rev. Father Nugent, who had the 'unfortunate' task of administering to the spiritual needs of a total of 12,420 inmates, the majority of whom were women. Rev. Caine did not point out that the difference between the respective proportions of Protestant and Catholic women was only a matter of 5.4 per cent, rather he presented the raw data – 4,742 Catholic women and 1,931 Protestant women – and highlighted his finding that, amongst Catholics, 'in fact more females than males' were incarcerated. Given his forceful comments concerning the greater depravity of intemperance in women, it is impossible to avoid his unspoken conclusion: that Catholics were more depraved then Protestants.[18] In one instance only was there a protest against this depiction of female drunkards as being *more* depraved than their male counterparts. In the September 1877 edition of *IT* an article entitled, 'A Woman's Protest and Impeachment', decried the sexual double standard with regards to alcohol:

We intend to have one standard of morality in the country and that is God's standard. There is no sex in guilt, in crime. It is as bad for a man to get drunk as for a woman. "Oh! young men," it is said, "must sow their wild oats," but let it be remembered that whatsoever a man's [sic] sows that shall he also reap . . . The law of nature and of God is inexorable, and a public sentiment must be created that shall require conformity thereto on the part of men as well as of women . . . [19]

This was not, however, the consensus on the issue. For most temperance writers, female drunkenness was more morally depraved than male intemperance.

The tragedy of female drunkenness, the ease with which women could fall into intemperance, and the measures necessary to remedy this, were all topics of temperance fiction. Again, these were most frequently penned by female authors. The realm of 'scientific' and medical opinion was reserved, of course, for male temperance advocates. Women activists employed the 'evidence' of the horrors of female drunkenness (which appeared in temperance literature in a highly repetitive fashion) produced by the male 'experts' in their prescriptive temperance tales.

In a serialised story by Mrs. M. A. Paull, 'Our Bill at the Grocer's', with the subtitle 'Founded on Fact', the plight of a young husband and father, Anthony, whose wife has become an alcoholic was described. The wife had deserted her husband and small children and Anthony told his elder brother of his troubles:

Oh, James! that you should have come to see my home deserted, myself bereaved, my children worse than motherless. . . . My house didn't look like this when you saw it last, . . . there never was a better mistress of a poor man's home than she was before she took to the drink, and she never would have gone to the public-house in the beginning; she was above it. It all come of the grocers selling the drink; curses on the wicked law, I say, that ever enable them to do it: it has ruined one good woman, anyway . . . she has brought shame not only upon me, but upon the innocent children of our love.[20]

Anthony told his brother of how he gave his wife money to purchase boots for their handicapped child and how, in an act that was the ultimate betrayal of her womanhood, she bought liquor with it instead. Needless to say it all ended in tears. Anthony continued:

. . . it was nearly midnight when she reeled into the house, a loathsome, drunken woman; instead of the honoured, sober, industrious wife I had loved and cherished . . . if ever strong drink made an incarnate fiend out of a gentle, loving woman, it was done then. I could hardly trace in that fiery-eyed, sensual, bold-faced woman the idol of my early manhood, the beloved, the trusted, tender wife of latter days.[21]

There was no redemption for Anthony's wife. She had subverted the moral order and betrayed her role as wife and mother. For a woman who stepped outside the boundaries of this model of female piety there was little hope. The author of 'Womanly Influence' explains that she had:

. . . known cases of men who, without seeking God's grace have by force of their own strong will, become sober men again; but very rarely of a woman. Womanly nature is more highly strung, and has so much the more need of God's restraining grace to keep them, and to rest on for stability . . . [22]

This theme is brought home time and again in temperance literature; men can have 'Narrow Escapes' and return to the straight and narrow, but it is next to impossible for 'fallen women' to be redeemed. In the reports of temperance missionaries who visited jails and distributed temperance literature, in the testimonials of those who ran homes for intemperate women, and, of course, in temperance fiction, the belief that women were nearly impossible to 'rescue' was repeatedly stressed.

In the tragic temperance poem, 'A Woman's Story', by Rosina H. Sadler, the moral that alcohol reduces women to 'un-women' comes across in a poignant yet deeply misogynistic way. The wife and mother in the story falls ill with fever and during her recovery is prescribed brandy (temperance literature devoted scores of articles to castigating those in the medical profession who prescribed alcohol as a medicine) and becomes a hopeless alcoholic. Her infant son dies of neglect and then her husband falls prey to the peculiar malady that afflicted those living in a household where 'drink' was present:

> From the time of the death of our baby,
> My husband had seemed to fade,
> And soon he, like our little child,
> On his bed of death was laid.
> They said of decline he was dying;
> I knew 'twas the work of his wife;
> I knew it was I who had killed him,
> For whom I'd have laid down my life.
> I knew that his heart, so good and true,
> Was crushed with its sense of shame
> For the sin and vice of the woman
> To whom he had given his name.[23]

The full spectrum of female behaviour within this construction is thus revealed, from the ideal of the woman who has sacrificed all for those she loves to its perverted mirror image – the woman who has sacrificed the one she loves because of her all-consuming love of alcohol. When using her 'moral suasion' and 'gentle influence' a woman was the ultimate warrior in the evangelical crusade against sin. Once she was lost to sin herself, and remember, this could happen very easily because of women's physical and moral weakness, she was the ultimate sinner, bringing down not only herself, but also her husband, her children, her community and her nation. Woman's influence was a two-edged sword; it could earn her the highest commendation or the most damning indictment.

IV

Lurking in the background of this construction of evangelical womanhood was the sometimes dark and shadowy, sometimes comic, but always distorted presence of Irish Catholic women. In large circulation periodicals like the *ITLJ*, which praised Catholic temperance effort and rarely made blatantly sectarian comments, the presence of the drunken Irish Catholic woman was only found in the reports of 'experts', like Rev. Caine, who used the veil of science to cover any sectarian ugliness. In fiction, especially in the *IT*, Protestants were not so circumspect. In a play called 'Comparisons', John Bull, a sanctimonious reformer and the 'feckless' Paddy Erin meet several times. Paddy's wife Biddy is everything evangelical women were not. The Erins' home was filthy – John Bull helpfully suggests that 'a pailful of white-wash for your walls is far better than a skinful of whisky for your bodies.'[24] Paddy replies that his 'jewel' Biddy is of the opinion that 'Bread may be the staff of loife but whisky's loife itself.'[25] Instead of gently advocating moderation, Biddy Erin encourages her family to drink. Unlike Johnny McCree's wife, who refused to chide or scold her husband, Biddy delights in upbraiding the hapless Paddy. She shrewishly scolds him about his bad manners, ignores his opinions, and generally dominates every scene she is in. Unlike the silent and gentle heroines of evangelical temperance tales, Biddy Erin never holds her tongue. She leaves the stage as she entered, on a cloud of words and oaths, chasing after a goat who, Biddy says, is like her master Paddy, 'there's no taching her manners.'[26] Although Biddy Erin was, ostensibly, a comic figure, in her intemperant and domineering personality there was an image of womanhood that evangelical Protestants loathed and perhaps feared. In Biddy's bragging about her 'darlin' son who might one day 'go and obstruct the Parliament – whatever that manes – and get a great name for himself and all the Erins,'[27] we see the concern of 'patriotic' templars about the influence mothers of the Biddy model were having over the men of Catholic Ireland. Perhaps the creation of the Biddy Erin type as the anti-thesis of evangelical womanhood – as a sort of negative reference point – made conservative evangelicals who were fearful of the Catholic majority, enforce even more rigorously this definition of themselves and their women as diametrically opposed to those whom they feared.

V

In article after article enlisting the support of women for the temperance cause, it is stated that women are intemperance's greatest victims. Women were said to suffer the most because of 'drink'. In 'An Appeal for Women's Influence and Aid' the author states:

Ever and anon we read of wife-beating and murder associated with drink; but only a case here and there comes to light. Vast is the number of wives and mothers, daughters and sisters, who have suffered silently, no ear hearing what was said to them, no eye seeing what they had to endure. Oh! the misery that females have endured through Intemperance – the broken hearts, the wasted frames, the down-trodden love, the disappointed hopes, the crushing woe. Oh! woman! if thou could'st but see the thousandth part of what this direful drink has done unto thy sisters in our land . . . thou would'st raise thy voice of warning, and employ thy most persuasive power to turn men from it, as from the cup of misery and death.[28]

While this appeal was chiefly to women's much lauded natural compassion, the following emphasised the more practical concern of self-interest. In this editorial article it was proclaimed that:

Nowhere, however, is the evil more painfully felt than within the domestic circle – "woman's kingdom, her state, her world." Where the female sex exercises its most refined and sacred influences, there the bane of intemperance is most keenly felt; and hence it has been well remarked, that "woman is the greatest relative sufferer from the national vice." If there were no other reason than this why the ladies should throw their influence into the Total Abstinence cause, we cannot help thinking it as an all sufficient one. Self-defence, and the defence of all that is dear, should enlist every woman in the ranks of personal abstinence.[29]

It would be a grave error to interpret these statements simply as manifestations of evangelical self-interest and social control. There can be little doubt that alcoholism caused women and children great suffering. Moreover, while paternalism, class-prejudice and self-interest may have informed the evangelical temperance movement in Ulster, one should not be too quick to dismiss out of hand motives of compassion and earnest Christian love. One has only to read the testimonials of female temperance workers, making allowances for sentimental Victorian language, to see the deep concern that these women felt for those they called the 'victims of drink'.

As the quotations that have been presented demonstrate, both men, chiefly clergymen but also laymen, and women contributed extensively to this model of evangelical female piety. Naturally, a major question that arises is 'Why did this alliance of interests occur?' The material cited provides several suggestions. The clergy's obvious enthusiasm in presenting women as naturally more pious and loving than men, may seem odd at first, but when we realise the importance of women's contribution to the strength and growth of evangelical congregations under adverse, secularising conditions, this phenomenon seems less peculiar. Women, as the 'chief victims of drink', may have needed temperance, but the temperance cause, as its advocates readily admitted, needed women. This construction of female piety was not static, it did change gradually over time, but there was no abrupt reworking of its basic elements.

The following passage contains a description of one important incident that created dissonance in this otherwise harmonious picture. The work of female anti-alcohol advocates in the United States was well publicised in Irish temperance literature and the arrival in Belfast for a series of meetings in 1874 of Mrs. Stewart, the leader of the 'women's whisky war' in Ohio, and her associates, was greeted with a great deal of fanfare. Anna Maria Hall, an English temperance advocate, enthused in the *Alliance News* that:

The work these heroic women are doing in Ohio, and in other States of America, is, of a surety, woman's work; they are doing it, as women ought to do it always and in every cause, not by usurping to men, but by the weapons that are essentially theirs – by persuasion and prayer. God give them fruit of the seed they are planting.'[30]

Those who eagerly anticipated the arrival in the British Isles of these American temperance 'heroines' frequently battled the impression that what the American women were doing – denouncing male clergy for inaction and holding hymn-singing and prayer sessions adjacent to or inside saloons and bars in order to shut them down – was somehow unwomanly. According to the construction just seen, with its emphasis on gentle suasion and domestic influence, they clearly were outside of evangelical gender orthodoxy. Yet the American activists and their Irish supporters went to great lengths to convince others, and perhaps to convince themselves, that this was not the case. Every article emphasised that these women were not usurping male authority, that they were not fearsome 'Amazons'. Why all of this concern? As Westerkamp pointed out in her study of female puritan prophetesses, dissonance is created when those who by gender definition should have no authority: women (I would amend this to say limited authority), become spiritually empowered.[31] In this case the American women who headed 'God's call' gained spiritual authority. As we shall see, this was a very disturbing thing for Ulster evangelicals, for Amazonian women would be out of place in the construction of female piety as it evolved in Ulster.

A flurry of letters and articles appeared in *ITLJ* in anticipation of the American women's arrival. The following letter from America is a good indicator of the radical nature of the women's crusade there:

Some call it imprudent, others injudicious; many speak with open contempt . . . They would do good, but quietly; close the stores, but orderly; use persuasion, but not prayers. Let your women be "keepers at home." They tell us it makes them brazen-faced, takes away their dignity, makes the young bold, gives them a domineering manner and a haughty appearance. The lovers of order tremble, but progression marches onward . . . [32]

When the American women arrived in London, Francis Craig wrote an advance report for temperance activists in Ireland. Craig's admiring description of 'Mother' Stewart seeks to conform this radical woman to the evangelical model of piety:

Her voice is sweet, and, though not loud, is clear, and some times penetrating . . . One's heart goes out to Mother Stewart, standing there pleading for help in her righteous cause . . . her eye flashes, her ardent feelings and aspirations heighten the colour in her face; now and then the voice will falter just a little to prove how womanly she is.[33]

At the Annual Soiree of the Irish Temperance League, held in Belfast in April 1876, Mrs. Stewart was the keynote speaker. She had these inspiring words to say:

The time was come when the Master called His handmaidens to take a stand against this giant curse. The gentlemen friends of the Temperance cause had laboured for years against great opposition and discouragement, but the missing link was the women. Now, if the Lord would only put it into the hearts of the women of Ireland to rise up and say this iniquity shall stop, it would be stopped. (Applause.) Although men had had a prejudice against women taking any public part in this movement, still they had acknowledged woman's influence in this direction . . . They had felt that they were helpless; they had seen their dear ones sacrificed; they had seen hearts broken and homes desolated, yet felt powerless, everyone saying, "No; a woman would be out of her place doing anything." But they must learn this lesson – "The servant is not above his master." They had exalted the idea of womanhood to an improper and false standard. The true woman was a true follower of the Master, ready to go and help and relieve suffering anywhere.[34]

This was a frontal assault on the construction that temperance journals were promoting. Mrs. Stewart recognised that relegation to the domestic sphere was not 'natural' or divinely ordained, but that it was an 'idea of womanhood'. She attacked what she saw as a 'false standard' a century before feminist historians theorised about gender as a social construct.

Yet 'Mother' Stewart understood her own role was an orthodox one, it was the evangelical *status quo* that she felt was deficient. Her orthodoxy lay in her being spiritually empowered not by her own strength, but by God's:

It was time that all obstruction was removed out of the way, and let the women come forward and help as they could. It was not for her to advise – that was God's work. When He saw them ready He would put it into the hearts of His handmaidens . . . The Lord sent His handmaidens out in their weakness, but in His strength and power, to shock the Christian world up to a sense of their condition and what they were coming to . . . She called upon them, in the name of the souls that were perishing in their island, to rise up in the might that God had given them and fight this iniquity. It was laid upon her sisters to go forth and take a stand that they never had done before . . . [35]

How did the Ulster evangelicals respond to this challenge to their accepted construction of female piety? This call for women to leave their gradualism and 'gentle suasion' and to 'rise up in the might of God' went unheeded. The words of Mrs. Margaret Byers, a ubiquitous presence in women's education and reform movements in the province, give us an indication of why this was so. She had the following comments to make when delivering the 1878 annual report of the Belfast Women's Temperance Association[36]:

This year your committee has to report nothing specially new in the working of the Women's Temperance Association. Its plans and operations have been carried on as heretofore in a quiet, unobtrusive way. Its action has been none the less powerful for good because it has never been characterised by anything that was startling or sensational . . . [37]

This was an unequivocal repudiation of Mrs. Stewart's call for women to operate, under godly influence, outside of the gender orthodoxy for evangelical women. The American woman's call to 'shock' Christians into awareness of the evils of intemperance was rejected by the province's single most influential evangelical woman. She stated that work with

female prisoners was popular with the women of the BWTA
because they were:

... deeply touched by the degraded condition of poor women, the
victims of intemperance. Cast out by society, disowned frequently by
their own kindred ... to give these unfortunate sisters one more
chance of recovering themselves, is a proper outlet for womanly
compassion ... [38]

Clearly, 'proper outlets for womanly compassion' did not
include critiquing the failures of the Church hierarchy or
staging demonstrations masquerading as hymn-sings on the
doorsteps of public-houses. That this was the consensus
among Ulster laywomen is indicated by their adoption of a
gradualist approach to the temperance cause. They continued to use their moral influence within their own homes and
among other women. But why? Some indication of Mrs.
Byers' reasons may be found in the latter part of her report.
Here she attributes the daughters of a famous anti-slavery
advocate with a significant influence over his political and
social activities:

In the same way, many a statesman, and many an author, many a
professional man, and many a man of business, has had his flagging
zeal in temperance work stimulated by the gentle approval and tender sympathy of her who, though she may shrink from public work,
accomplishes, it may be, more by her personal influence at her own
fireside.[39]

VI

This powerful alliance between evangelical clergy and
women gave a certain measure of satisfaction to both of its
constituent groups. For women, the tangible benefits of this
construction might, at first, seem difficult to discern. The
manner in which the temperance crusade was implemented
in Ulster ensured that women activists only gradually
enlarged their sphere of activity, from their own homes, to
the homes of other women, to public places where they could
assist other women.

Yet, this ideology of evangelical femininity was a restrictive one. Male elites could take comfort in the thought that their women were imbibing a set of prescriptions and sanctions that warned of the dangers of stepping outside of conventional gender orthodoxy. This gave male temperance advocates power over the women in their ranks. The women were taught that submission to the dictates of the male hierarchy – both clerical and lay – was in their best interests and, moreover, that this submission was divinely ordained.

[1] The poem 'On Seeing a Woman Drunk' was published in Aug. 1894 issue of the *Irish Temperance League Journal* (hereafter *ITLJ*) and in June 1907 edition of *Everybody's Monthly* (hereafter *EM*). This article is largely based on a sixty year run of the Irish Temperance League's publications. The *ITLJ* was published from 1863–1903 and *EM* existed from 1906–40.

[2] Marilyn Westerkamp, 'Puritan patriarchy and the problem of revelation' in *Journal of Interdisciplinary History* (Winter 1993), p. 573.

[3] 'Ladies Temperance Union Annual Report', *ITLJ*, xxii, no. 5 (May 1884), p. 59.

[4] 'Woman's Work', *ITLJ*, ix, no. 2 (Feb. 1881), p. 20.

[5] Ibid.

[6] J. E. McConaughy, 'Home and Mother', reprinted in *ITLJ*, ix, no. 6 (Apr. 1871), p. 54.

[7] 'Hints to Females', *ITLJ*, ix, no. 3 (Mar. 1881), p. 36.

[8] Rev. E. E. Wilmot, 'Johnny McCree', *ITLJ*, x, no. 1 (Jan. 1872), p. 11.

[9] 'Words for Wives', *ITLJ*, i , no. 1 (Feb. 1863), p. 15.

[10] Isabella Shaw of Belfast, a temperance and women's rights activist, wrote a poem 'on a true story' for the *Irish Templar* (hereafter *IT*), vi, no.1 (Mar.1882), p. 13, that is typical of 'true to life' temperance poetry which takes abuse and blood as central motifs:

> And instead of a kindly greeting
> She is struck a cowardly blow,
> And she reels and falls insensible,
> Then the life-red blood begins to flow
>
> And gush in a crimson tide,
> Till the baby resting on her breast
> Is almost choked in its mother's blood,
> As close to her heart it's press'd

> Then shun the sparkling wine cup,
> Look not when it is red;
> Touch not the gambler's dice box,
> You see to what it led . . .
>
> Changing man into a demon,
> Killing a loving wife,
> Spreading death and desolation,
> Causing tears, and blood, and strife.

[11] Mrs. Bewsher, 'A Narrow Escape,' *ITLJ*, xvi, no. 7 (July 1878), p. 84. A very similar tale, 'A Priceless Jewel,' in *IT*, iii, no. 10 (Dec. 1879), tells of a wife who accuses her drunken husband of killing her: ' "Look my husband what you have done" . . . she made a last dying effort to save him from his tyrannic foe.' However this story has a different twist, as the wife is not an innocent victim. She tells her daughter Nell, 'but I am justly punished . . . On our marriage day . . . [I] handed him the wine to toast our future health, and – my God, it has come to this.'

[12] 'What Love Can Do', *ITLJ*, xii, no. 1 (Jan. 1874), p. 14. 'The Baby in the Brown Cottage', *IT*, v, no. 1 (Mar.1881), pp 9–12, has the same theme of self-sacrificing female children (ages seven and ten they took sole responsibility for their baby brother), with a dead Christian mother and a drunken father. The children restore the father and 'God used them as a means of keeping his feet in the safe ways of sobriety.' In all of the stories that I have found where children rescue their father, the family is of the labouring classes. Why were bourgeois men never rescued by their children in temperance tales?

[13] *ITLJ*, i, no. 2 (Feb. 1863), p. 15.

[14] M. L., 'Woman's Rights', *IT*, iv, no. 12 (Feb. 1881), p. 183.

[15] Rev. John Pyper, 'Belfast Ladies' Temperance Union', *ITLJ*, xiv, no. 3 (Mar. 1876), p. 37.

[16] 'An Appeal for Woman's Influence and Aid', *ITLJ*, xii, no. 10 (Oct. 1874), pp 153–54.

[17] 'The British Association' in ibid., p. 158.

[18] 'Report of a paper given by the Rev. William Caine' in ibid., pp 159–60.

[19] Annie, 'A Woman's Protest and Impeachment', *IT*, i, no. 7 (Sept. 1877), p. 128.

[20] Mrs. M. A. Paull, 'Our Bill at the Grocers', *ITLJ*, xii, no. 10 (Oct. 1874), p. 162.

[21] Ibid.

[22] 'Womanly Influence', *ITLJ*, ixx , no. 12 (Mar. 1881), p. 29.

[23] Rosina H. Sadler, 'A Woman's Story', *ITLJ*, xx, no. 6 (June 1882), p. 73.

[24] Rev. H. T. Basford, 'Comparisons', *IT*, no. 5 (July 1881), pp 70–2 and v, no. 7 (Sept. 1881), pp 99–102.

[25] Ibid.

[26] Ibid.

[27] Ibid.

[28] 'An Appeal for Woman's Influence and Aid', *ITLJ*, xii, no. 10 (Oct. 1874), p. 153.

[29] Rev. John Pyper, 'Belfast Ladies' Temperance Union', *ITLJ*, xiv, no. 3 (Mar. 1876), p. 37.

[30] 'Address to the Women of America', *ITLJ*, xii, no. 6 (June 1874), p. 95.

[31] Westerkamp, 'Puritan', p. 573.

[32] 'Temperance Work in Ohio', *ITLJ*, xii, no. 10 (Sept. 1874), pp 126–27.

[33] 'Mrs. Stewart's Visit', *ITLJ*, xii, no. 4 (Apr. 1874), p. 66.

[34] 'Report of the Annual Conference', *ITLJ*, xii, no. 5 (May 1874), p. 73.

[35] Ibid.

[36] Hereafter BWTA.

[37] 'Annual Report of BWTA', *ITLJ*, xvi, no. 6 (June 1878), p. 78. For further information on Margaret Byers, see Alison Jordan, *Margaret Byers: pioneer of women's education and founder of Victoria College, Belfast* (Belfast, n.d.).

[38] Ibid., *ITLJ*.

[39] Ibid.

THE GENESIS OF CONVENT FOUNDATIONS AND THEIR INSTITUTIONS IN ULSTER

1840–1920

MARIE O'CONNELL

I

Convent foundations flourished in Ulster from the middle of the nineteenth century, with nuns becoming a familiar sight in the cities and towns of Ulster. This article traces the remarkable proliferation of convents across the landscape of the seven Catholic dioceses of the north of Ireland in the period 1840–1920. Using diocesan divisions, the number of convents, their breakdown by religious order and their social functions are presented. Particular reference is made to two Belfast convents.

The proliferation of convent foundations between 1840 and 1920 in Ulster was part of a general trend in the Catholic church in Ireland at this time. Archbishop (later Cardinal) Paul Cullen was the driving force at the head of this religious regeneration in Irish catholicism until his death in 1878. As an ultramontanist, Cullen contributed to the growing influence of the pope in Irish catholicism. The collapse of traditional regimes in mainland Europe along with rapidly improving systems of communication, innovations in postal services, railways and shipping, increased his ability to supervise the Church more efficiently. Cullen was determined to improve the internal discipline of the Irish Church and bring it into line with European catholicism.[1] Following the potato famine in the mid-1840s the population of Ireland dropped considerably. As a result, a programme of improvement was possible within the Irish Catholic church. New and more ornamental churches were built, increasingly elaborate vestments worn, and more frequent sacraments and religious ceremonies established. In 1840 the ratio of priests to parishioners in Ireland stood at 1:3,500; by 1870 the ratio had dropped to 1:1250.[2] These improving conditions were reflected in the growing numbers of female religious. In 1800 there were as few as 120 nuns in all of Ireland; by 1851 this figure had risen to 1,500 and multiplied still further to include a significant 8,000 women by the end of the nineteenth century.[3] For women from respectable backgrounds, joining a convent was, apart from marriage and motherhood, one of the few occupations open to them. By the 1911 census, nuns as a category of professional occupation outnumbered teachers, midwives and nurses.[4]

The growth and strengthening of the Catholic middle classes during this era with their improving economic condition meant that the Catholic church was able to improve its status in Irish society. As a result of Cullen and the ultramontanists, this influence was a conservative one which inculcated a specific perception of women and their role in society. Eibhlin Breathnach has stated:

The notion of women's role and nature prevalent at the time [referring to nineteenth-century Ireland] was derived from two influences, one rooted in the Catholic devotion to Our Lady, virgin and mother which also encompassed the polar opposite figure of Eve. The other was drawn from the Victorian ideal of service and devotion to men, personified by the sombre persona of Victoria herself.[5]

The behavioural stereotypes for Irish women were clear cut: the devoted wife and mother; the chaste virgin, remaining either unmarried or as a member of a religious community; or the outcast sinner as Eve. To reinforce these feminine ideals there was a constant flow of pastoral warnings from the Church informing the populace of the dangers of succumbing to 'temptation'. Sex was equated with sin and in an age when a deluge of foreign magazines, books, and newspapers began to erode traditional standards of morality, public statements of Catholic policy became increasingly strident.

Post-famine Ireland witnessed an unprecedented rise in the number of young women joining convents due not only to the pressures imposed on women in regard to their behaviour, but also to the economic condition of Ireland and its impact on female employment. In pre-famine times women accounted for half of the total non-agricultural labour force and were to a large extent economically independent. J. J. Lee has argued that the famine destroyed much of the domestic industry women relied on, as well as increasing the amount of domestic work they were required to do. This led to a deterioration in their economic status and as a result marriage rates fell. Without the prospect of economic independence or marital security, large numbers of women emigrated (about 50 per cent of the total number of emigrants). Many others joined convents. All these women were the victims of an increasingly male dominated society and of the image of women it was projecting – as dutiful, passive, obedient and sexless.[6]

Restrictive models of female behaviour promoted by a morally conservative church hierarchy, combined with worsening economic opportunities to push more and more young women into the conventual life. This was a trend experienced throughout Catholic Europe. In 1850 there were 72 convents in the Netherlands; by 1900 there were 423. France had 31,000 female religious in 1831; by 1878 that number had swelled to 127,000.[7] These increases reflected the growing number of women experiencing vocations to a religious life. In Ireland the emerging Catholic middle classes welcomed vocations among their female relatives as a symbol of prestige. There is also a possible link between the falling marriage rate and the growth in vocations. Women may have entered convents to escape restrictive stereotypes and to find alternative forms of economic security.

Religious sisters embarked upon a variety of social, educational, and medical occupations and were responsible for a wide range of institutions, for example: poor schools; night schools; teacher training colleges; orphanages; homes for the old and infirm; workhouses; reformatories; and hospitals. Yet few clergymen acknowledged the professional, practical, and difficult nature of their work. In fact, they consciously denied women access to the power structures within the Church. The male hierarchy controlled those aspects of female convent organisations which could threaten their hegemony. This tight reign went so far as to include the wording of a female order's constitution. For instance, the 'Propaganda Fides' of the Sisters of Mercy Congregation in 1840 stated:

Constitutions cannot be said to be complete when they lack those positive prescriptions for observation of rule [guidelines of the order] which are so necessary for religious communities, *especially of women*, whence to remove doubt, disquietude and perplexity of soul in subjects, and to moderate within certain limits the authority of superiors.[8] (my emphasis)

These were the words of the central body in Rome governing constitutions of Catholic religious communities all over the world. It expressed the male hierarchy's belief that women could not exercise power judiciously or without encountering problems. It also expressed the hierarchy's fear of female religious power in the Church – a fear which would grow as convents spread throughout Europe and Ireland.

Armagh, Clogher, Derry, Down and Connor, Dromore, Kilmore and Raphoe – the seven Catholic dioceses of Ulster – shared in a massive expansion in the number of new convents from the middle of the nineteenth to the twentieth centuries. This growth was already firmly established by the time Paul Cullen became a cardinal in 1866 and the convents proved an integral component in raising the profile of catholicism which was occurring all over Ireland in the post-famine era. Convents facilitated the development of a widespread system of education for the Catholic population of the north, as well as providing female agents of social welfare in areas like orphanages, workhouses, hospitals, old people's homes and female reformatories.

In the pre-famine years the hierarchies of the northern dioceses expressed a desire to see convents established in their districts. As early as 1840 the *Irish Catholic Directory and Almanack* contained petitions from bishops of four of the northern dioceses – Clogher, Kilmore, Raphoe and Down and Connor – requesting female religious congregations to establish branch houses in the north.[9] Rt. Rev. Cornelius Denvir, Bishop of Down and Connor, stated 'we would rejoice to see the introduction here of those religious orders which have added so much to the sacred cause of solid education, true charity and extensive usefulness in other districts.'[10] At this time there were only two such establishments, both of which were located in Drogheda: the Sienna Dominican Convent, Lawrence Gate; and the Presentation Convent, Fair Street. (Map 1) The 1837 *ICDA* described the two convents in these terms: 'In Drogheda there are two convents, the religious ladies of which devote their time and labours to the glory of God and the good of their neighbours'. Both convents ran schools for the children of the city, marking the beginning of a long association between northern convents and education.

Recent historiography has failed to consider the situation of convents in Ulster in their own right.[11] However, the convent system flourished in Ulster and had similar characteristics to those in the rest of Ireland. In Ulster, as in the rest of Ireland, female orders needed the express permission of the local bishop to establish a religious community. In most cases the mother house convent would not set up a new foundation until a specific request came from a bishop. In 1853 Dr. Denvir, Bishop of Down and Connor, sent a deputation of clergy and local businessmen to Dublin's Mercy Convent in Baggot Street to make a formal request for the foundation of a Mercy convent and poor school in Belfast. The Superior of the convent, Mother M. Vincent Whitty agreed and on the 16 January 1854 three Mercy sisters moved from Dublin to Belfast. They were Sr. M. Philomena Maguire, Sr. M. Ignatius Grolly and Sr. Mary Liston: the first nuns in Belfast. They

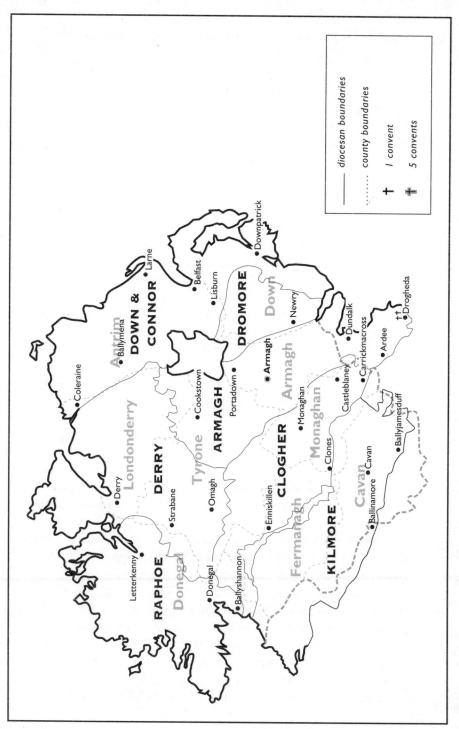

MAP I The distribution of convents in the north of Ireland, 1840.

Legend:
— *diocesan boundaries*
···· *county boundaries*
✝ *1 convent*
✝✝ *5 convents*

Coleraine
Larne
Ballymena
Belfast
Lisburn
Downpatrick
Newry
Drogheda ✝✝
Dundalk
Ardee
Derry
Cookstown
Portadown
Armagh
Carrickmacross
Castleblaney
Strabane
Omagh
Monaghan
Ballyjamesduff
Letterkenny
Enniskillen
Clones
Cavan
Ballinamore
Donegal
Ballyshannon

ANTRIM
DOWN & CONNOR
DROMORE
Down
Armagh
ARMAGH
Londonderry
DERRY
Tyrone
CLOGHER
Monaghan
Fermanagh
Cavan
KILMORE
Donegal
RAPHOE

were joined the following day by three more Dublin Mercy sisters. This small group of pioneers immediately set up a school and then began visiting prisoners and the sick, together with running a night school for the local working women.[12] A permanent convent was eventually set up in premises called St. Paul's located on the Crumlin Road, Belfast. From the original six sisters the numbers rose very quickly. Between the years 1895–1920 there were 64 new entrants to this one convent. The optimum growth period was between 1895 and 1905 when 15 new recruits started their novitiate.[13] The same invitation from a local bishop occurred in the case of the Dominican Sisters in Belfast. This time it was Dr. Dorrian who went, as Bishop of Down and Connor, to the Dominican mother house in Cabra near Dublin in 1868 to request a Dominican convent for Belfast. He hoped to ease the situation regarding female education in the rapidly expanding and largely Catholic area of west Belfast. In March 1870 seven Dominican sisters arrived from Cabra and set up a convent on the Falls Road. Four months later they were managing and teaching in St. Mary's Convent Boarding School. The following year they also set up their own national or poor school called St. Catherine's.[14] By 1928 they were running their own teacher training college and there were 38 sisters working and living in this congregation, representing more than a four-fold increase.[15]

Dependent on the male-dominated Catholic hierarchy to grant them permission to expand, convents were also reliant on the generosity of wealthy patrons to financially support these new congregations. Ulster's middle-class Catholics, the number of which expanded rapidly in the mid- to late nineteenth century, were willing contributors, not just of recruits to the religious life but also of money and property. For example, James Duffy, a wealthy Belfast businessman, upon his death in 1854 left a sum of £1000 for the purpose of, as he wrote 'establishing, purchasing and maintaining a suitable house and premises as an institution to be conducted by a group of females of a religious order professing the Catholic faith and the care and religious education of poor female children.'[16] It was this bequest which facilitated the establishment of the Mercy congregation in Belfast. However, dependence on wealthy patrons was never very large. To a certain extent, convents and their schools were financially self-reliant. The main sources of income for the convents were large dowries and money paid to the nuns by the state for their teaching responsibilities.[17] Schools were partially financed by the government as part of the National Education system and school fees accounted for the remainder. Dowries were used primarily for the personal maintenance of each nun.[18] Dowries from new entrants to the Belfast Mercy convent peaked in 1905.[19] In that year the average contribution from each of the three entrants in 1905 was £336, accounting for a total of over £1,000. From 1895–1900 there were fifteen new entrants and twelve more in the period from 1901–05.[20] In 1910 dowries still averaged £320 each. Only 5 per cent of the new entrants brought no dowry.[21] These women would have been from poorer families and would have been educated to a lower level than the other sisters. The Mercy order, along with the Dominicans and the other congregations of female religious divided their new recruits into either lay or choir sisters. The lay sister would have been from the poorer sections of Ulster society and would have had duties pertaining to the upkeep of the house and school: cleaning, cooking and washing. The choir sister was usually well educated and would have contributed a substantial dowry on entering. Her duties were of a professional nature; teacher, nurse, administrator, or supervisor. It was 1954 before the Dominican order relinquished this policy of lay/choir division and the other orders soon followed suit. In the meantime, the dowries which the choir sisters brought to the convents provided the financial security necessary to run their numerous institutions. In any case, the increase in the number of convents in Ulster indicated that money was not a barrier to expansion.

II

The only convent founded in Ulster in the 1840s was a convent of Poor Clares in Newry, in the diocese of Dromore. In the subsequent decade ten new convents were established.

Throughout Ireland the years 1860–70 were called the, 'missionary decade' because of the substantial increase in the number of new foundations. This growth was also true of the north. Here, from 1840–1920 the average increase in the number of convents was seven per ten years. In the missionary decade the increase was fifteen. (Figure 1)

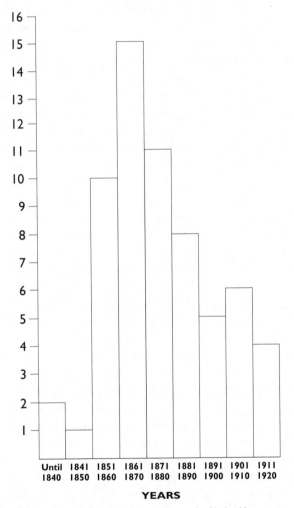

YEARS

FIGURE 1   The growth of convents in the north of Ireland by census decade, 1840-1920.

Source: *Marie O'Connell, 'Convents in the north of Ireland from the mid-nineteenth to the mid-twentieth centuries', unpub. M.A. diss., Queen's University of Belfast, 1992.*

In addition to this numerical increase was the emergence of a distinct geographical distribution of convents along an east-west divide. Looking at the maps, it is possible to see that the majority of convents were established in the eastern dioceses of Down and Connor and Armagh. This trend reflected the commercial, industrialised and prosperous nature of the east coast, centred on the port and city of Belfast where the catholic middle classes were concentrated. The wealth generated by this region meant that its inhabitants could afford to support and sustain a religious community.

Another characteristic of convent distribution in Ulster was the prevalence of the Mercy order. (Figure 2) Mercy congregations accounted for nine of the fifteen new convents in the 1860s. Catherine McAuley, a wealthy Dublin woman, had established a community of women who shared their goods, took private vows and conducted various philanthropic endeavours. In 1828 they were granted diocesan approval as a secular institute but the independence these women enjoyed created some hostility amongst the Catholic hierarchy. McAuley was persuaded to style her community as a religious congregation and the rules and constitutions of the order were adopted by the congregation in 1840.[22] This connection with Rome offered the new order permanence, donations and recruits, allowing it to continue its expansion throughout Ireland and set up twenty-eight new convents in Ulster by 1920. (Figure 2) Quite often several Mercy convents were founded in one diocese in the same year. In Down and Connor convents were opened in Blackmore, Belfast and Downpatrick in 1866; Kilmore's Belturbet and Ballyjamesduff convents date from 1869; Dromore's Rostrevor and Lurgan gained new convents in 1867 while Warrenpoint and Kilmore Street, Newry opened in 1889.

As well as demonstrating the 'wealth' of Catholic support, this tendency to concentrate on one diocese suggests the importance of an invitation from the presiding bishop. Once the initial convent had been established in the diocese, others were able to form much more easily. This resulted in a tendency of some orders to focus almost exclusively on one diocese. This is most marked with the St. Louis order which

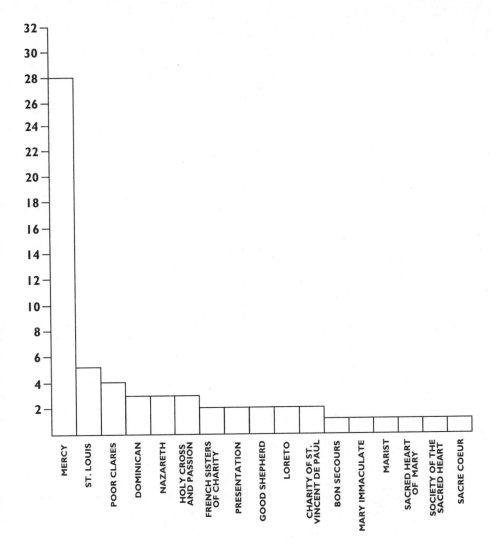

FIGURE 2   The distribution of convents, by order, in the north of
Ireland, 1840-1920.

Source: *O'Connell, 'Convents in the north of Ireland'.*

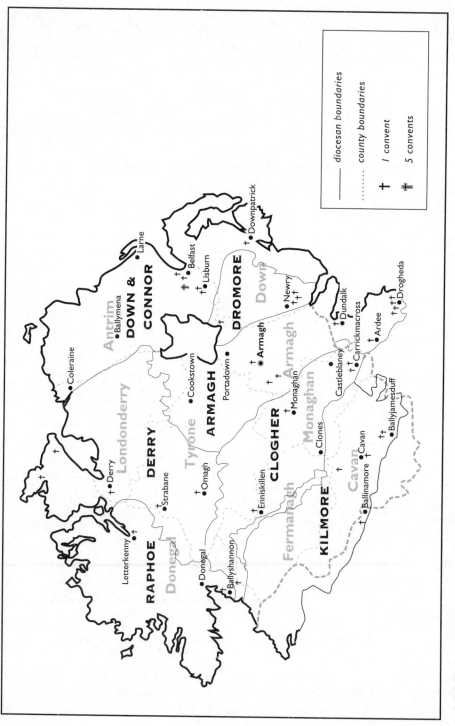

MAP 2   *The distribution of convents in the north of Ireland, 1880.*

set up four of their five congregations in Clogher diocese between 1859 and 1904, with their Middletown convent located in the Armagh diocese. Within three years of each other, two of the Poor Clares' four convents were set up in the Kilmore diocese: in Cavan in 1865; and in Ballyjamesduff in 1868. Two of the three Nazareth convents were in Down and Connor: Ballynafeigh and Ravenhill Road, both in Belfast. Between 1900 and 1913 all of the Holy Cross and Passion convents were set up in this diocese. The Dominican order had two convents in Down and Connor and one in Armagh. Both convents of the Presentation Sisters were in Armagh.

Another trend which is clear in the spread of convents in the north concerns the primacy of two dioceses – Down and Connor and Armagh – in the concentration of convent foundations. (Maps 2 and 3) These were the two most prosperous dioceses. Belfast was the centre of an industrial district dominated by linen mills and shipbuilding and the city's economic importance helps explain the concentration of convents around it. In 1840 there were no convents in Belfast but by 1880 there were seven and by 1920 the figure had increased to eleven. Armagh had a prosperous agricultural base and also enjoyed the reputation of being the spiritual centre of Ireland and archdiocese for the Catholic Church. Five out of the six orders with only one convent in the north were located in either Down and Connor or Armagh. Most orders with multiple convents had at least one congregation in each of these two primary dioceses. Out of a total of seventeen orders represented in Ireland, ten had branches in Down and Connor and nine in Armagh. Only two orders – the Marist and Loreto orders – did not set up in either of the two primary dioceses. But these account for only three out of the 62 convents which were established in the north between 1840 and 1920. Convent distribution reinforced the religious importance of Armagh and Belfast in Catholic missionary efforts.

III

Convents reflected the diversity of social activity which also characterised their southern co-religionists. The emphasis in the convents was most definitely upon education, with over two-thirds (42 out of 62) of the convents connected with schools in some form. This parallels the situation elsewhere in Ireland where as early as 1860, 84 per cent of convents were involved in schools.[23] Only five of the seventeen orders of the north were not involved with education: Nazareth; Good Shepherd; Marist; Mary Immaculate; and Bon Secours. These orders were more concerned with social welfare issues like orphanages, laundries and prison visiting. Taken together, they accounted for eight of the 62 convents, or less than ten per cent. Cities, however, attracted an equal balance of the social welfare oriented and teaching congregations. For example, in Belfast (See Appendix, Table 1) the Mercy Convent, Crumlin Road, the Dominicans, the Holy Cross and Passion and the Charity of St. Vincent de Paul all provided educational establishments. The Good Shepherd, the two convents of Nazareth sisters, and the Mercy Convent, Sussex Place had no such involvement. The Good Shepherd Convent, Blackmore, Belfast provided a 'Magdalene Penitentiary', a laundry which acted as a reformatory for women.[24] The 1879 *ICDA* stated, 'the penitents who apply for admission keep a laundry on which they are wholly dependent for the support of the inmates.'[25] The women would have mostly been young and pregnant and the directory makes this place sound more like a prison than a home for young women. The Mercy Convent, Crumlin Road also ran a reformatory and laundry for a short time and the Mercy Convent of Sussex Place, Belfast ran the Mater Hospital or infirmary. One of the Nazareth convents provided an old people's home at Blackmore. One report stated that it was a home, 'for old and infirmed men and women of all religions'.[26] In 1876, the Bon Secours sisters, Alfred Street, Belfast claimed to 'attend the sick of all denominations'.[27] The other Nazareth convent set up an orphanage in 1917 – only the second one run by nuns in the Down and Connor diocese. The Mercy sisters of the Crumlin Road had established an orphanage by 1865. The city of Belfast was well looked after in both education and social welfare. The smaller towns were fortunate to house even one teaching congregation. In Down and Connor eleven of the eighteen convents were concerned with education.

The Armagh diocese by 1920 had witnessed the establishment of fourteen convents, twelve of which were concerned with teaching. (See Appendix, Table 2) The French Sisters of Charity, Drogheda and the Poor Clares of Keady, together with the sisters of St. Vincent de Paul, Drogheda, the Presentation Convent, Portadown and the Mercy Convent of Cookstown all ran night schools for working women. These five, in addition to four in Down and Connor and one in Derry, account for half of the night schools run by nuns in the north of Ireland at this time. These were all located in large population centres where, with their more buoyant economies and burgeoning industries, working women were to be found. The night schools of Down and Connor were all concentrated in the city of Belfast where many women worked in the mills and were receptive to the idea of night school lessons. The Sisters of Charity of St.Vincent de Paul, in Armagh diocese also ran an industrial school for their district of Drogheda. The only orphanage of the diocese was the St. Louis Convent of Middletown where the sisters also had a boarding school and poor school.[28] Only the Sisters of Mercy, Ardee were involved in nursing. This congregation was set up originally in 1865 when three sisters took charge of the local workhouse hospital.[29] Again, the emphasis within this diocese was educational, and the wealth of the diocese meant that the educational convents thrived. This wealth was also shown by the lack of sisters working in workhouses or in female reformatories.

Apart from Down and Connor and Armagh, the other dioceses in Ulster suffered from a variety of disadvantages which made the widespread foundation of convents more difficult. After 1870 Raphoe witnessed no expansion in its number of convents. In 1856 one Loreto convent was founded and in 1867 a Mercy congregation was set up. Part of the explanation for this was that the diocese lacked modern communications, had very little commerce or industry and was removed from the major centres of industrialisation on the east coast. It was thus unable to sustain an extensive network of convents. For the convents which were established, their activity reflects the poverty of the region. (See Appendix, Table 3) The Mercy Convent in Ballyshannon operated, along with a House of Mercy, a large poor school, orphanage, and workhouse hospital from 1893.[30] Branch houses in Stranorlar and Glenties, unable to attain independent status until after 1920, were connected to workhouses and in Donegal Town to a national or poor school.[31] However, in 1865, the *ICDA* announced, 'the institute of Loreto, Letterkenny for the education of the upper and middle classes of females',[32] providing a select day school with boarding facilities. The sisters also had a poor school but the main emphasis was upon the select school.

Derry diocese was also removed from the prosperity of the east but by 1920 eight convents had been set up. (See Appendix, Table 4) Four of the convents were in Londonderry city itself and were attracted by a combination of factors including the thriving shirt industry, sea port and a substantial Catholic population. As with Belfast, about half the convents were concerned with social welfare work and half with education. The two Mercy convents operated a select school and two free schools together with a night school for the women of the shirt factories. The Nazareth sisters from 1893 supervised an orphanage and the Good Shepherd sisters managed a laundry and female reformatory, one of only four in the entire province.[33] Londonderry's social needs were well catered for in comparison to more rural areas. The other convents in the diocese, such as the Loreto convent, Omagh and the Mercy convent, Strabane focused their attention on education, the latter offering instruction in the form of 'a superior school for young ladies'.[34] The Strabane school taught 130 boarders besides operating a large free school. The sisters also ran a female orphanage and an industrial school from 1879.[35] The preponderance of Mercy convents (they represented five out of the eight convents in the Derry diocese), reflects their willingness to work in poor, rural regions populated with small farmers and artisans. In such regions the Mercy nuns were pioneers in the education of the local Catholic population.

Despite predominantly Catholic populations in the western half of the province, convents clustered in the dioceses of the northeast. Such was the case in the diocese of Clogher and Kilmore, where the majority of the convents were located in towns close to the east coast. (Map 3) In Clogher, six of the eight convents were involved primarily with education. (See Appendix, Table 5) The Mercy Convent of Enniskillen conducted an industrial school from 1858, 'dispensing to hundreds of female children the blessing of a sound religious, moral and industrial education, the immense advantages of which are already manifest in the town and neighbourhood'.[36] Clogher convents combined their educational duties with practical work. The St. Louis Convent, Monaghan, as well as running a school, managed one of the four reformatories in the province. The Mercy sisters in Castleblayney, besides their poor school, visited the local prisons and sick poor. Other convents focused exclusively on social relief efforts. The Mercy order ran all three of the convent-managed workhouses in Ulster, one of which was set up in 1905 in Ballyshannon.[37] Here the sisters dealt with destitute families and old people. In Clogher there were no convents concerned with night schools, orphanages, hospitals or homes for the old, which normally relied on larger and richer centres of Catholic population to sustain them financially.

Kilmore, a diocese located in the poorer midlands of Ulster, was isolated from the industrial north-east. Like Clogher, its six convents were clustered in the eastern end of the diocese – including four Mercy congregations and two Poor Clares. The low level of educational provision and social welfare efforts in the diocese was an indication of the general poverty of the Catholic population. (See Appendix, Table 6) There were no boarding or select schools in the region. The Poor Clares were able to sustain poor schools only in Ballyjamesduff and Cavan, although in the latter case they did run an industrial school as well. This was in contrast to Dromore diocese, which, although it was half the size, was

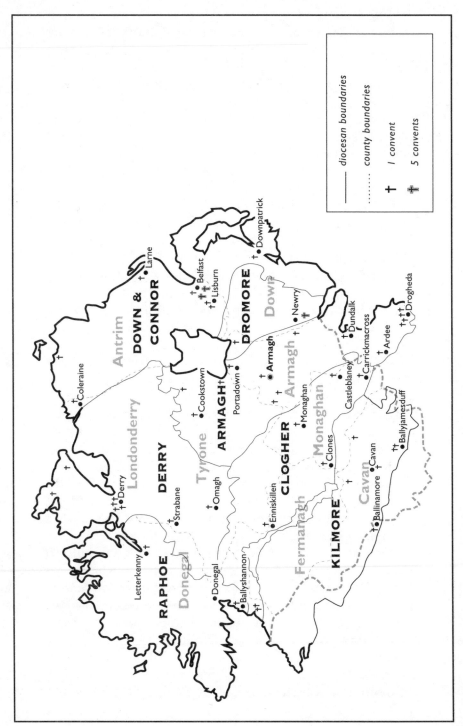

MAP 3   The distribution of convents in the north of Ireland, 1920.

able to maintain six convents, five of which concentrated exclusively on education. But what Dromore gained educationally, they lost out to Kilmore's social activity where two Mercy convents were concerned with infirmaries. The Belturbet Mercy convent established a fever hospital in 1869 and later ran a county infirmary. The hospital of the Mercy sisters, Ballinamore, opened in 1873 but had closed down by 1920, most probably due to lack of funding.

The Dromore diocese is sandwiched neatly between the two primary dioceses of Down and Connor and Armagh and gained convents because of this. Between 1843–89 five Mercy convents and one Poor Clare convent had been established, three of which were based in Newry. (See Appendix, Table 7) Only the Mercy sisters of Warrenpoint did not involve themselves in education. Newry's position as a large and prosperous Catholic town ensured it was able to sustain three boarding schools and two poor schools.

IV

Looking at the distribution of convents by order, it is possible to see that in general, most of the orders were engaged in a wide range of activities. Only four of the congregations of sisters ran schools without some form of social welfare work: the Dominicans; the Presentation sisters; the Poor Clares; and the Loreto sisters. These account for just eleven convents by 1920. The Loreto sisters only ran poor and boarding schools, while the Presentation and Dominican sisters also controlled night classes for working women. The Poor Clares ran industrial schools, as well as free, boarding and night schools. Most of the congregations, therefore, did some form of social work. At the very least the congregations visited the sick, including the Sacre Coeur, the French Sisters of Charity, the Holy Cross and Passion Sisters, and the Sisters of Charity of St. Vincent de Paul. Only the Sacre Coeur sisters supplemented this activity with a poor school and a boarding school. The French Sisters of Charity, the Sisters of Charity of St. Vincent de Paul, together with the Holy Cross and Passion Sisters did not run any select or boarding schools but ran free or national schools, night schools and industrial schools. The

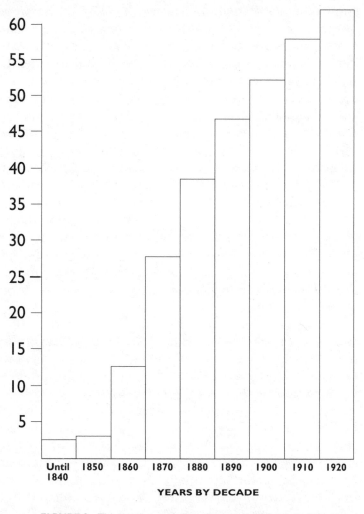

FIGURE 3   The cumulative number of convents in the seven dioceses of the north of Ireland to 1920.

Source: *O'Connell, 'Convents in the north of Ireland'.*

two congregations with the most varied agenda were the Mercy and the St. Louis sisters. They were involved in poor schools and boarding schools as well as orphanages, reformatories and visiting the sick. In addition, the Mercy sisters also ran industrial and night schools, together with workhouses and hospitals. The Mercy sisters were a more dynamic group than any of the other orders in terms of the range and capability of their work. Of the seventeen orders represented in Ulster only five were not involved in educational work: the Good Shepherd sisters who ran reformatories; the Bon Secours sisters who visited the sick and old; the Nazareth sisters who were involved with orphanages and old peoples' homes; the Marist and Mary Immaculate orders.

To conclude, over the course of the nineteenth century the number of convents increased in Ulster, with the years 1860–70 standing out as the most successful decade (Figure 3) The trend was towards a concentration of convents around the eastern side of the region, where Belfast industries and the port facilitated the growth of a prosperous middle class who were able and willing to finance educational and social relief efforts. Convents empowered women to work as professionals in a society which considered the ideal context for women to be motherhood and the home. The convent was a place of security and order, as well as a place of professional and spiritual fulfilment. At this time, when the Catholic church was flourishing both in Ireland and in Europe, convents provided women with a wide range of work. The spread of convents occurred at a time when other opportunities for female work were becoming more restrictive.

Convents in Ulster succeeded in providing health care, social welfare and education for a mass of people who had no alternative provisions. The exceptional success of the Mercy congregations is especially marked. The years after partition created a whole new set of challenges for the female religious of Ulster. The study of nuns in the north is a wide one which merits much more research.

---

[1] Sean Connolly, *Religion and society in nineteenth century Ireland* (Dundalk, 1985), p. 15.

[2] These figures are taken from Patrick Corish, *The Irish catholic experience* (Dublin, 1985), p. 199 and J.J. Lee, 'Women and the church since the famine', in Margaret MacCurtain and Donncha Ó Corráin, (eds.), *Women in Irish society: the historical dimension* (Dublin, 1979), pp 37–9. For similar analysis see Emmet Larkin, *The historical dimensions of Irish catholicism* (Washington, 1984), pp 58–9.

[3] Tony Fahey, 'Nuns in the catholic church in Ireland in the nineteenth century', in Mary Cullen, (ed.), *Girls don't do honours: Irish women in education in the nineteenth and twentieth centuries* (Dublin, 1987), p. 7 and Lee, 'Women', pp 39–40.

[4] Fahey, 'Nuns', p. 15.

[5] Eibhlín Breathnach, 'Charting new waters: women's experience in higher education, 1879–1908' in Mary Cullen, (ed.), *Girls don't do honours: Irish women in education in the nineteenth and twentieth centuries* (Dublin, 1987), pp 56–7.

[6] Lee, 'Women', pp 37–42.

[7] Fahey, 'Nuns', p. 7.

[8] Catriona Clear, 'The limits of female autonomy: nuns in nineteenth century Ireland' in Maria Luddy and Cliona Murphy, (eds.), *Women surviving: studies in Irish women's history in the 19th and 20th centuries* (Swords, 1990), p. 19.

[9] *Irish Catholic Directory and Almanack* (hereafter *ICDA*) 1840 (Dublin, 1839), pp 238–40, 242.

[10] Ibid., p. 240.

[11] Recent research has not considered the role of convents in Ulster in any great detail. Catriona Clear makes passing reference to Ulster convents in 'The limits of female autonomy', pp 24–5 and Fahey mentions Belfast only in relation to urbanisation's impact on the establishment of convents, 'Nuns', p. 16. The only known work on Ulster nuns is by Linda-May Ballard, 'Some aspects of tradition among female religious in Ulster' in *Ulster Folklife* 38 (1992), pp 68–78.

[12] *Convent of Our Lady of Mercy St. Paul's, 1854 to 1954* (Belfast, 1954), p. 55.

[13] Marie O'Connell, 'Convents in the north of Ireland from the mid-nineteenth to the mid-twentieth centuries', unpub. M.A. diss.,The Queen's University, Belfast (1992), p. 79.

[14] Monsignor O'Laverty, *History of the diocese of Down and Connor* (Belfast, 1850), pp 440–41.

[15] *Weavings: a celebration of Dominican women* (n.p., n.d.), pp 25–30. Available in the library of the Dominican convent, Falls Road, Belfast.

[16] Last will and testament of James Duffy, 20 Sept. 1855. Roman Catholic Diocesan Centre, Somerton Road, Belfast.

[17] O'Connell, 'Convents', p. 60.

[18] For a more extensive discussion of dowries see Clear, *Nuns in nineteenth-century Ireland* (Dublin, 1987), pp 70, 87–8 and Fahey, 'Nuns', p. 14.

[19] O'Connell, 'Convents', p. 79.

[20] Record of entrants to St. Paul's Convent, Crumlin Road, Belfast, 1895–1919, St. Paul's Convent, Belfast.

[21] O'Connell, 'Convents', p. 79.

[22] Clear, *Nuns,* pp 50–1.

[23] Ibid., p. 104.

[24] *ICDA,* 1870, p. 88.

[25] Ibid., 1879, p. 136.

[26] Ibid., 1876, p. 136.

[27] Ibid.

[28] Ibid., 1867, p. 123.

[29] Ibid., 1880, p. 121.

[30] Ibid., 1891, p. 129.

[31] Ibid., 1907, p. 136.

[32] Ibid., 1865, p. 161.

[33] The others were run by the Mercy sisters, Belfast; Good Shepherd sisters, Belfast and St. Louis sisters in Monaghan.

[34] *ICDA*, 1897, p. 129.

[35] Ibid.

[36] *ICDA*, 1858, p. 150.

[37] The others were in Belturbet (Kilmore), dating from 1869 and Ballyshannon (Raphoe), established in 1867.

APPENDIX

A LIST, BY DIOCESES, OF THE INSTITUTES RUN BY AND THE WORK DONE BY CONVENTS IN ULSTER BETWEEN 1840 AND 1920.

Source: O'Connell, 'Convents in the north of Ireland';
Irish Catholic Directory and Almanack (ICDA)

TABLE I   Down & Connor

CONVENT NAME, WITH FIRST *ICDA* LISTING	Select Pay and Boarding Schools	Free or Poor Schools	Night Schools for Women	Industrial Schools	Orphan-ages	Work-houses	Hospitals and Infirmaries	Homes for Old	Reform-atories/ Laundry	Visit sick, prisons and old
Mercy, Crumlin Rd., Belfast (1854)	●	●		●	●				●	
Mercy, Blackmore, Belfast (1866)										
Mercy, Downpatrick (1866)	●									
Good Shepherd, Blackmore, Belfast (1868)									●	
Dominican, Falls Rd., Belfast (1870)	●	●	●							
Sacre Coeur, Lisburn (1871)	●	●								●
Bon Secours, Belfast (1876)										●
Sacred Heart of Mary, Lisburn (1878)	●	●								●
Nazareth, Ballynafeigh, Belfast (1876)								●		
Mercy, Sussex Pl., Belfast (1883)							●			
Holy Cross and Passion, Belfast (1900)		●	●							●
Charity of St.Vincent De Paul, Belfast (1900)		●	●							
Mercy, Whiteabby (1901)										
Holy Cross and Passion, Larne (1906)		●								
Holy Cross and Passion, Ballycastle (1913)		●								●
Dominican, Portstewart (1917)	●	●								
Nazareth, Ravenhill Rd., Belfast (1917)					●					
French Sisters of Charity, Belfast (1865)		●	●							●

TABLE 2 Armagh

CONVENT NAME, WITH FIRST *ICDA* LISTING	Select Pay and Boarding Schools	Free or Poor Schools	Night Schools for Women	Industrial Schools	Orphan-ages	Work-houses	Hospitals and Infirmaries	Homes for Old	Reform-atories/ Laundry	Visit sick, prisons and old
Dominican, Drogheda (*pre*1837)	●	●								
Presentation, Drogheda (*pre*1837)	●	●								
Society of the Sacred Heart, Armagh (1851)	●	●								
Mercy, Dundalk (1856)	●	●								
French Sisters of Charity, Drogheda (1857)			●							●
Mercy, Ardee (1865)	●	●					●			
Poor Clares, Keady (1871)		●	●							
Charity of St. Vincent de Paul, Drogheda (1876)			●	●						
St. Louis, Middletown (1876)	●	●			●					
Presentation, Portadown (1882)	●	●	●							●
Mercy, Cookstown (1889)	●	●	●							
Mercy, Bessbrook (1891)										
Mercy, Dungannon (1896)	●	●								
Mary Immaculate, Magherafelt (1890)										

TABLE 3 Raphoe

	Select pay and boarding Schools	Free or Poor Schools	Night Schools for Women	Industrial Schools	Orphan-ages	Work Houses	Hospitals and Infirmaries	Homes for old	Reform-atories/ laundry	Visit sick prisons and old
Loreto, Letterkenny (1856)	●	●								
Mercy, Ballyshannon (1867)		●			●	●	●			

TABLE 4 Derry

	Select pay and boarding Schools	Free or Poor Schools	Night Schools for Women	Industrial Schools	Orphan-ages	Work Houses	Hospitals and Infirmaries	Homes for old	Reform-atories/ laundry	Visit sick prisons and old
Mercy, Pump St., Derry (1852)	●	●								
Loreto, Omagh (1857)	●	●								
Mercy, Moville (1865)										
Mercy, Strabane (1872)	●	●		●	●					
Mercy, Carndonagh (1874)										
Nazareth, Derry (1893)					●					
Mercy, St. Peter's, Derry (1905)		●	●							
Good Shepherd, Waterside, Derry (1920)									●	

TABLE 5   Clogher

CONVENT NAME, WITH FIRST *ICDA* LISTING	Select Pay and Boarding Schools	Free or Poor Schools	Night Schools for Women	Industrial Schools	Orphanages	Workhouses	Hospitals and Infirmaries	Homes for Old	Reformatories/ Laundry	Visit sick, prisons and old
Mercy, Enniskillen (1858)				●						●
St. Louis, Bundoran (1859)	●									
St. Louis, Monaghan (1861)	●	●							●	●
Marist, Carrickmacross (1876)										
St. Louis, Carrickmacross (1890)	●	●								
St. Louis, Clones (1904)		●								
Mercy, Castleblaney (1908)		●								●
Mercy, Ballyshannon (1905)						●				

TABLE 6   Kilmore

CONVENT NAME, WITH FIRST *ICDA* LISTING	Select Pay and Boarding Schools	Free or Poor Schools	Night Schools for Women	Industrial Schools	Orphanages	Workhouses	Hospitals and Infirmaries	Homes for Old	Reformatories/ Laundry	Visit sick, prisons and old
Poor Clares, Cavan (1865)		●		●						
Poor Clares, Ballyjamesduff (1868)		●								
Mercy, Belturbet (1869)						●	●			
Mercy, Ballyjamesduff (1869)										
Mercy, Ballinamore (1873)							●			
Mercy, Cootehill (1881)										

TABLE 7   Dromore

CONVENT NAME, WITH FIRST *ICDA* LISTING	Select Pay and Boarding Schools	Free or Poor Schools	Night Schools for Women	Industrial Schools	Orphanages	Workhouses	Hospitals and Infirmaries	Homes for Old	Reformatories/ Laundry	Visit sick, prisons and old
Poor Clares, Newry (1843)	●	●								
Mercy, Canal St., Newry (1856)	●	●								
Mercy, Rostrevor (1867)	●	●								
Mercy, Lurgan (1867)	●	●								
Mercy, Warrenpoint (1889)										
Mercy, Kilmore St., Newry (1889)	●									

INDEX